The Recall's Broken Promise

How Big Money Still Runs California Politics

By
Derek Cressman

The Poplar Institute

The Recall's Broken Promise
How Big Money Still Runs California Politics

by Derek Cressman

Published by
The Poplar Institute
2320 D St. #203
Sacramento, CA 95816

http://www.PoplarInstitute.org
info@PoplarInstitute.org

First Printing May 2007

ISBN -13: 978-0-9786405-0-7 (pbk.)
ISBN -10: 0-9786405-0-0

Printed in the United States of America

Library of Congress Control Number: 2006906405

Cover design by Brion Sausser, www.BookCoverDesigner.com

Printed in the United States of America.

People who have more money should be free to buy more cars, more homes, and more gizmos than the rest of us. They should not be able to buy more democracy.

—Bill Moyers

All political power is inherent in the people. Government is instituted for their protection, security, and benefit, and they have the right to alter or reform it when the public good may require.

—California Constitution of 1849

In memory of Susan Birmingham

CONTENTS

INTRODUCTION

The Promise

Californians Find Hope in the Recall

On August 6, 2003, Arnold Schwarzenegger appeared on *The Tonight Show* with Jay Leno, supposedly to explain why he had chosen not to run for governor in California's historic recall election. Arnold had been dropping hints for years that he wanted to run for governor, and months earlier had met with Karl Rove in the White House to help grease the skids for a potential campaign. When the petition to recall Governor Gray Davis was nearly qualified to appear on the ballot, Arnold had said, "If the state needs me, and if there's no one I think is better, then I will run."[1]

Yet on July 28, *Fox News* reported that a source close to the actor had told them, "Arnold Schwarzenegger won't seek the California governor's office in conjunction with a recall election set for October."[2] Rumors were flying that Schwarzenegger was deferring to his friend Richard Riordan, the former mayor of Los Angeles, because his wife, Maria Shriver, did not want Arnold to run.

On the show, Arnold told his buddy Jay, "The politicians are fiddling, fumbling and failing. The man that is failing the people more than anyone is Gray Davis." That wasn't news. A majority of Californians thought the same thing. Then Arnold continued, "He is failing them terribly, and this is why he needs to be recalled and this is why I am going to run for governor of the state of California."

Wowza! The audience went nuts. Somebody was announcing a candidacy for office on *The Tonight Show*, unusual to begin with.

> ***"As you know, I don't need to take any money from anybody. I have plenty of money myself. I will make the decisions for the people."***
> ***—Arnold Schwarzenegger***

The fact that it was Arnold Schwarzenegger was all the more enthralling.

Arnold said the decision to run was the most difficult choice he'd made in his life, other than deciding to get a bikini wax in 1978. Already voters could tell that he was going to be a different sort of candidate.

Even Arnold's closest advisors did not know he was planning to announce his candidacy on *The Tonight Show*. His words that evening were his own, before his handlers could carefully craft his words.

"The biggest problem we have is that Sacramento is being run by special interests," Schwarzenegger declared. "I will go to Sacramento and clean house."

Then came the biggest promise of Arnold's campaign: "As you know, I don't need to take any money from anybody. I have plenty of money myself. I will make the decisions for the people." Arnold's spin masters would later try to take back this promise, explaining that he really didn't mean he wouldn't take *any* money from anybody. But to millions of Americans watching that evening, that promise was a big reason to believe; believe not only in Arnold, but in the recall as an historic moment. Had you suggested to anyone watching that Arnold Schwarzenegger would go on to take more money from powerful interests than any candidate in the history of California, indeed more than any non-presidential candidate in the history of America, you'd have been dismissed as a cynic—this guy was *different.*

Like voters everywhere, Californians were sick and tired of big money calling the shots in politics. Trial lawyers and gaming tribes gave money and got friendly politicians elected who did exactly what they wanted. Big corporations and developers got special favors and tax breaks while the rest of us got socked with tuition hikes, higher car taxes, and government spending on boondoggles that seemed to benefit narrow private financial interests instead of the broader public good.

For the first time in ages, voters saw a figure that could be entirely free of special-interest influence. Newspapers estimated that Arnold was worth at least $100 million, and probably more than $200 million. He was a charismatic hero with celebrity status that guaranteed him nearly unlimited access to the media. Arnold could have won the recall election without spending a dime, just based on his popularity, charm, and ability to command public attention. To the extent that he did want to run TV ads, Arnold really did have enough money to pay for the ads himself. Others had done it. John Corzine had spent $65 million of his own fortune to run for the U.S. Senate in New Jersey and Michael Bloomberg spent even more to become mayor of New York. Businessman Al Checchi had self-financed an expensive campaign for California governor in 1998 and former eBay exec Steve Westly would attempt a similar feat in 2006.

Millionaire candidates who finance their own campaigns are a mixed bag for democracy. On the one hand, they have an unfair

"I don't want to take . . . any campaign contributions, from the special interests. Because as soon as you do that, as soon as you say OK, give me this money and I will do this, this, and that for you, you are selling out."
—Arnold Schwarzenegger

advantage over their opponents. There is something distinctly undemocratic about using massive amounts of money to buy your way into office. The land of opportunity once prided itself on the fact that anyone could become president, no matter how humble his or her upbringing. We now live in a country where at least 40 percent of U.S. senators are millionaires.

On the other hand, when candidates entirely fund their own campaigns, voters at least know that they are not beholden to anyone else. That's an upside that (for some people) more than offsets the inherent inequity that exists when millionaires use their financial clout to trounce non-wealthy opponents. Moreover, millionaire candidates appear to come from all over the political spectrum, so they don't necessarily advantage one side or the other. John Corzine, in New Jersey, is a proud liberal. Steve Forbes, who spent $37 million of his own money running for president against George W. Bush in the Republican primary of 2000, is a die-hard conservative, as is Bill Simon, who self-financed his own bid for the California governorship in 2002. Then there are folks like Bloomberg and Schwarzenegger who fall somewhere in the middle. And let's not forget about Ross Perot, who would never have made such an impact on American politics had he not been willing to part with $65 million of his own money to give to the cause.

Arnold tapped into voters' frustration with big money in politics, making it a major theme of his campaign. "The people of this state do not trust their government," he said. "They feel it is corrupted by dirty money, closed doors and back room dealing. They see the contributions go in, the favors go out, and they're punished with wasteful spending and high taxes."[3] This was a mantra he would repeat again and again during the campaign. One of Arnold's ads said, "Special interests have a stranglehold on Sacramento. . . . Here's how it works: Money comes in—favors go out. The people lose. We need to send a message: Game over."[4]

As the campaign progressed, Arnold backed away from his promise not to take money from anyone. He said that what he really meant was that he wouldn't take any money from "special interests."

Arnold told listeners on a talk radio show, "I want to be a governor who is for the people, for everyone. . . . Therefore I don't want to take any contributions, any campaign contributions, from the special interests. Because as soon as you do that, as soon as you say OK, give me this money and I will do this, this, and that for you, you are selling out."[5]

In explaining who he would accept funds from, Arnold said "I take money from [the] little grocery store, or the little shoe store, or the guy that owns the real estate company, or something like that. But most of my contributions, 90 percent of them, are just from regular people."[6]

Any group of regular guys employed by the state of California, however, qualified as Arnold's definition of a special interest if they were part of a union. "You cannot expect to represent the people of California if you are taking money from a union, and you know that down the line you are going to sit across the table from them," he explained.[7]

After returning a $2,500 check from the Los Angeles Deputy Sheriffs, he explained, "We realized this was a conflict of interest. As soon as you take their money, you owe them something. It's an old rule: campaign contributions come in, favors go out, and the people are hurting."[8]

Always one to understand the value of a good prop, Schwarzenegger barnstormed the state with a broom in his hand and told voters that if they elected him he would sweep the special interests from Sacramento. The day before the recall, he staged a rally in Sacramento. "We are here to clean house," declared Arnold. "We are here to sweep out the bureaucracy. We are here to sweep out the special interests, and we are here, number one, to sweep out Gray Davis."

Arnold brought Twisted Sister singer Dee Snider up to sing the rock anthem, "We're Not Gonna Take It." Arnold then predicted, "When I come up here to Sacramento and take over this office, special interests are going to go crazy. They know I am here to kick some serious butt."[9]

Arnold turned his lack of political experience into an asset, telling voters that he was not a career politician in the pockets of special interests. A third of probable voters said the fact that he had never held elected office made them more likely to vote for Schwarzenegger.[10] He was a competitor with a can-do mentality that would get things done.

The day after he was elected, Arnold promised to devote himself entirely to his new job, saying, "The people of California want me to be the governor, and I would do that and nothing else. I will work as the governor. I will work as much as I can, even if it is around the clock. There will be no time for movies or anything else. I will pay full attention to this job."[11] Based on that statement, voters would hardly imagine that only days later Schwarzenegger would sign a contract to edit muscle magazines—while governor—that would pay him as much as $8 million.

The same discontent that fueled the recall of Gray Davis created an opening for voters to finally believe in change. In taking matters into their own hands by recalling a sitting governor, voters saw they could indeed make a difference. Mark Baldassare, a pollster of the Public Policy Institute of California, described voters as "upbeat about the notion of being part of this process, of the political process, the public policy-making process."[12] Half of the people he polled said that the recall made them more interested in politics generally. Baldassare attributed much of this to Schwarzenegger: "Without him as an option, a lot of people would have stayed home angry."[13]

In that same moment of negative energy focused at Davis, voters dared to give their trust to someone else. Arnold recognized the special trust he had been given. In his acceptance speech on election night, he told his audience:

> Today California has given me the greatest gift of all. You've given me your trust by voting for me. Thank you very much to all the people of California for giving me their great trust. And let me tell you something. I will do everything I can to live up to that trust. I will not fail you. I will not disappoint you. And I will not let you down. . . . For the people to win, politics as usual must lose. . . . I want to be

> the people's governor.[14]

Schwarzenegger continued this same theme of reform in his inaugural address:

> Today is a new day in California. I did not seek this office to do things the way they've always been done. What I care about is restoring your confidence in your government. . . . This election was not about replacing one man. It was not replacing one party. It was about changing the entire political climate of our state.[15]

It was the dawn of a new era in California—or at least that's how it felt at the time. Arnold Schwarzenegger is a man of remarkable talent, energy, and charisma. As a moderate Republican who was married to a well-known Democrat, he had the ability to reach out to both conservatives and liberals to find common ground and get things done. Arnold was poised to continue the legacy of Republican reformers such as President Teddy Roosevelt, who championed a ban on corporate contributions to federal candidates in 1907, and California Governor Hiram Johnson, who successfully called for the creation of the initiative, referendum, and recall process in California as a way of standing up to corporate robber barons at the dawn of the last century.

More than any politician in America, Arnold Schwarzenegger owed his first election to his promise to clean up government and to take on special interests. Voters were angry enough to remove a sitting governor during the recall. In promising to be different, Schwarzenegger set a high bar for himself.

But how well has Arnold Schwarzenegger lived up to the promise that most Californians felt the recall would deliver? I'll attempt to answer that question by taking a look at both the specific promises Schwarzenegger made during his campaign and the larger political context of the recall election. We'll examine the money Arnold has taken as governor, the ties to powerful business interests his administration had created, and the conflicts between Arnold's personal finances and his decisions as governor. Finally,

I'll examine what Arnold has done to try to reform the system and point out the obstacles he has faced from members of both political parties.

As the director of the non-profit, non-partisan group TheRestofUs.org from 2003–2006, I chronicled record levels of money that flowed into California politics from big business and other private interests during Arnold's term in office. At times, TheRestofUs.org was involved as a participant, doing what we could to curb the role of big money, or at least make politicians play by the rules.

This book will not examine how Governor Schwarzenegger has performed on every issue or answer the question of whether he has been a good governor overall. There are certainly many taxpayer groups, business leaders, and other interests who would say that Schwarzenegger performed well as governor. Environmentalists give him mixed reviews. There are others, including nurses and teachers, who would say that he has short-changed them or backed out of promises he made. But we will for the most part not get into that.

Rather, we will focus our attention on the topic of Arnold's promise, and his real potential, to improve democracy in California and make government more accountable to the people. Readers will draw their own conclusions, but on balance I believe that Arnold has, so far, not lived up to the promise of the recall election. Nor have other politicians.

When it comes to reform from 2003–2006, Arnold and the California legislature not only fell short of the mark, they took us in the wrong direction. Big money, from a handful of private interests, plays a bigger role in California politics today than it ever has. Now that he has been re-elected, time remains for Arnold to take bold steps to reduce the power of big money in politics.

Because Arnold Schwarzenegger is an international celebrity, his election as governor of California generated worldwide attention. While this book has a special importance to Californians, it contains lessons for all Americans. Most of us share a frustration with special interest money in politics. We've seen headlines about lobbyist Jack Abramoff wining and dining members of Congress and Representative Duke Cunningham resigning after pleading guilty to earmarking defense contracts in exchange for bribes. Former House Majority Leader Tom DeLay stepped down after being charged with illegally funneling corporate contributions into Texas political races, an act that is perfectly legal in California. While the culture of corruption was one significant reason Republicans lost control of Congress, Democrats are not immune. Congressman William Jefferson has been videotaped by the FBI accepting $100,000 in marked bills that later turned up in his freezer. The scandals that recently rocked the U.S. Congress involved not only outright bribery, but also the successful coup that powerful interests have staged by using campaign cash to elect politicians who will do their bidding. Clearly, Americans face no shortage of reasons for concern about the role of big money in politics.

The story of money in California politics can provide valuable tips for citizens across the country. Likewise, citizens in other states have been much more successful than California in reforming their government and curbing the power of special interests, so there is much Californians can learn. Chapter 15 will present some ideas for improving the current system.

One central theme of this book is the new trend emerging in California politics to combine candidate campaigns and ballot initiative campaigns. Our story is one of a celebrity governor, accompanied by a set of powerful interests and their clever consultants, fundamentally altering politics in the Golden State. More so than ever before, money from large donors dominates the process. As the rock band The Who put it, "meet the new boss, same as the old boss."

Most of all, this book is intended to inspire ordinary citizens to take matters into our own hands. Rather than leaving it up to the politicians to clean up their own act—which is simply not going to happen—there are things that we can and must do to take back our government from the fat cats. The final chapter suggests some initial steps we can take. But first, let's begin with a look backward to the Gray Davis administration to understand why California voters were fed up with money in politics and why they elected Schwarzenegger to do something about it.

CHAPTER 1

THE PREDECESSOR

Gray Davis and Big Money Set the Stage

Many non-Californians, who initially failed to appreciate the enthusiasm that voters had for Arnold Schwarzenegger and the recall election, never fully understood the frustration that Californians felt with Gray Davis and the entire political system he represented. The recall was a sane response to the insane politics that preceded it. While some voter dissatisfaction derived from the personality of Gray Davis, his handling of the energy crisis, and California's serious budget imbalance, much of it stemmed from the fundamentals of modern day political campaigns. Sadly, there are too many politicians in too many states that have too much in common with Gray Davis. Politicians everywhere would be wise to consider the California recall as a shot across the bow from regular folks who are mad as hell about big money in politics. The politicians should set to work to seriously revamp the way campaigns are financed in other states and in Congress. If they don't, the anger that fueled the recall will one day surface in other states as well.

The Consummate Politician vs. the Millionaires

Gray Davis was the classic example of a new breed of career politician. While men who devote their entire career to politics were once known as public servants, Davis more than anyone helped change that perception. By the end of his reign as governor, he was perceived as serving private interests who funded his campaigns rather than serving the public at large.

After serving as chief of staff to Governor Jerry Brown from 1975 to 1981, Davis ran for the California Assembly and won. Four years later, he moved one step up the ladder to state controller. In 1995, he moved up one more rung to lieutenant governor. By 1998, he was ready to run for governor. That campaign proved to be a turning point in California politics, further augmenting the role of truly massive amounts of money in influencing elections. In 1996, Bill Clinton had paved the way for a new influx of huge contributions at the federal level by expanding a so-called "soft-money" loophole that allowed him to raise unlimited sums of money for the Democratic Party and then use that money to promote his re-election. Gray Davis observed Clinton's success and emulated it in California.

Davis ran in the Democratic primary against Al Checchi and Jane Harman, both of whom were rich. Harman would spend $17 million on her campaign. Checchi spent $39 million—more money than anyone had ever spent on any race for governor at the time. Checchi's net worth was estimated at over a half billion dollars. He had made most of it as a corporate takeover artist, with his most famous exploit being a buyout of Northwest Airlines. Jane Harman's money came from her husband, Sidney Harman, co-founder of the stereo company Harman Kardon. She had spent $2 million to buy herself a seat in Congress in 1992, but was looking to move up in the world.

While it may be hard for many to believe in retrospect (based upon his performance as governor) Davis was seen as the progressive, grassroots candidate in the race. With six weeks to go in the election, he was considered the underdog with little chance of winning. As one academic who studied this race told me, "everyone, I mean *everyone*, followed Checchi and no one paid attention to Davis."[1] Jane Harman got traction only after Diane Feinstein decided not to run.

Having worked for the government for most of his life, Davis did not have a deep personal bank account to draw on. Instead, he became adept at asking other people to give him their money.

Al Checchi began airing ads in November 1997, earlier than any candidate had ever done before. He spent millions promoting himself and trashing Jane Harman with negative ads. In all, Checchi ran more than 40 different ads. His campaign produced another 60 more that were junked after voters responded negatively when they were shown the ads in shopping mall test groups. The effect of Checchi's ads was to both lower Harman's standing in the polls and drag down Checchi with her because voters were turned off by the mudslinging. Davis was the beneficiary. He responded with a series of ads that claimed he had "experience money can't buy." One ad proclaimed:

> When you're alone in the governor's office, all the money in the world won't buy you what you need to make the tough decisions. Gray Davis. Chief of Staff to Governor Jerry Brown, Assemblyman, Controller, Lt. Governor. The *San Jose Mercury News* called him "perhaps the best trained governor in waiting California has ever produced." Pro-choice. For the death penalty. A lifelong leader on education. Endorsed by nearly every law enforcement group in California. Gray Davis. Democrat for governor. Experience money can't buy.[2]

Davis won the race handily, garnering 35 percent of the vote while Checchi received only 13 percent and Harman 12 percent. Dan Lungren captured the Republican nomination with 34 percent.

Davis raised $9 million for the primary, more than anyone had ever raised for a similar race. Yet he was outspent dramatically in this campaign by opponents who did not need to raise money due to their own deep pockets. Even though he won, his consultants walked away from the experience concluding, "money still matters."[3]

Davis conducted a steady, if lackluster campaign for the general election. "Boring is back. Boring might even be beautiful!" he declared at a rally with Vice President Al Gore, who knew a thing or two about the subject.[4] Davis may have cared deeply about the issues facing California, but he certainly didn't project it. For a while, the plain vanilla style worked well for him. There wasn't much to like, but there wasn't much to dislike either.

Davis went on to win the general election handily, defeating Dan Lungren 59 percent to 39 percent. Given that Republican governors had ruled California for the past 16 years, it was an embarrassment for Lungren and a triumph for Davis. Perhaps not coincidentally, this was also the first election in 12 years where the Democrat had outspent the Republican candidate for governor.

Davis apparently concluded from the near-death experience with Checchi that he must always be prepared to run against another millionaire candidate, perhaps one with more skill and experience than Checchi. To prepare for such a day, Davis began fundraising immediately after taking office. Al Checchi contributed to Gray Davis's metamorphosis into a Frankenstein fundraiser. In that sense, Checchi set in place a chain of events that would lead to the California recall.

Non-Stop Fundraising

In his first year as governor, Davis raked in money at a pace of about a million dollars a month. That comes to nearly $33,000 per day.

To keep the money flowing, Davis took a calculated middle road position on practically every issue. This meant that both corporate and labor interests constantly felt the need to keep him on their side. As one lobbyist put it coyly when asked why her company gave to Davis, "We support candidates who are reasonable when it comes to our industry. It doesn't mean they always agree with us. But when they don't, they disagree reasonably."[5] Another explained, "With this governor, you know you're not going to get everything you want. But if you want anything, you know you have to ante up. . . . On every issue he drives right down the center, and that allows him to collect money from both sides. Nobody is out of the picture. Nobody is protected. Everybody has to invest."[6]

Corporate donors may have concluded that it was unlikely that a Republican would win office and that Gray Davis was the friendliest Democrat they were likely to see. They wanted to keep him around as long as possible. While labor didn't get everything they wanted, Davis was probably more sympathetic than a self-funded millionaire, having won office without their help, would have been.

Business vs. Labor

During the years Davis was governor, donors that are directly identified with several major business interests gave 17 percent of the funds raised by California candidates, as tracked by a national campaign finance database. Because corporations are fictitious entities that are given special powers by the state to achieve important economic goals, many states have concluded it is inappropriate for corporations to use those advantages for political purposes. Twenty states, and the federal government, ban corporate contributions to candidates entirely. In these states, individuals who support corporate agendas, like CEOs and other corporate execs, are free to make individual contributions and band together collectively through political organizations to make pro-corporate viewpoints known, but they must do so as people, not through the corporation. But California allows corporations to use money from customers and shareholders in its corporate treasury to make contributions to candidates.

Over the same three election cycles, labor groups have given six percent of the money raised by California candidates. These organizations represent about 17 percent of California workers. The labor money has the redeeming value of being raised in small contributions by large numbers of people. Unlike corporations, labor unions are formed in part for political purposes and their members vote on the political leadership of their organization, so they have a more credible claim to spend money in politics than corporations do.

Business vs. Labor Political Contributions in California[7]

	2000	2002	2004	3 cycle total	
Total Tracked	213,573,865	335,171,768	521,203,849	1,069,949,482	
Labor	17,830,984	35,621,576	13,026,583	66,479,143	6 %
General business	7,985,968	16,172,952	6,319,851	30,478,771	3 %
Finance, Ins., Real Estate	15,867,971	47,297,883	15,460,448	78,626,302	7 %
Communications Electronics	5,999,460	14,066,761	4,343,287	24,409,508	2 %
Energy Natural Res.	4,965,921	5,413,863	3,496,405	13,876,189	1 %
Construction	2,707,962	9,100,204	3,324,262	15,132,428	1 %
Transportation	1,463,043	4,214,315	2,314,732	7,992,090	1 %
Agriculture	2,543,806	6,904,263	2,638,862	12,086,931	1 %
Total Business	41,534,131	103,170,241	37,897,847	182,602,219	17 %

Consumers and taxpayers lack similar vehicles that workers in a labor union have to collectively pool their small donations in order to have a big impact. Individuals can make voluntary contributions to taxpayer and consumer organizations, but there is no way for citizens to vote collectively in their role as taxpayers or consumers to jointly fund an organization to promote these broad interests. As a result, issues that impact citizens in their roles as consumers and taxpayers often get short shrift in Sacramento when they butt up against labor. Labor often appears unduly powerful compared to those interests, but it is the corporate money that most greatly distorts the process, while consumer and taxpayer interests are disproportionately weak.

Throughout Davis's career as governor, incidents kept emerging in which he had sided with a private interest over the public interest, often after the private interest had given him money. Davis and his staff repeatedly swore that fundraising had no impact on any policy decisions made by the governor, a pledge that Arnold Schwarzenegger would repeat often. "There is an absolute separation between politics and policy," said Davis spokesman Roger Salazar. "The governor doesn't base his decisions on contributions—never has, never will."[8] But it really didn't matter. The donors got what they wanted: a politician in office who did what was good for them. Whether he did it because he agreed with them or because he was taking their money made no difference. Big money keeps politicians in office who are accountable to big donors and keeps out politicians who stand up for the public good.

One example is TOSCO. This polluter gave Davis $10,000 on March 23, 2001. Why? One reason might be that the state water board, appointed by Davis, had issued a ruling on March 7 that allowed the company to discharge five times more dioxin into the San Francisco Bay than was previously permitted. The board also intervened to oppose a bill in the legislature that would have cracked down on water pollution. All in all, TOSCO gave Davis $55,000. Clearly there was something about the man that they liked.

In another incident, the Metabolic Company, a manufacturer of dietary supplements, gave Davis $100,000 in two installments. Why? Nine days before the contributions, legislators had introduced a bill to require Metabolic and other producers of appetite suppressing supplements to put labels on their packages telling consumers whether they contained ephedrine. When the bill reached the desk of Gray Davis, he vetoed it. The federal Food and Drug Administration has since banned ephedrine because it may cause strokes and heart attacks. It's not hard to imagine why companies like Metabolic would have wanted to keep Gray Davis in the governor's office.

Hollywood mogul Stephen Bing dropped a cool quarter million bucks on Gray Davis, and other Hollywood interests kicked in another $250,000 and change. Davis signed at least three bills that were supported by the filmmaking industry to keep movie producers from going out of state.

Banking giant Citigroup donated a total of $200,000 to Davis between 2001 and 2003. A $75,000 contribution came right before Citigroup sued the state of California over a law that required it to tell its customers how long it would take them to pay off credit card balances if they only made the minimum payment each month.

Bankers know how to invest money so that it makes more money, and political contributions are no different. Bob Stern, president of the Center for Governmental Studies asked, "What do they want for that big investment? My assumption is that the return will be enormous if they get what they want."[9]

Davis grew bolder and bolder in his requests for campaign cash. In one meeting with Wayne Johnson of the California Teachers Association, he went too far. The CTA had given Davis $1.3 million to help him win election in 1998, but relations between Davis and the teachers had become strained since then. Johnson related the conversation with Davis to the press: "We were just sitting there and talking and he, just out of the blue, says 'you know, I really need a million dollars from you guys.'" Johnson went public with the story, to Gray's embarrassment, and then withheld significant support for Davis in 2002. In apparent retaliation, Davis killed a bill that the teachers' union wanted that would have given each teacher more control over the textbooks used in their classroom. One teacher representative expressed his outrage by saying, "Let Gray go out and ring his own damn doorbells. No way in hell we're gonna be his ground troops. Not this time. Not ever again."[10]

The Oracle Debacle

Perhaps the biggest fundraising scandal to rock the Davis administration came when his administration awarded a $95 million database management contract to the Oracle Corporation without going through a competitive bidding process. State audits found that the contract was a disaster—it cost an extra $41 million rather than saving the state $111 million, as Oracle had promised it would. Things looked even worse for Davis when it came to light that Oracle lobbyist Ravi Mehta had given Davis technology aide Arun Baheti a $25,000 campaign contribution in a Sacramento bar just days after Davis approved the contract. Ironically, Mehta was the former head of the California Fair Political Practices Commission (FPPC). He was forced to resign in 1997 after making comments to lobbyists that trashed campaign contribution limits.

Oracle fired Mehta and Davis fired Baheti and three other aides involved in the deal while returning the campaign contribution, but the damage was done.

The public had been given a glimpse of how things worked in Sacramento and was more than ready to believe that this was not an isolated incident but rather business as usual. Contributors at times appeared to be buying policy outright. At other times, wealthy interests were simply helping elect, or re-elect, an agreeable "public servant." Either way, the public always seemed to lose out.

The Fundraising Arms Race

It all added up to record-shattering levels of political fundraising. In 1978, Jerry Brown and Evelle Younger spent a combined $5.7 million on their campaigns for governor. By 1990, Pete Wilson spent $16 million to Diane Feinstein's $13 million, a combined total of $29 million. Gray Davis and Dan Lungren spent a combined $52.5 million in 1998, and this was on top of the $39 million spent by Checchi and $17 million spent by Harman in the primary. That's more than $100 million spent to elect the governor of one state. Davis had helped propel big money fundraising to ten times what it had been just two decades before. The chart of the following page compiled by the California secretary of state tells the story.

Increased fundraising could theoretically have been the result of California's growing population and a greater number of people wanting to give small donations to candidates. But, in fact, just the opposite was happening. In Pete Wilson's 1994 race, he collected $1.3 million in contributions that came in amounts under $100. Wilson had an average contribution that was under $1,000. Eight years later, Gray Davis and his challenger Bill Simon's average contributions were both more than $5,000. Davis raised less than $500,000 from regular people in amounts under $100—far less than Wilson had.

Jim Knox, then an advocate for the campaign reform group

Campaign Fundraising and Spending by Candidates for Governor in the 1978–1998 General Elections

YEAR	CANDIDATE	RECEIPTS	EXPENDITURES
1978	**Brown, Jerry (D)***	$ 3,485,328	$ 3,435,034
	Younger, Evelle (R)	$2,324,400	$2,274,772
	TOTAL	$ 5,809,728	$ 5,709,806
1982	Bradley, Tom (D)	$6,627,492	$6,803,633
	Deukmejian, George (R)	$ 5,143,967	$ 4,972,389
	TOTAL	$11,771,459	$11,776,022
1986	Bradley, Tom (D)	$5,767,675	$6,137,522
	Deukmejian, George (R)*	$ 4,774,842	$ 9,565,125
	TOTAL	$10,542,517	$15,702,647
1990	Feinstein, Dianne (D)	$12,718,038	$13,227,930
	Wilson, Pete (R)	$12,205,291	$16,028,590
	TOTAL	$24,923,329	$29,256,520
1994	Brown, Kathleen (D)	$9,294,145	$12,251,634
	Wilson, Pete (R)*	$14,828,808	$19,555,243
	TOTAL	$24,122,953	$31,806,877
1998	**Davis, Gray (D)**	$25,757,912	$28,642,125
	Lungren, Dan (R)	$20,768,942	$23,845,008
	TOTAL	$46,526,854	$52,487,133

* = Incumbent
Bold = winner
Source: California Secretary of State

California Common Cause, said the increasing size in contributions was squeezing small donors out of the game. "Quite frankly, it is a major factor contributing to the disengagement and alienation of people from the political process," Knox commented. "The message the voters get is that their contributions don't matter."[11]

The *Los Angeles Times* noted that "the engaged citizen who gives $10, $20, even a few hundred dollars has become an anachronism."[12]

Davis was making the fundraising done by Wilson or any other politician look quaint. His 2002 campaign had 93 different donors who gave $100,000. But even *that* looked like small potatoes compared to the 28 donors who gave $250,000 and 13 others who gave more than a half-million bucks.

$ $ $

DONOR PROFILE: Jerry Perenchio was the CEO and owner of Univision, the largest Spanish-language network in the U.S. Experts predicted he would make $1.3 billion on the planned sale of Univision in 2006. *Business Week* described Perenchio as having an "iron grip" on America's 40 million Hispanics due to his media empire. His networks repeatedly beat out the major U.S. networks for ratings in the 18-49 year old category.

Along with his wife, Perenchio is the largest landholder in Malibu, an elite coastal village north of Los Angeles. He lives in the house that the mountaineer Jed and his oil-rich family reveled in during the 1960s sitcom *The Beverly Hillbillies*. Nancy Reagan lives next door. Perenchio built a secret, unauthorized, 10-acre golf course in Malibu that he hid for years from the California Costal Commission by claiming it was a jogging trail and building a massive wall around it. Aerial photography finally revealed the truth. Local activists complain that the golf course dumped pesticides like Roundup into local wetlands and sued Perenchio when the government refused to intervene.

Perenchio is one of California's fattest political fat cats, having given more than $14 million to California candidates from 1999 to 2005. He gave Gray Davis $775,000 while he was in office and later gave Arnold Schwarzenegger $2.25 million for his California Recovery Team and $1.5 million to Schwarzenegger's front group, Citizens to Save California. Perenchio covers his bets by giving to many opposing candidates for governor. He gave Cruz Bustamante $100,000 in 2003, Richard Riordan $500,000 and Bill Simon $200,000 in 2002. Along with his wife, Margaret, Perenchio has given more than $1.8 million to federal candidates and parties. He served as a Pioneer to the Bush 2004 campaign, raising more than $100,000 for the president. He also gave $4 million in 2004 to the federal electioneering group Progress for America which supported Republican efforts under the leadership of Karl Rove ally Tony Feather. Perenchio ranked 89 on the 2005 Forbes 400 list, with an estimated net worth of $2.6 billion.

$ $ $

An analysis of Davis's contributions done by the *San Francisco Chronicle*, dating from May 2002 and going back to his days as controller, found that labor unions had given him $7.3 million, followed closely by the real estate industry, which gave $6.3 million. At least 14 other industries had contributed more than a million dollars to Davis over his career, including Hollywood ($4.9 million), banks ($4.6 million), health care providers ($3.4 million), telecommunications firms ($2.8 million), insurance companies ($2.4 million), and the energy industry ($2.1 million.) Indian tribes and other gambling interests gave $1.5 million.[13] All these interests had private financial stakes that were affected by the actions of California government and all of them saw giving money to Davis as a way to further those private interests.

Davis's constant fundraising undermined voters' faith in him personally and in California government in general. As the *San Francisco Chronicle* editorialized two years after Davis was elected governor, "For all his political skill in other areas, Davis seems to have a tin ear when it comes to public perception of his fundraising frenzy. His tactics create the image of a cash-hungry governor who has chosen to enlist big interests rather than grassroots voters in his political army."[14] The following spring, national reformer Senator John McCain came to California and denounced Davis's $26 million in fundraising as "disgraceful."[15]

Opposing Reform

It would have been one thing had Davis simply played as hard as he could under the current rules of the game. Given that he could face opponents who could spend tens of millions of dollars, it would have been unfair to ask Davis to hold himself to a higher standard than other politicians and disadvantage himself by not raising money that was after all perfectly legal for him to accept. But Davis also worked to prevent changes in the rules that might have reduced the role of big money in politics.

In 2000, Silicon Valley millionaire Ron Unz spent more than a million bucks to qualify a campaign finance reform proposal for the ballot, Proposition 25. Unz had bankrolled the successful Prop 187 a few years earlier to ban bilingual education in California's schools. He was looking to run for the U.S. Senate himself, and the campaign finance initiative was a way to burnish his credentials.

In some ways, the Unz measure was flawed. It set limits on contributions to candidates at $3,000 for legislative races and $5,000 for statewide races. These were higher than limits set by most states and obviously still way beyond the reach of 99 percent of Californians who could maybe afford to give $50 or at most $100 bucks if they really felt strongly about a candidate.

But Unz was reluctant to set lower limits because of the fact that contribution limits do make it harder for candidates such as Gray Davis to compete with millionaire candidates such as Al Checci, or Ron Unz for that matter. This is because the current Supreme Court interpretation of the Constitution is that you cannot place any limits on millionaire candidates spending their own money to buy themselves credible campaigns, and sometimes successful ones. In the infamous 1976 case *Buckley v. Valeo*, the Supreme Court allowed limits on contributions that a candidate like Davis can accept but it threw out a law that set limits on what candidate can spend overall.

In setting limits low enough to really return politics to the average citizen, Unz might have looked self serving. He'd be free to spend as much as he wanted to if he ever ran for governor, while others could collect smaller amounts from their donors. But Unz added in other measures, like providing public funds for ballot measures that agreed to abide by spending limits.

Davis organized conference calls of lobbyists and business executives and asked them to contribute money to kill Prop 25, telling them that if it passed it would be easier for consumer groups to win ballot measures against them. Davis triumphed as Prop 25 went down to defeat with only 35 percent of the vote.

The Energy "Crisis"

Davis's lack of credibility as a governor who would stand up for ordinary citizens against powerful interests proved devastating to his ability to address the biggest crisis he faced while in office: the California blackouts and out-of-control electricity price increases of 2001. Davis had done nothing to cause the crisis, but he also failed to solve it.

California had deregulated its energy markets with a bill passed in 1996 by a Democratic legislature and signed by Republican Governor Pete Wilson. Consumer groups such as the

Foundation for Taxpayer and Consumer Rights opposed the deal, but it passed nearly unanimously.

Enron, the now bankrupt and disgraced energy company, used massive campaign contributions to pave the way for the deregulation for energy markets in California and across America. Twenty-four states had deregulated in the course of four years. Enron invested $1.1 million in contributions to state and local candidates to make it happen. Enron's Jeffrey Skilling had come to California in 1994 to testify before the legislature that deregulation could save almost nine billion dollars. He told legislators that with the money saved, "you can triple the number of police officers in Los Angeles, San Francisco, Oakland, and San Diego. . . . The stakes are huge and every minute that we delay bringing competitive markets to California allows the meter to keep ticking."[16]

It sounded too good to be true.

It was.

In 2001, when the deregulation began taking effect, prices began to skyrocket in California. The problem began in San Diego, but eventually spread across most of the state. Even in winter months that typically had lower demands for electricity, energy shortages caused California to adopt a policy of rolling blackouts to keep its electricity grid from crashing entirely.

Federal and state investigators later learned that the energy "crisis" was not a crisis at all, but rather the result of market manipulation by Enron and other energy traders. Through schemes with names like "Fat Boy" and "Get Shorty," energy traders would buy gobs of California's power and ship it out of state. When the artificial shortage they had created caused prices to spike in California, they turned around and re-imported power back into the state. Other schemes involved intentionally shutting down power plants for bogus maintenance operations to create fake shortages that again drove prices through the roof.

As the crisis mounted, Enron and others waged a full-out public relations campaign to deflect blame away from themselves and instead fault California's failure to completely deregulate all of its markets. Vice President Dick Cheney joined them by scoffing that California deserved what it was getting after decades of strong environmental protections had kept companies from building new power plants. He derided conservation as nothing more than a personal virtue, not a serious means for dealing with energy policy.

According to Davis spokesman Steve Maviglio, Enron CEO Ken Lay spoke with Davis "many, many times" over the course of the crisis.[17] Lay also met with Arnold Schwarzenegger in secret discussions, although neither side to this day has revealed what was said.[18] Likewise, Lay was invited to meet with Vice President Cheney on his energy task force. Cheney went all the way to the Supreme Court to prevent the watchdog group Judicial Watch from learning the details of what Lay and Cheney discussed.

Energy companies like Enron reaped obscene profits while Californians got ripped off and Gray Davis saw his career go up in smoke. A disastrous end to Gray Davis was not only a boon to Arnold Schwarzenegger, who had begun talking about a 2006 run for governor as early as 2002. It also benefited George W. Bush because Davis had been widely seen as a potential Democratic contender to run against Bush for the presidency in 2004. Further, the faked energy shortage helped drum up political support for Bush's national energy plan that called for increased domestic energy production through drilling in the Arctic National Wildlife Refuge and offshore oil exploration.

Davis opponents certainly took the opportunity of the energy crisis to drag him through the mud. In 2001, American Taxpayers Association, a group run by Republican consultant Scott Reed, unleashed $1.8 million worth of ads blaming Davis for the rolling blackouts. The ads, called "Gray-outs, from Gray Davis" asserted that the governor was at fault for the crisis. While the ads did not urge voters to defeat Davis in the next election, Davis thought they were clearly politically motivated. Davis sued ATA to force them to disclose who had funded the ads, but the courts ruled against him.

In February 2002, *Newsweek* magazine reported that the ads were entirely paid for by Reliant Energy, one of the companies later found to be manipulating California's energy market. Reliant eventually agreed to a $50 million settlement with the Federal Electricity Regulatory Commission.

Whatever the cause of the energy shortage, Davis was slow to respond. In March of 2001 when the legislature was gridlocked on policy to address the energy shortage, Davis was in Palm Springs at a fundraiser. During the first six months of 2001, he maintained his million-dollars-a-month fundraising pace. During six different days when blackouts struck, Davis reported tens of thousands of dollars flowing into his campaign coffers.

Davis had received $600,000 from Enron and other energy companies in the two years before the energy shortage; other California politicians had raised $3.4 million more. All but one of 118 legislators in office during that time had taken money from energy companies. Southern California Edison alone had given $989,000 to California candidates for the 2000 election. Energy firms spent another six million dollars on lobbying during that period. Earlier in the 1990s, Davis had received $97,500 out of Enron's $438,000 in donations to politicians in California.

By 2001, the energy companies were vigorously lobbying Davis to say that the problem was with California's law, not their own reckless and criminal behavior. His penchant for taking the middle road and offending nobody may have kept him from taking bold action. Davis raised rates on consumers an average of 30 percent.

When in Doubt, Hire a Consultant

One move that Davis did take was to hire public relation gurus Mark Fabiani and Chris Lehane. This team had helped Bill Clinton finesse his way out of the Monica Lewinski scandal and had served as advisors to Al Gore's 2000 presidential campaign. They had become known as the go-to guys whenever a politician was in trouble, but they also did work for many corporate clients.

Although they had absolutely no expertise in energy issues, Davis brought Fabiani and Lehane onto the California state payroll for a whopping $30,000 a month as consultants to help manage the energy crisis. Normally, when new high-ranking employees are added to the government payroll, they fill out forms to disclose their financial interests. This allows news reporters and the public to investigate whether state officials have any personal financial conflicts of interest that might impair their ability to do their job.

Fabiani and Lehane had failed to file personal disclosure forms. We soon learned what Fabiani and Lehane had been hiding. They had both been on the payroll of Southern California Edison within months of being hired by Davis to handle the energy crisis. On June 22, 2001, I stood at a press conference with Republican Secretary of State Bill Jones and demanded that they file. I stated:

> Based on their recent disclosures, it certainly appears that Fabiani and Lehane have received substantial compensation from Southern California Edison and are now engaged as government officials promoting a policy that is clearly in Edison's self-interest. At a minimum, these individuals should be placed on the governor's campaign payroll, as others have previously suggested.
>
> But the larger issue is whether it's even appropriate for consultants with close business ties to the energy industry to be invited into the governor's office to help craft energy policy. How can the public know that these individuals are acting in the interest of California ratepayers and taxpayers when they are clearly tied to the private interests of a utility company? On this issue in particular, it's important for the governor not to blur the line between the public interest and private interests.[19]

How did Governor Davis expect to have any credibility in dealing with California's skyrocketing energy prices when he was bringing the industry's hired guns into his own administration to run the show?

Davis's poll ratings fell through the floor. By May 2001, only

36 percent of voters approved of how he was handling his job as governor.

The energy "crisis" came to an end when the Federal Energy Regulatory Commission agreed to impose price caps on the California energy market. Davis had been calling on FERC to do this for months, but to no avail. Patrick Wood III, whom Enron CEO Ken Lay had recommended for the spot to President Bush, chaired FERC. Within weeks of the FERC ruling, California had plenty of energy and Enron's financial house of cards began to collapse around it, now that it could no longer make outrageous profits in California to cover up its other financial fraud.

Enron's demise came too late to save Gray Davis. Voters believed he was ineffective in solving the problem and continued to see him in the pockets of big donors. As one Democratic consultant put it, "the voters have a snapshot of him in their mind from the time of the energy crisis and they don't like what they see. They see a governor who did very little to prepare them or warn them of what was coming, and they were left saying, 'How the hell did this happen?'"[20] Worse, the long-term contracts that Davis had signed to buy power at inflated prices were putting a significant strain on California's budget.

When Davis became governor, California enjoyed a budget surplus. By 2002, that had turned into a deficit of $34.6 billion. The combination of the energy crisis and the bursting of the Internet stock price bubble left California in a huge bind. It was yet another reason for voters to turn away from him.

Non-Davis Scandals Rock California as Well

It bears remembering that Davis was not alone in fueling voter disgust with California government. In 2002, Republican Insurance Commissioner Chuck Quackenbush resigned his office to avoid almost certain impeachment. Quackenbush had let 21st Century Insurance and other companies off with very light penalties of $100,000 after they had ripped off consumers following an earthquake in Northridge. The insurance companies then paid $6 million into a nonprofit entity that Quackenbush controlled. That nonprofit paid for TV ads that featured Quackenbush in a transparent attempt to boost his name recognition to help him run for higher office.

Voters also held the legislature in low regard after observing that politicians got into office primarily by toeing the line that big donors laid down. Energy companies had given $3.4 million to legislators and spent another $6 million lobbying them. Southern California Edison had given Assemblyman Rod Wright tens of thousands in campaign dollars, making them his largest single contributor. Edison spent $20,000 to take Wright on trips to South Africa and Europe, accompanied by their lobbyist. On one trip, Wright spent $7,000 in campaign funds on jewelry, which he listed as "campaign paraphernalia" on his disclosure forms.

With all this going against him, it might have been seen as a miracle that Gray Davis was re-elected in 2002. But rather than the hand of the almighty, it had more to do with the power of the campaign dollar. Quite simply, Davis won re-election by using his campaign war chest to take out his most viable opponent during the Republican primary.

Dirty Pool in the 2002 Republican Primary

Three men were chomping at the bit to take on Davis in 2002: Secretary of State Bill Jones, Los Angeles Mayor Richard Riordan, and investment banker Bill Simon. Jones was well respected and had significant experience in statewide politics, but he was not backed by wealthy donors and therefore was quickly seen as non-viable by the media. Bill Simon was a political neophyte, whose only claim to office was that his father had served in the Nixon administration. However, Simon had a personal net worth estimated in the hundreds of millions and he was prepared to spend lots of it on his campaign. Nearly all political observers on both the right and the left saw Riordan as the most qualified and most credible challenger to Gray Davis. Davis quickly came to the same conclusion.

In a move unprecedented in California politics, or anywhere else for that matter, Davis spent $12 million on TV ads in the Republican primary—almost as much as Riordan and Simon spent combined. Davis, in fact, spent more money to influence the Californian Republican primary than anybody else had spent to influence any Republican gubernatorial primary in the country. Davis's ads attacked Riordan for taking positions that Davis also held, such as being supportive of abortion and favoring gun control. Davis knew that attacking Riordan for these positions would hurt him with conservative voters in the Republican primary.

Voters were positively turned off. Emil Bernstein, a retired professor of biology, summed up public sentiment well with a submission to the *Sacramento Bee*:

> We, the people, are fed up with lies and broken promises. Why vote for either candidate when all are thick as thieves?
>
> Most of the candidates are men and women who sell their services to the highest bidders. How can candidates for offices, from the lowest municipal to the highest executive and legislative branches of government, talk to us about our democratic responsibilities when they spend millions on their campaigns, precluding all but the most powerful and well-connected from running? Gray Davis, for example, spent more money trying to influence the Republican Party outcome in the primary than other, lesser-known third party candidates could collect in a lifetime.[21]

Bernstein concluded that the only logical response was to boycott the election.

When the primary was over, Simon had beaten Riordan 49 percent to 31 percent. Bill Jones managed a mere 17 percent. Turnout was only 35 percent—the Davis attack ads had worked to keep many Republican voters home in disgust. One Republican campaign expert predicted that Davis would win the general election by 20 percentage points.[22]

Simon's fundraising could not keep pace with Gray Davis, as he lagged behind Davis right from the primary. Simon took a big hit in the fall, when the *Wall Street Journal* ran a story suggesting that he might have benefited from illegal tax shelters.

A Lackluster Victory

In the end, things worked as Davis had planned. His chief strategist, Garry South, had explained, "this is not going to be Gray Davis versus an opponent with no name. The voters are going to have to choose between Gray Davis and Bill Simon, and in the end they will choose Davis."[23] Davis won re-election in November 2002 with 47.4 percent of the vote compared to Bill Simon's 42.4 percent. Green Party candidate Peter Camejo garnered a surprising 5.3 percent even though Davis had refused to participate in any debates with Camejo present. The recall, however, would upset South's calculus. In that election, it really would be Gray Davis versus an opponent with no name. The first part of the recall was simply an up or down vote on whether or not Gray Davis should remain governor.

Davis was anything but triumphant. In 1998, he had received 4.8 million votes. In 2002, he earned only 3.5 million. Matt Welch, a free-lance writer from Los Angeles summed up the victory like this:

> He is a public official so despised, his own supporters call him "distinctly loathsome." He is a human being so colorless and stiff, people he describes as "great friends" (or "buen amigos") say they barely know him. He ran a campaign so dreary that turnout reached an all-time low, while third-party candidates made historic gains. He was a Democrat incumbent so weak that after outspending his inexperienced Republican challenger, Bill Simon, by two to one, in a state where Democrats enjoy an advantage of 1.4 million

> registered voters, he won by only 330,000 votes.
>
> Yet California Governor Gray Davis emerged from Tuesday's elections as arguably the most successful major Democratic politician in the United States and an early front-runner for his party's 2004 presidential nomination.[24]

Guess again.

CHAPTER 2

Total Recall

Californians Fire Their Governor

By February 5, 2003, Ted Costa had seen enough of Gray Davis. Davis had served just 30 days of his second term when Costa filed a petition to recall the governor. The recall would send a shock wave through California politics and put politicians across the country on notice that citizens were prepared to take serious measures to shake up a government that had lost their trust. It would pave the way for a bodybuilder and actor with no political experience to oust one of the most seasoned politicians in America. It would create a political climate conducive to significant political reform, if politicians were ready to embrace it.

Costa directs the People's Advocate, a taxpayer group that carries the legacy of Paul Gann, who along with Howard Jarvis led the effort to enact Proposition 13 in 1978. Prop 13 cut property taxes by 60 percent and made it harder for government to increase property taxes in the future. The effort also re-ignited the modern era of ballot initiative politics. Costa's recall petition listed the huge budget deficit, the increase in the car tax, the loss of jobs, and the role of special interests in the Davis administration as reasons for voters to fire their governor.

While filing a recall petition so soon after Davis had won re-election struck some as sour grapes, many Californians did not see Davis's November 2002 victory as legitimate. He had barely beaten Bill Simon, a political rookie, who made huge blunders during his campaign. Had Davis not spent $12 million to defeat Richard Riordan in the Republican primary, it is quite likely that Riordan would have gone on to defeat Davis in the general election. For many voters, the best man had not in fact won. Even Peter Schrag, an editorial writer who detests both the recall and initiative process, acknowledged that Davis had contributed to the "anything goes atmosphere" in California politics by his meddling in the Republican primary.[1]

Costa's filing did not immediately alarm Governor Davis. Few people in the political establishment gave it much thought at all. Every California governor for the past 30 years had faced a recall attempt; Davis had already seen two recall petitions come and go during his first term. Two California legislators had been recalled in 1995, but you had to go back to 1914 to find the next example of a successful recall of any California legislator. Only one governor in the history of the United States had ever been recalled—Lynn J. Frazier from North Dakota back in the 1920s.

History of the Recall

The recall appeared at the very initial stages of democracy in America but its origins may date back to the ancient Greeks. The colony of Massachusetts included a recall provision in its charter, as of 1631. A couple of other states included the recall as part of their state constitutions, enacted after the revolution. The Articles of Confederation, which predated the current United States Constitution, contained provisions for recall as well, although they were not utilized.[2]

But even in America's early days, the recall was a contentious idea that was hotly debated between two schools of thought that continue to argue about it today. One school, the populists, take seriously the Declaration of Independence's "We the People" and the promise of a government *of* the people and *by* the people as laid out in President Lincoln's Gettysburg Address. These small "d" democrats believe in the basic premise of democracy: that citizens are inherently sovereign and have not only the right but indeed the best collective wisdom to govern themselves. The opposing school, the elites, believe in government *for* the people, but one run by qualified experts. These small "r" republicans fear a direct democracy and instead champion a representative republic where the people play some role in selecting educated and experienced decision-makers who run the country based upon their good conscience, not upon the whims of the uneducated masses. Most citizens see some merit to both of these opposing viewpoints. Our modern-day government is a combination of both approaches.

Even back at our nation's founding, populist thinkers favored the recall because it gave the people the ability to hold their representatives accountable between elections. John Lansing, an Anti-Federalist who opposed the Constitution as too elitist, said that U.S. Senators "will lose their respect for the power from whom they receive their existence, and consequently disregard the great object for which they are instituted" without the ability of states to recall them.[3]

Alexander Hamilton headed the elites, known as Federalists at the time. He feared the recall for exactly the same reason. The recall "will render the senator a slave to all the capricious humors among the people," he said.[4] Hamilton wanted politicians to be free to govern without political pressure from their constituents.

During the Constitutional Convention of 1787, the Federalists successfully eliminated the recall features that had been in the Articles of Confederation. In the post–Revolutionary War government under the Articles of Confederation, the recall had been limited to a state legislature's ability to recall that state's U.S. senators. The people, who did not directly elect U.S. senators, had no role. During the debate over ratification of the Constitution, the lack of a recall was one reason that some Anti-Federalists opposed it. Rhode Island, the last colony to ratify the Constitution, called for an amendment to establish the recall process as part of its decision to join the union. Virginia's legislature later proposed constitutional amendments to create a recall, but eventually the idea lost steam.

At the dawn of the 20th century, populists revived the idea of the recall along with other tools of direct democracy like the citizens initiative and referendum. In California, John Randolph Haynes championed the concepts of citizen initiative and recall by forming the Direct Legislation League of Los Angeles in 1900. Haynes reportedly took his inspiration from Switzerland. Haynes told a charter commission, "inefficiency, extravagance, and corruption characterize the management of city affairs by and for interested cliques, while the mass of the citizens are helpless 'til the next election."[5]

By 1903, Los Angeles had adopted a recall process as part of its city charter and in 1909 voters kicked out the corrupt Los Angeles Mayor A.C. Harper in the first California local recall election.

Populists formed the Lincoln–Roosevelt League to promote a statewide California recall process in 1905 as one of many responses to the ironclad grip on power held by the Southern Pacific Railroad and rampant corruption in state and local politics. As one reformer put it:

> There was only one kind of politics [in California] and that was corrupt politics. It didn't matter whether a man was a Republican or a Democrat. The Southern Pacific Railroad controlled both parties, and he either had to stay out of the game altogether or play it with the railroad.[6]

The Lincoln–Roosevelt League recruited Hiram Johnson to run for governor in 1910. He had prosecuted corruption cases that convicted San Francisco boss Abraham Reuf. The Democrats ran Theodore Bell, who also opposed Southern Pacific. Reformers believed that a Republican had a better chance of winning so they convinced Johnson to compete in the Republican primary. Johnson made the creation of the initiative process and the recall the centerpiece of his governorship. In his inaugural address, Johnson said:

> While I do not by any means believe the initiative, the referendum, and the recall are the panacea for all our political ills, they do give to the electorate the power of action when desired, and they do place in the hands of the people the means by which they may protect themselves.[7]

Progressives believed in the recall and initiative process philosophically, but now that they had their own man in as governor, they might have been tempted to try to hold on to power. But to the contrary, the progressives saw the recall as their own insurance policy in case the Southern Pacific Railroad managed to put their own politicians back in office. The legislature readily approved the initiative and referendum process and, after much debate about applying the recall to judges (and deciding to do so), eventually adopted the recall, with 106 legislators voting in favor and only 14 opposed. In 1911, voters approved constitutional amendments to establish the recall and the citizens initiative in a special election that Hiram Johnson had called for that purpose.

Initial Skepticism

By 2003, the idea of the recall was largely forgotten. Voters were not enthused about the idea. In April of 2003, 67 percent of voters had an unfavorable opinion of Governor Gray Davis but 59 percent of them said that recalling him was a bad idea. To qualify for the ballot, Costa and his People's Advocate organization needed to gather signatures equal to 12 percent of the votes cast in the last election. That amounted to 897,156 valid signatures—a daunting task.

Even Republican leaders at first dismissed the idea of recalling Davis as either pie in the sky or irresponsible. The *Washington Post* reported, "The Republican gadflies promoting it lacked cash and public support. Even many GOP leaders scoffed at their audacious goal. Recall the newly re-elected Democratic governor in a state his party dominates? Dream on."[8]

Bill Whalen, of the conservative Hoover Institute, asked, "Why recall Davis at this critical juncture in state history? And won't dumping him in this manner just lower the level of discourse of state politics? . . . If Davis is recalled and replaced with a Republican governor, will Democrats target GOP lawmakers and engage in a tit-for-tat retaliation? Will Republicans then feel forced to respond in kind?"[9]

The elites were getting nervous.

Issa Steps Up

Congressman Darrell Issa forever changed the dynamic of recalls in California by giving the People's Advocate a much-needed boost on May 15, 2003. Issa announced that he would personally dump hundreds of thousands of dollars into a signature gathering effort to qualify the recall petition. California's electorate has grown so huge that using direct mail and paid signature gatherers have become necessary to qualify initiative petitions for the ballot. Issa's commitment would provide much of the fuel that the Costa effort needed to qualify the recall.

Earlier in life, Darrell Issa made a small fortune by selling car alarms. It is possible he knew a thing or two about the need for such devices, as when he was 27, he and his brother were charged with a felony count of stealing a Mercedes. The charges were later dropped, but perhaps that's where Issa got the idea that it would be really neat to have sirens going off on every street in America whenever somebody touched anyone else's car.

"When people ask me why I got into the car alarm business, I tell them the truth. It was because my brother was a car thief," said Issa.[10] Gray Davis operatives made sure to leak this information to the press as the recall petition gained momentum.

Issa entered politics in 1998 when he spent $10 million of his own money to run for the U.S. Senate. He lost the Republican primary to Matt Fong, who went on to lose to Barbara Boxer in the general election. Issa also championed Proposition 187, an effort to deny state benefits to illegal aliens. In 2000, Issa bought himself a seat in Congress by spending $3.6 million of his own money to defeat Peter Kouvelis, who spent only $20,000. But Issa's ambitions were higher than a seat in the U.S. House of Representatives. He would eventually spend $1.71 million to qualify the recall petition and then another $2.3 million on his own campaign to replace Gray Davis as governor.

Momentum Builds

By May 25, 2003, Ted Costa announced that he had turned in 18,000 signatures on the recall petition. A tiny amount, but Issa's inflow of cash meant that more would be coming. The Davis administration began taking the recall seriously.

On May 29, Davis ally Raquelle de la Rocha filed a complaint at the Federal Election Commission alleging that Issa had violated federal campaign finance laws by using money from one of the corporations he owned, Greene Properties, to fund the recall, and by soliciting large contributions to the recall from other donors.

The newly passed Bipartisan Campaign Reform Act prevented federal officeholders, such as Issa, from soliciting any funds beyond what they were legally allowed to solicit for their own campaigns. Federal law has banned candidates from receiving corporate contributions for more than a hundred years, and the new changes in the law prevented federal officials from raising contributions of more than $5,000 for state campaigns.

In her FEC complaint, de la Rocha argued that Issa had effectively solicited his own corporation to give money and that because donors he had spoken to had given amounts greater than $5,000, Issa had violated the law. Issa argued (1) that he had taken care not to ask for any specific amounts for the recall, and (2) since he controlled Greene Properties and California law did not prohibit corporate contributions to recall campaigns, he was therefore operating within the law. The FEC initially found reason to believe that Issa had technically violated federal campaign finance rules, but by a 4-to-1 vote decided on November 2, 2005, to take no action against him because the commissioners believed that the funds actually were Issa's personal money. However, the idea that elected officials should face limits on the funds they can raise from others to influence ballot campaigns would resurface later in California politics when members of Congress wanted to raise funds to defeat an initiative to reform the process for drawing political districts.

To stave off the recall, Gray Davis began doing what he

did best, asking for cash. By early June 2003, Davis had raised $344,000 to oppose the recall drive, including $50,000 from Jerry Perenchio.

Davis allies began circulating a counter-petition calling for Davis to stay in office. While the document had no legal effect, their purpose was to hire so many professional signature gatherers that there wouldn't be enough people left for the recall proponents to hire. Rather than hoping that citizens simply wouldn't sign, Davis was again up to his old tricks of using money to try to prevent voters from having a meaningful opportunity to support or oppose his rule.

Davis allies also ramped up the Chicken Little rhetoric about the disastrous consequences of recalling a sitting governor. "We're telling voters this is a choice between democracy and anarchy," said Dan Terry of the firefighters union, who was leading efforts to defeat the recall.[11] Democrats tried to spin the numbers by saying it was impossible for the proponents to make it. "It will be impossible for them to keep up the astronomical pace that they're claiming," said Carroll Wills, who headed up a pro-Davis group, Taxpayers Against the Governor's Recall.[12]

But it was far from impossible. By June 12, recall proponents were claiming to have 700,000 signatures turned in, with more being processed daily. A majority of voters now told pollsters that they favored the recall and only 21 percent approved of Gray Davis.[13] Signatures began pouring in over the Internet with recall organizers claiming that 20 percent of their signatures came in from petitions sought via the web and e-mail.

Davis had committed no crime, but many voters were ready to be done with him anyhow. Among ten reasons to recall Gray Davis, one group listed his special interest fundraising as reason number one:

> **1) Very Questionable Fund-raising**
> Last year, Republican gubernatorial candidate Bill Simon ran television spots during his campaign against Davis in which average Californians were depicted approaching Davis's secretary. Each asks

> to speak to the governor and is turned away in favor of a shady man bearing a briefcase of cash. Finally, a small boy approaches with his piggy bank. The secretary takes the bank, holds it up and shakes it, and tells him, "Keep saving, kid."
>
> The ad may actually have been an understatement.
>
> In January 2002, Davis signed off on an astounding 34 percent pay increase for state corrections officers. Just weeks later, the prison guards' union contributed $251,000 to Davis's campaign. Their contribution, argues former state GOP chairman Shawn Steel, "bought the prison-guard union of 26,000 a billion-dollar pay increase over the next six years."[14]

Other reasons for voters' disgust included Davis's handling of the California energy crisis, the budget deficit and how Davis had manipulated the numbers about it, and the tripling of the car tax. But even more profoundly, voters were beginning to feel like the recall could be the one tool they had to express their profound dissatisfaction with everything that was broken with California's political system.

Finally, they had the politicians running scared.

Timing

The question soon became not *whether* Gray Davis would face a recall election, but *when*. The California constitution required the lieutenant governor to call a special election within 60 to 80 days for a recall if a petition with sufficient signatures was turned in by September 3, 2003. Otherwise, the recall would be on the March 2, 2004, ballot.

If nothing else, a spring election would mean Davis could stay in office for another half year. Political pundits also generally believed that Davis would fare better in the spring of 2004 because the Democratic presidential primary would be held at the same time. George W. Bush would be running unopposed in the Republican primary. This would mean that voter turnout would tilt strongly Democratic, favoring Davis in the recall.

Prominent Democrats tried to slow the progress of the recall petition by announcing that they would not run in an election to replace Davis should he be recalled. State Treasurer Phil Angelides, State Attorney General Bill Lockyer, and U.S. Senator Diane Feinstein all announced in late June that they had no intentions of running. Democratic National Committee Chairman Terry McAuliffe warned on July 17, "I want the folks here in California to know that we are not going to have another Democrat on the ballot."[15]

The not-so-subtle threat to Democratic voters who were thinking about signing the recall petition was that if they really did it, they would have to choose between only Republicans to be the next governor.

Rick Hasen, a respected law professor who specializes in election law, published a column cautioning voters to consider problems of a recall election before signing a recall petition:

> First, if a majority of voters decide to recall Davis, his successor will be chosen at the same election by merely a plurality of the voters. The plurality rule means that if there are 20 candidates on the ballot, the candidate with the greatest number of votes becomes the next governor, even if that candidate polled only 10 percent or 20 percent of the votes. There are no primaries, no runoffs. . . .
>
> Second, in the campaign for and against the recall, usual campaign contribution limits are off. Anyone can give as much as they want for or against the recall, raising concerns about the potential for corruption. . . . Do we really want Davis and his opponents to be out there raising even more money? . . .

> Third, California voters may be left with no credible Democratic candidates on the ballot. . . . [and]
>
> Fourth, the form of the ballot may be confusing to voters.[16]

Hasen was certainly correct regarding his first two points. Should a majority of voters want to oust Davis, his replacement would be chosen on the same ballot. There would be multiple candidates (far more than 20) and the winner could be chosen by a slim plurality. It would be odd indeed if 45 percent of the voters wanted to keep Gray Davis as governor, but being short of a majority he would be booted from office only to be replaced by someone backed by only 15 or 20 percent of voters. Campaign contribution limits didn't apply to campaigns for or against the recall because, bizarrely, it was considered a ballot question instead of a candidate contest.

But people weren't scared. On June 16, 2003, Costa and his allies had a total of 376,000 signatures turned in. Ten days later it was up to 625,000 turned in with another 240,000 being processed. By July 8, Costa said he would be suspending his signature drive because he had enough. By July 14, he claimed to have turned in 1.6 million signatures, a number that eventually grew to 2.1 million signatures.

Gentlemen, Start Your Engines

On July 23, Secretary of State Kevin Shelley announced that election officials had certified 1,356,408 signatures on the recall petition—well above the 897,156 needed to qualify. The recall was on and scheduled for October 7.

The floodgates of democracy burst open as 247 candidates filed to run for governor. Gary Coleman from TV's *Different Strokes* tossed his hat in the ring, as did porn star Mary Carey, *Hustler* publisher Larry Flynt, retired meat packer Joel Britton, and physician Ronald Freidman. While many of these candidates weren't seen by either themselves or voters as serious, others were. Recall financier Darrell Issa joined the fray, and Bill Simon signed up for a second attempt at beating Davis.

On August 5, conservative state Senator Tom McClintock announced his candidacy. He proved to be a formidable, credible candidate that provided a real alternative for many voters on the right.

The next day, Lieutenant Governor Cruz Bustamante and Insurance Commissioner John Garamendi, both Democrats, announced they would run as replacement candidates should the recall be successful. This broke the former Democratic Party vow to refuse to offer any candidates. Garamendi would drop out two days later, clearing the field for Bustamante to be the sole Democratic alternative.

August 6 brought arguably the most suspenseful and exciting day of the short recall campaign. Arnold Schwarzenegger appeared on *The Tonight Show* and surprised the world by announcing that he would indeed run. Suddenly, anything seemed possible.

Darrell Issa bowed out the day after Schwarzenegger's entry, as did former Los Angeles Mayor Richard Riordan.

On the last day of filing, August 9, former baseball commissioner Peter Ueberroth filed papers to run as a Republican and poured in his own money to back a campaign. Writer Arianna Huffington announced her independent candidacy with the statement:

> I am running for governor to break the hold that special interests have on Sacramento. To give the voters of California an independent, progressive leader. My opinions are not for sale, and my support will not be on the auction block. I am also running because I believe that the only way things are going to change is if We the People become outraged—and mobilized to remake our democracy.

What Have Those Darn Voters Done Now?

The experts had a field day poking fun at voters who had been stupid enough to bring the "circus" politics of the recall upon themselves. Caltech professor Michael Alvarez said, "One way or another, it's going to be a mess," to have so many candidates on the ballot.[17] Leon Panetta, a former White House budget director and congressman, blamed voters for making California impossible for anyone to govern by passing so many ballot initiatives that tied the hands of politicians:

> I don't think there's any question it's democracy run amok. Our whole system of government is based on the theory that you elect leaders who then have to exercise good judgment to direct the state or direct the country. Now what you have is the worst fears of our forefathers. Instead of allowing our elective leaders to make these decisions, the people have taken matters into their own hands—and not to good effect.[18]

Bruce Cain, a political scientist at UC Berkeley, charged months before the election took place, and before anything could have gone wrong, that "California's recall laws, like Florida's recount procedures, were an accident waiting to happen." Cain suggested that California raise the signature threshold for qualifying recall petitions to make the process less "user friendly."[19] One could practically hear early elites like Alexander Hamilton rolling over in their graves at how disastrous American politics had become with mob rule running roughshod over enlightened rulers who were trying to do the right thing for the people.

Experts made dire predictions of lower voter turnout, plurality winners, long lines due to fewer polling places, confused voters who couldn't understand the lengthy ballot, and spoiled election results due to hanging chads and malfunctioning touch screen voting machines. Given the problems in administering the previous presidential election in Florida, the concerns were not unwarranted. Just what had the people gotten themselves into?

The possibility that someone could win with a relatively small share of the vote was very real indeed. One solution would have been to hold a runoff election between the top two candidates, but the California constitution did not provide for runoffs in recall elections. The city of San Francisco had eliminated the need for separate runoff elections to achieve a majority winner by adopting a system of Instant Runoff Voting. This allowed voters to rank three candidates in order of preference on one initial ballot. A computer could then conduct a virtual runoff by using people's ranked choices. Instant Runoff Voting would have led to a majority winner in the recall, but there was no way for the legislature to enact this change in time for the October election. Nor is there any indication that the legislature would have adopted this change—politicians seemed to prefer antiquated voting systems that make the recall process less workable.

Big Money Campaigns

While money in politics was chief among the reasons why people were upset with Gray Davis, the recall began looking like business as usual. Arnold Schwarzenegger pumped $10 million of his own money into his campaign. Four of the ten million came in the form of loans that his spokesman said would be repaid by donors after the campaign was over. Watchdogs like Jim Knox of California Common Cause complained that this would deprive voters of knowing who many of Arnold's financial backers were. "This prevents the public from knowing the identity of a candidate's financial backers until after the election, and also creates the impression that those contributions will be more influential," he wrote in an e-mail to reporters.[20]

Schwarzenegger replied by saying that voters would just have to take his word that his donors would all be wholesome people:

> You know something, when the voters vote for me they're voting for me because they trust me. Always when you vote for somebody you have to have trust. I will always let anyone know whatever checks come in. They can see it. What does it matter if they read it now? . . . If it is before or after the election, the rules will stay the same. I will not take money from the special interests, from any of the unions, or Indian gaming.[21]

But trust is something that must be earned and Arnold was already giving voters reason to doubt that trust. Despite his initial statement that he had enough money and wouldn't need to ask other people for money, Arnold raised $16 million from other donors. These included:

- Donald Bren, head of the Irvine Company, and his wife each gave Arnold $21,200. Real estate and developer interests wound up accounting for 14 percent of Schwarzenegger's campaign donations.[22]

- The Hilmar Cheese Company kicked in $21,200. Hilmar had major interests with the state ranging from milk pricing to regulation of pollution from its plant.

- Car dealers gave a total of $800,000 to Arnold's committees. His promise to repeal the car tax was appealing to them because it would spur new sales.

- Paul Folino of the tech company Emulex gave Arnold $100,000 for his pro-recall campaign. Schwarzenegger subsequently tapped Folino as an economic advisor on his campaign. Folino had also contributed to Arnold's Prop 49 ballot campaign in 2002.

- Tim Blixseth of Rancho Mirage gave Arnold $100,000 for his pro-recall committee. Blixseth's firm, Yellowstone

Development LLC, had faced numerous fines and sanctions from environmental agencies in Montana for polluting the Gallatin River and filling in wetlands without permits. One had to wonder why someone like this wanted Arnold in the governor's office. In reference to Schwarzenegger's pledge not to take money from special interests, Sierra Club spokesman Carl Zichella said, "as far as we're concerned, they don't come any more special than guys like Tim Blixseth."[23]

$ $ $

DONOR PROFILE: Alex Spanos, a major real estate and apartment developer from Stockton and owner of the San Diego Chargers, gave $200,000 to Arnold's pro-recall committees. Since 1999, Spanos has given more than $8.75 million to California political committees. Spanos gave more than $300,000 to Bill Simon's 2002 campaign, $2.25 million to Schwarzenegger's California Recovery Team, and $2.8 million to the California Republican Party. His family has given an additional $2 million to federal candidates and parties. He raised more than $100,000 for George W. Bush in 2000 and more than $250,000 in 2004. In 2004, he also gave $5 million to the national electioneering group Progress for America that helped Republican candidates. In addition to giving cash, Mr. Spanos makes his corporate jet available to politicians for luxurious travel. Spanos received $78 million in taxpayer funds to renovate the Charger's stadium in 1997. In 2004, *Forbes* estimated his net worth at $1.1 billion, placing him at 320 of the 400 richest Americans.

$ $ $

Arnold tried to explain away the contradiction between his

campaign promises and his fundraising reality. Schwarzenegger stuck to his rhetoric that, "Any of those kinds of real big, powerful special interests, if you take money from them, you owe them something." But then Arnold claimed that taking money from corporations wasn't a problem because, "I don't promise anyone anything. There's no strings attached to anything."[24]

Larry Noble of the Center for Responsive Politics described Arnold's dance as:

> Defining a special interest as 'somebody who supports my opponent.' Corporations are also concerned about actions by the state, environmental regulation, safety regulations, taxes. He's saying that he, unlike anybody else, just will not be influenced by it. But they're all contributing because they want something.[25]

Schwarzenegger spared no expense on his campaign. He hired some 80 campaign staff and traveled the state on corporate jets while other candidates traveled Southwest Airlines. In a foreshadowing of disappointments still to come, the *Santa Maria Times* editorialized just days before the election that:

> Schwarzenegger, in a slick political move, is borrowing campaign funds from a Beverly Hills bank, which gives him a very favorable interest rate. His spokesman said the loans will be repaid by contributors—after he wins the election—which means the actor is saving his special-interest linkage until he becomes governor.
>
> And that from a guy who promised early on that he would finance his own campaign so as not to be beholden to special interests. So much for early promises.
>
> It's revealing how non-traditional candidates become more like the people they want to replace as the campaign moves toward conclusion.[26]

Cruz Bustamante came under even heavier critique than Schwarzenegger for the massive amounts of money he raised from Indian tribes flush with money from their casino operations. During the first week of September 2003, Bustamante raised $2 million from a single tribe, the Viejas. All in all, of the $14 million Cruz raised for his candidate and ballot campaigns, $8.2 million came from tribes. When the figure was lower early in the campaign, Arianna Huffington asked, "Does anyone think they've given him $3 million expecting nothing in return?"[27] Bustamante announced that he favored lifting both the cap on the number of slot machines any tribe's casino could operate as well as a moratorium that was hampering about 35 tribes who wanted to open up new gambling operations. Nelson Rose, of Whittier College, said that the tribes' contributions amounted to "such a cheap bet. In return they get a monopoly on a casino industry that this year alone is going to make $4 billion or $5 billion."[28] Even assuming that Bustamante truly wanted to help the tribes and did not change his policy position due to their donations, their contributions to him were a key part of his strategy for being elected.

Schwarzenegger hit Bustamante hard for his links to the tribes. He aired an ad saying that the tribes "make billions, yet pay no taxes and virtually nothing to the state. . . . It's time for them to pay their fair share. . . . I don't play that game. Give me your vote, and I guarantee you things will change."[29]

Schwarzenegger spokesman Todd Harris said that Arnold meant no disrespect for Indians. "The people have a right to expect their politicians won't be bought and paid for by the highest bidder. This ad is not about the tribes. This ad is about the politicians."[30]

Arnold's staff confirmed privately that the ad was a success and that their polling numbers showed "strong movement on the recall question and toward Arnold when that ad aired."[31] One month after the campaign began, Bustamante was leading Schwarzenegger by a margin of 35 percent to 22 percent, but he went downhill fast.[32] Bob Stern suggested that the tribes had squandered some of their traditional goodwill with the voters by spending so much money on politics. "They have acted like a traditional special interest and they were regarded as different before this," he said. "People have a lot of sympathy for the tribes, but when they act like a traditional special interest, the sympathy goes."[33] The same held true for politicians that sided with the tribes.

For all their success in raising huge sums of money, neither Bustamante nor Schwarzenegger held a candle to Arianna Huffington and Tom McClintock by another measure. If the number of people willing to make a contribution to a candidate's campaign is one test of the true level of public support for a candidate, then those two were winning the race hands down. As of August 23, here were the numbers of donors each candidate had received contributions from:

Arianna Huffington	2,258 contributors
Tom McClintock	1,158 contributors
Arnold Schwarzenegger	426 contributors
Peter Ueberroth	250 contributors
Cruz Bustamante	155 contributors

By the end of the campaign, both Schwarzenegger and Bustamante had gained ground in the number of their donors, but it remained the case that McClintock had a few more supporters than Arnold, and Huffington had more than Bustamante. The following chart lists the top contenders by number of donors as of the end of the campaign, total spent by the end of the year (which includes donations received after the election was over to pay off debts) and the average contribution per donor. Bustamante's

	Donors Through 10/7/06	$ Raised Through 10/7/06	$ Spent Through 12/31/06	Avg. $/ Donor
Schwarzenegger	5,143	$18,829,066	$21,915,465	$3,661
McClintock	5,298	$1,962,618	$2,323,135	$370
Huffington	3,119	$833,685	$1,092,384	$267
Bustamante	2,693	$5,816,501	$14,440,520	$2,160
Camejo	274	$45,865	$76,395	$167

spending includes the spending of his No on 54 committee, which featured Bustamante in its ads.

However, because Huffington and McClintock raised most of their money from regular people who could only afford to give small contributions, the real fundraising edge went to those candidates who could raise huge chunks of cash from wealthier donors and special interests.

The massive spending helped make the case for changing the rules. Paul Ryan, at the time a colleague of Bob Stern's at the Center for Governmental Studies, said, "The millionaires are helping to raise public awareness of the need for campaign finance reform. Until we institute systems of public financing at every level of government, we will continue to see a prominent role by millionaires and a very significant advantage for those wealthy individuals."[34]

Figuring Out the Details

The problems involved with administering an honest and accurate election also threatened to doom the recall. After the 2000 presidential election, California Secretary of State Bill Jones had ordered counties to phase out the punchcard voting machines that led to the problems of hanging chads and endless recounts in Florida. However, by 2003, most counties had not yet completed the transition. There was a strong possibility that many people's votes would not be accurately counted due to problems with the punchcard technology.

Perhaps worse, a few counties had replaced punchcards with touch screen machines, similar to an ATM. These machines could display ballots in many languages and were easier to use than punchcards for most voters, especially those with disabilities. Best of all, there were no hanging chads. But, as anyone who has ever had their computer freeze up due to a virus or other technical glitch knows, the problem was that these touch screen voting machines could fail. Unlike an ATM, these machines did not print out a paper receipt that would allow the voter to verify that the machine had in fact correctly captured their vote. Computer scientists warned that even a 15-year old could hack into some of these systems and vote multiple times, and that the lack of a paper trail would make a recount impossible in the event of a computer malfunction. County clerks could only respond that by pointing out potential problems with the new machines, "the scientists are undermining people's confidence in democracy."[35]

Due to concerns about the punchcard machines, a three-judge panel of the Ninth Circuit Court of Appeals suspended the recall election on September 16. The ACLU had filed a lawsuit alleging that 40,000 votes would be wrongly counted due to the punchcards and that California must postpone the recall until the following spring election. The judges were telling the world's sixth largest economy, home of Silicon Valley and the undisputed leader in technology, that it was too inept to hold an election. This was a boon for Gray Davis, who was appearing to make some progress in the polls.

Pundits and opinion leaders had different takes on the judge's ruling. The *Sacramento Bee* and *New York Times* applauded the decision. The *Bee* said, "the decision by the Ninth U.S. Circuit Court of Appeals to delay the recall election is a good sign that we have learned the big lesson of the Florida recount debacle of 2000."[36] The *Times* concluded, "It is a serious matter for a court to stop an election, but the federal appeals court that put off California's gubernatorial recall did the right thing."[37]

But the *Los Angeles Times* decried it, saying the cure was worse than the disease. The *Times* objected to the ruling because Los Angeles County Registrar Connie McCormack said it would be impossible for her to hold the recall election in the spring because she was also holding a presidential primary.

The nation that had put a man on the moon couldn't figure out how to hold two elections at once.

Yale Law Professor Bruce Ackerman, generally known as a liberal, provided a concise critique of the ruling. The court's action was simply unfair:

> By suddenly changing the finish line, the three-judge panel of the United States Court of Appeals for the Ninth Circuit disrupts the core First Amendment freedom to present a coherent political message to voters. Worse yet, the decision disrupts the First Amendment interests of the millions of Californians who have participated in the recall effort. State law promised them a quick election if they completed their petitions by an August deadline. . . . The Ninth Circuit enjoined the Oct. 7 election because of imperfections in the voting systems, even though they were the same systems that elected Davis in the first place—not once but twice. For some reason, the systems that put him in office are somehow not good enough to remove him from office.[38]

The folks in the black robes had second thoughts. On September 22, eleven judges of the Ninth Circuit Court of Appeals got together and reversed the order postponing the recall. This did not appear to be a partisan ruling; Democratic presidents had appointed eight of the eleven judges. The election moved forward as scheduled.

The Non-Disaster

A funny thing had happened along the way to the electoral disaster that experts had forecast for the California recall: democracy worked.

While the number of candidates who filed was indeed unwieldy, it turned out to be more of a blessing than a problem. The field of 247 applicants was immediately pared down to 135 after the rest failed to meet the basic signature qualifications. Candidates then began conducting their own self-selecting "primaries" as they looked at the polls and saw they had no chance of winning. Darrell Issa dropped out of the race the day after Arnold Schwarzenegger announced. Bill Simon dropped out of the race on August 23, followed shortly thereafter by Peter Ueberroth on September 9.

Prominent Democrats stayed off the ballot to give their Lieutenant Governor Cruz Bustamante a clean shot at replacing Davis should the recall succeed. Arianna Huffington dropped out of the race on September 30 and urged a no vote on the recall, but not until she had made a significant contribution to the debate. Tom McClintock stayed in the whole way, despite cries from Republicans to clear the field for Schwarzenegger. As a result, voters got real choices on Election Day for the first time in ages.

While big money played too large a role in the recall, its impact was considerably less than in most elections due to the massive amounts of news coverage that in many ways overwhelmed the paid advertising of the candidates. We learned that when important things are really at stake in an election and the media does its job, voters rise to the challenge and closely follow politics.

Media outlets and universities hosted a series of debates that were arguably better than anything staged in modern day politics. Unlike presidential debates that now screen out independent and third party candidates, the debate forums invited any candidate that was polling at ten percent support or more to attend. Voters got to hear from a variety of well-reasoned viewpoints that ranged from the principled conservatism of Tom McClintock, to the unbridled reform platform of Arianna Huffington, to Green Party candidate Peter Camejo's thoughtful positions on the environment and international justice. Arnold Schwarzenegger skipped the first three candidate debates, but rather than canceling them or refusing to cover them like media outlets normally do, they provided an empty chair to represent Schwarzenegger and allocated his time to the other candidates.

Arnold did participate in the final debate, although as a condition for doing so he insisted that all the questions be given to him ahead of time. Tom McClintock's campaign chair, John Feliz charged that "this should not be called a debate, it's a scripted forum."[39] Nonetheless, millions of voters watched as the event was carried live in California and repeated on cable news channels across the country as well as far off places like England and Japan. Some 500 reporters covered the debate and more people in

California watched it than the season opener of *The West Wing*.[40] More than nine out of ten voters reported viewing or reading about the debates and 64 percent said they were helpful in their decisions. A similar number reported seeing candidate TV ads, but only a quarter said that the ads were influential in their decision-making.[41] It was enough to make many people think that we could hold elections where candidates spend a whole lot less money if they'd only spend more time debating each other so that voters could really see what they were all about.

Arianna Huffington built upon voters' frustration with money in politics by making a proposal to enact full public financing of elections a centerpiece of her campaign. The states of Arizona and Maine had already adopted similar plans, which awarded public funds to qualified candidates who agree to completely abandon any fundraising from private interests. Huffington even filed a ballot initiative to enact this clean money system in the middle of her campaign. Much to her surprise, Cruz Bustamante endorsed the idea during the final debate. It was beginning to look like a new day for California politics.

As the recall campaign unfolded, a few pundits actually began sticking up for California voters and defending them from the ridicule that the national press was heaping on them for the crazy recall they had started. Bob Stern and Tracy Westen of the Center for Governmental Studies cheered the increased media attention to politics, saying:

> What all this means is that candidates won't be able to control the message through their own TV and radio spots as they could in the past. And they will get much more free exposure on TV and radio as well as in the print media than ever before. In all, campaign money will play less of a role for the candidates and for the voters. . . . This is the way that we had hoped elections would be: big turnout, free media, discussions around the water cooler, less emphasis on raising money and lots of ideas being debated. So instead of lamenting the recall election, let's celebrate it for reducing the

> importance of campaign money and increasing our interest in politics.[42]

State Librarian Kevin Starr had joined in the initial ridicule of the recall but then changed his mind:

> The atmosphere surrounding the recall election had deteriorated into a political circus. When a *Times* reporter asked me to answer the rising chorus of laughter and mockery directed at California, I threw my towel into the ring. This time, the Golden State had gone over the top. I couldn't defend it any longer.
>
> But I'm now retrieving my towel. The circus has become a grand opera. . . . Yes, Schwarzenegger's entry into the race was unorthodox, but he is a formidable political figure, as are Cruz Bustamante, Arianna Huffington, Bill Simon, Peter Ueberroth, Tom McClintock and Peter Camejo. Collectively, they suggest how rich our political resources are; in a real way, their candidacies honor California. . . .
>
> What seems to be going on in California, then, is not a political sideshow—and nothing to be defensive about.[43]

Finally, Bob Bauer, an election lawyer in Washington, D.C., who usually represents Democratic interests, wrote the following in the *Washington Post*:

> One cannot help noting the profound dissatisfaction expressed by media commentators with the recall process in California. This is what we hear—that it is "bizarre," a "circus" and, in one notable formulation, a "tragedy" masquerading as farce.

Yet, Bauer asked readers to consider the following benefits:

- **Competition**. Due to the great number of candidates and the low barriers of entry.

- **Limited partisanship**, because candidates could run as independents.

- **Short duration**, instead of the normal never-ending campaign.

- **Intense engagement by the electorate.**

- **Intense engagement by the media**.

- **And a "backlash against politics as usual.** The recall is being self-consciously directed against all of the purported ills of the last general election: heavy fund-raising, the role of special interests and negative advertising. This recall could be viewed as a virtual referendum on all of the evils of political campaigning as depicted in the reform movement."[44]

When October 7 came, the voters went to the polls. Disaster did not strike. Turnout was high, elections machines worked, and voters made their voice heard loud and clear. At the end of the day, they had voted to recall Governor Gray Davis and replace him with Arnold Schwarzenegger.

The sky did not fall. California politics did not turn into an ugly match of revenge recalls where Democrats suddenly tried to oust Schwarzenegger or other officeholders. A wave of recalls did not sweep the nation. Instead, democracy had run its course. Many Democrats were upset at the results, but many were not. According to exit polls, 25 percent of Democrats and 54 percent of independents had voted for the recall. Twenty-three percent of Democrats had even voted for Schwarzenegger.[45] Democratic Attorney General Bill Lockyer even admitted to voting for Arnold. Independents had given him 46 percent of their vote.

While Arnold did fall short of a majority win, his 48 percent gave him a reasonable mandate. Indeed, Arnold's 4.2 million votes amounted to 700,000 more than Davis had received in 2002 and Davis had won that race with only 47 percent of the vote. Tom McClintock received 13.5 percent of the vote. Had either instant runoffs or traditional runoffs been in place, these voters would likely have chosen Schwarzenegger over Bustamante in a rematch between these top two candidates.

Arnold had won, and in doing so he was taking steps to unite a terribly divided and bitter California. Three quarters of voters walked away from the experience feeling like it was a good thing that people had the ability to recall their elected officials. Half of the people surveyed in a poll said the recall had made them more enthusiastic about politics. People were beginning to believe in their government again for the first time in a long time, an outcome that none of the elite naysayers would ever have predicted could come of an unruly tactic like a recall election.

CHAPTER 3

THE MONEYMOON

Arnold Courts Democrats and Big Donors

When the dust of the recall had finally settled, things were looking up for California. Nationally, people continued to poke fun at Californians for electing an actor as governor, apparently forgetting California had done the same thing with Ronald Reagan. The jokes and fake Austrian accents seemed endless. But within the state, citizens were optimistic. The Golden State emerged proudly from a bizarre election with 135 candidates on the ballot and rules that would have allowed someone to win with less than 20 percent of the vote. To its citizens, California looked like a respectable-looking democracy where people had taken matters into their own hands and cleaned house.

The message to politicians everywhere was clear: "shape up or ship out!" Both Arnold and the Democrats in the legislature heard part of the message; they knew that voters wanted them to work together and avoid useless partisan bickering. But neither the Democrats nor Arnold heard the voters' demand to reduce the role of money in politics. Of if they did hear, they chose to ignore it.

Arnold Schwarzenegger emerged from the recall as a hero, winning a commanding victory and demonstrating strong support among Republican, Independent, and even Democratic voters. Democratic legislators were eager to work with Schwarzenegger lest he use his popularity against them in the next election. Nobody wanted to be the next Gray Davis. Even a Hollywood movie script could not have set up Arnold so well to succeed.

Arnold set a tone of cooperation and vowed to work with

both Democrats and Republicans in the legislature to get things done—just like the people wanted. Arnold struck a nonpartisan tone, saying he didn't care what people's ideologies were, he just wanted results. He also took some bold initial steps like repealing the car tax and terminating a proposal that would have allowed illegal immigrants to get driver's licenses.

Arnold was a man of action. He deemed himself the "Governator" and he was prepared to make things happen.

The Arnold Amendment

Schwarzenegger's initial popularity was so great that it wasn't long before people began talking seriously about amending the United States Constitution to allow U.S. citizens who were born on foreign soil but had been naturalized citizens for more than 20 years, such as Schwarzenegger, to run for president.

Orrin Hatch, a U.S. senator from Utah, had introduced just such an amendment on July 10, 2003, just weeks before Schwarzenegger announced his candidacy on *The Tonight Show*. Hatch said his amendment was not specifically designed for Schwarzenegger, but the two men are friends and Arnold had campaigned for Hatch in Utah.

The case for prohibiting bona fide U.S. citizens from running for president is dated at best. When the Constitution was adopted, some of the framers were concerned about rumors that Prussian or British royalty were planning to infiltrate the colonies, perhaps with a relative of King George to make a bid for the presidency. At the time, there was no uniform definition of citizenry as each colony was free to set its own rules. There were many Tory loyalists to England remaining in the colonies, and Austrian, Prussian, and Russian monarchies had in fact orchestrated a takeover of Poland, so at the time the fear may have been reasonable.

Even today, there might be valid reasons why Americans would not want foreign-born citizens to serve as president. Should we face a war with Austria, for instance, maybe we would conclude that we didn't want an Austrian-born person as our commander in chief. Arguably, the best defense against such a circumstance is voting. If voters were worried about a candidate's loyalty to America, we certainly wouldn't elect him or her.

But many believe that depriving ourselves of the opportunity to vote for somebody who might be the best person to lead our country is self-defeating. Looking beyond Schwarzenegger, we have had many talented foreign-born citizens serve our country that might well have been qualified for the presidency. Current Michigan Governor Jennifer Granholm was born in Canada. Henry Kissinger and Madeleine Albright have represented America as secretary of state without hindrance of their foreign birthplace. The list of foreign-born U.S. citizens who voters are barred from even considering for the presidency goes on and on, including Secretary of Labor Elaine Chao, Representative Peter Hoekstra, who chairs the House Intelligence Committee, and Florida Senator Mel Martinez who is general chairman of the Republican National Committee.

December of 2003 saw a brief buzz about the so-called Arnold Amendment, with stories running in the *San Francisco Chronicle* and *Scripps Howard News Service.* At TheRestofUs.org, we were excited too. While our primary mission was to reduce the role of big money in politics, we believe in promoting the people's right to run the country as they see fit, including voting for whomever they want to lead them. We purchased the Internet address of www.arnoldamendment.org and began building a website to educate citizens about such a constitutional amendment.

Lissa Morgenthaler-Jones, an Arnold donor from Silicon Valley, also set up a website, www.amendforarnold.com which began generating heavy traffic. Arnold played down any presidential ambitions, but earlier in his career when asked if he wanted to be president had said, "Yes, absolutely. Why not? With my way of thinking, you always shoot for the top."[1] His wife, Maria Shriver, was more negative. "Forget about it. It is not going to happen," she said, perhaps realizing that distancing the amendment from Arnold might be the only way for it to advance.[2]

Arnold Loses and Says, "Fantastic"

Arnold was on a roll, with nearly two-thirds of Californians approving of the job he was doing as governor. But it didn't take long for a few chinks in his armor to appear.

On January 26, 2004, Sacramento Superior Court Judge Loren McMaster ruled that a $4.5 million dollar loan that Schwarzenegger had given his campaign during the recall was illegal. The judge ordered Arnold to pay back the loan with his personal funds, not money he had raised from other donors.

Arnold's response? "Fantastic. We never wanted to raise money to pay it back."[3]

Come again? He was hoping he'd have to pay more money out of his own pocket? This was the first time that Arnold's credibility appeared to stretch a little thin.

Candidate loans to campaigns are problematic because when campaigns pay back those loans using money from private donors, the money goes straight into the candidate's own pocket. There's simply not much difference between that transaction and a bribe where a donor hands a politician a suitcase full of cash. Because of this concern, California law prohibits candidates from loaning more than $100,000 to their own campaigns.

The Fair Political Practices Commission had ruled in 2001, however, that candidates could take out loans from legitimate banking institutions so long as they do so at market rate. Political watchdogs condemned this practice because it meant that the donors who ultimately paid for a candidate's campaign wouldn't be disclosed until long after Election Day. In fact, those donors wouldn't even exist until the candidate had won office and began raising money to pay off his debt from donors eager to suck up to a new administration. Judge McMaster agreed with the watchdogs, saying "the public would not learn who financially contributed to the campaign until after the election, when it would be too late."[4]

This loan-payback technique is a particularly good way for lobbyists and other special interests that had backed another candidate in the election to win the good graces of the person who had won the election.

A final downside to these loans from a public policy point of view is that they are effectively only available to wealthy candidates. As Judge McMaster wrote, "The only persons who could obtain a loan on terms made available to defendant Schwarzenegger here—$4.5-million signature loan at prime—would have to be persons of independent wealth." Alternatively, loans might go to candidates with the ability to raise huge war chests, even if they lose, because they hold some other office. So, a California senate president could probably get a loan to run for attorney general because the bank would know that the senate president would still be in a position to raise big bucks should they lose their race for higher office. But for those candidates who aren't rich and powerful, a system of loan-financed campaigns just leaves them further in the dust.

Arnold's original excuse for taking out the loan was that he had been traveling on the campaign trail and hadn't been in Los Angeles to cut a personal check to his campaign. This is odd since the two bank loans were taken out, with Arnold's signature, in Los Angeles on September 19, a day when Schwarzenegger had no campaign events planned, and September 25, a day Schwarzenegger was in Los Angeles to receive the endorsement of Bill Simon. Schwarzenegger spokesman Rob Stutzman said that the papers hadn't necessarily been signed in Los Angeles or on the same date that the loans close, but you have to wonder how it was possible for some aide to bring Arnold some complicated bank papers to sign but impossible to bring him his checkbook.

Had Arnold in fact planned on paying back that loan out of his own pocket, he could certainly have done so long before January. Instead, he hired some high-priced lawyers and fought the effort to require him to pay back the loan. Judge McMaster ruled that the FPPC had been wrong in authorizing bank-backed loans to any candidate, and while he didn't fine Schwarzenegger for the violation, he did make clear that he needed to pay back the money out of his own wallet.

Lowell Finley, the lawyer who brought the suit against Schwarzenegger, was so incensed by Arnold's claim that losing the lawsuit was "fantastic" that he threatened to make public bank documents that he had received during the discovery phase of the lawsuit that implied Arnold would pay back the money with campaign funds he raised after the election. While the whole brouhaha eventually died down, it was the first indication that Arnold might not be quite as genuine a reformer as he had claimed to be.

Especially Interesting Campaign Cash

Other problems involving campaign cash began creeping up. Arnold had promised in the campaign not to take money from special interests. While his definition of special interest seemed to be a moving target, one group he had clearly said he would steer clear from was people with state contracts.

In December 2003, a consumer group revealed that Schwarzenegger had received a $50,000 campaign contribution from Affiliated Computer Services, Inc., a company with a contract with the controller's office to collect unclaimed property, as well as smaller state contracts. ACS had lobbied California to adopt its red-light camera technology to give people traffic tickets through the mail. Obviously, they had an interest in state government, and obviously Schwarzenegger had taken their money. On December 1, 2003, after the election, the company gave Schwarzenegger's Total Recall Committee $50,000. In September, the company had given $50,000 to the anti-recall committee, and previously had given $30,000 to Gray Davis. It looked like the very type of contribution that voters had found so troubling about Mr. Davis. ACS was now trying to get on the good side of the Schwarzenegger administration by helping him pay down his campaign debt.

Brent Wilkes, a computer and defense contractor in the San Diego area, contributed $22,300 to Schwarzenegger in September 2003. Wilkes' company, ADCS, held only a small contract with the state of California, doing most of its business with the federal government. But Wilkes was clearly angling to increase his business with the state. Schwarzenegger appointed Wilkes to the

Del Mar Racetrack Board in 2004 and the state Race Track Leasing Commission in 2005. Nobody knew it at the time, but Wilkes would later be named as one of the men who bribed Congressman Duke Cunningham in return for defense contracts. After Cunningham plead guilty to accepting bribes, Schwarzenegger asked Wilkes to step down from the boards, saying that any of his appointees must resign if they do anything that "is unlawful or not cool."[5] In February 2007, a grand jury charged Wilkes with providing Cunningham with boats, cash, vacations and even prostitutes as bribes.

In June 2004, an inexperienced Virginia-based computer company, CGIAMS, won a multi-million dollar contract to help California trim its five billion dollar purchasing bill. Two months prior to winning the contract, the company had given $25,000 to Schwarzenegger. CGIAMS had hired Schwarzenegger's chief fundraiser Marty Wilson as a political consultant. By spring of 2005, Democratic lawmakers were arguing that the company had saved the state little money and were calling for an audit of the program.[6] A California Senate investigation found that the company was supposed to have saved California $96 million but had only saved $8.5 million after nine months on the job. To those who had been around Sacramento a while, it smelled a little bit like the $25,000 that Gray Davis had received after giving a computer contract to Oracle.

$ $ $

DONOR PROFILE: The Irvine Company is one of the largest landowners and developers in California, tracing its roots back to a 185-square-mile land grant from the Mexican and Spanish governments in 1864. Several cities, including Newport Beach and Irvine, California, are now within the borders of the original Irvine ranch. Irvine gave more than $4 million to California political committees from 2000 to 2005, including $150,000 to Schwarzenegger's

California Recovery Team in 2004 and $250,000 to Citizens to Save California in 2005. Gray Davis raised more than $50,000 from Irvine. In addition to campaign contributions, Irvine has spent more than $2 million lobbying California decision-makers on dozens of bills since 2000. Donald Bren, the chairman of Irvine, is 38th on the Forbes 400 list, with an estimated net worth of $5.7 billion.

$ $ $

None of these contributions appeared to be illegal, but collectively they began undermining Schwarzenegger's claim that he didn't need anyone else's money because he was so rich and that he wouldn't take anything from anyone who had business with the state. Dan Schnur, a reform-minded Republican consultant who had run John McCain's 2000 presidential campaign in California, remarked near the end of June, "Voters didn't decide to trade in a boring governor for a celebrity governor, they decided to trade in a career politician for an outsider and reformer. Once he gets done with the necessary economic triage, I hope he'll get back to the reform agenda that got him elected." [7]

Big Bond Money

Big bucks really started rolling in by early 2004 when Schwarzenegger launched a huge campaign to pass two bond issues on the March ballot that were critical to his success as governor. In learning he could raise huge contributions for ballot campaigns, Schwarzenegger began walking down the path that Cruz Bustamante had blazed in raising money for his campaign against Prop 54 during the recall. It was a simple technique that allowed politicians to get around the restrictions on fundraising for their own campaigns.

The first bond question, Proposition 57, dealt with a $15 billion loan to cover a structural deficit that Schwarzenegger had inherited from past administrations. Rather than cut spending or raise taxes, Arnold wanted to borrow his way out of the problem. Proposition 58 was a budget cap measure intended to restrict future governors from doing the exact sort of deficit spending that Schwarzenegger was contemplating to dig California out of its budget hole. Arnold was going on a borrowing binge but then tearing up the credit card.

To pass these bond measures, Schwarzenegger created the California Recovery Team, a ballot committee that was able to work on multiple questions rather than just a single ballot measure. Showing that he could cross party lines, Schwarzenegger teamed up with Democratic Controller Steve Westly to raise money for the bonds campaign. Westly lent his name, but Arnold did the heavy lifting in fundraising.

And boy could he raise money. Arnold went to New York and joined with Governor Pataki to host a fundraiser on Wall Street where tickets ranged up to $500,000. Nobody could remember an event with prices that high, but Schwarzenegger's celebrity and charm opened up a whole new world of campaign cash. Blair Horner, who had tracked money in politics for two decades with the New York Public Interest Research Group (NYPIRG) told the *Los Angeles Times* that he had never seen solicitations of a half-million dollars before. "One Central Park West," he said of the address of one of the events. "That pretty much says it all; you're talking about one of the most elite ZIP codes in the country."[8]

It makes sense that Wall Street would be interested in helping to pass a $15 billion bond deal in California. Once the voters approved it, it would be the New York investment banks that underwrote the bonds, making millions in the process.

Back in 1994, when Kathleen Brown was running for governor of California, the bond industry's self-regulating group, the Municipal Securities Rulemaking Board, had passed internal rules that barred bond traders from doing business with any public entity for two years if the bond firm or any of its traders had made a contribution to any public official who helped issue the bond. But this prohibition didn't prevent other Wall Streeters from pouring huge chunks of cash into a campaign effort that would not only help the bond deal get passed but also bring the donors closer to Schwarzenegger.

Conservative California Republican Tom McClintock, who had run against Schwarzenegger in the recall and who opposed the bond deal as fiscally irresponsible, was also concerned. "If I was a New Yorker, I'd want to see those bonds passed. Wall Street types will be making all the money off the bonds," he observed.[9]

One of the New York events was held at the home of Robert Wood Johnson, a multi-billion dollar heir to the Johnson & Johnson fortune. Mr. Johnson personally gave Schwarzenegger's Recovery Team $25,000 and Johnson & Johnson would eventually kick in nearly $10 million to the pharmaceutical companies' California Initiative Fund. Johnson's donation appeared to be another violation of Schwarzenegger's promise not to take funds from interests with business before the state. Johnson & Johnson was registered to lobby on no less than nine pieces of legislation and negotiated with the state on issues like health care supplies for the Medi-Cal program.

Back in California, the Sacramento Kings owners, Joe and Gavin Maloof, got into the act by sponsoring a $25,000 ticket event for the governor. Donors were not only treated to box office seats with the Maloofs, they got to rub elbows with Arnold during the game. At the time, the Kings were angling for a new taxpayer-financed stadium in Sacramento.

All told, Schwarzenegger raised $5.3 million to pass Props 57 and 58 through his California Recovery Team out of the total $8.1 million raised to pass the measures. But Arnold didn't just raise money; he lent talent as well.

Schwarzenegger tapped Rick Claussen to run the campaign to pass the bond measures. Rick was one of two partners who had founded the public relations firm Goddard Claussen, which specialized in ballot campaigns and public opinion molding for corporate interests such as insurance companies and high-tech firms. Goddard Claussen's clients include General Motors, the Edison Electric Institute, and the National Association of

Broadcasters. Claussen's greatest claim to fame was his work to co-produce the "Harry and Louise" TV ads that helped torpedo former President Clinton's healthcare overhaul back in 1993. Mike Murphy, the political strategist who engineered Schwarzenegger's victory in the recall campaign also played a hand in shepherding the California Recovery Team.

With Arnold's charm, Wall Street's money, cooperation from the Democrats, and cunning from advisers like Claussen and Murphy, Props 57 and 58 passed with flying colors. They went from 33 percent and 49 percent in initial polling respectively to 50 and 55 percent support in pre-election polls to final passage of 63 and 71 percent.

Arnold had won his first major victory, boosting his popularity further and calming some of his early critics who had wondered if a body-builder turned actor had what it took to govern the world's sixth largest economy. In winning such a take-home victory, Arnold learned quickly that ballot initiatives could be an easy way for him to take himself and his agenda to the voters directly and come out ahead. Come fall 2004, he would again be heavily involved in ballot initiative politics.

The Chamber Keeps on Giving

In day-to-day governing, Schwarzenegger adopted a posture of moderation. He was pro-business, but also pro-environment. He was a Republican to be sure, but pro-choice. It was a winning formula for Arnold, and especially so for the California Chamber of Commerce.

Schwarzenegger had been the first candidate for governor that the Chamber had endorsed for statewide office in more than 100 years. During the campaign, he promised the Chamber he would "stand up to anti-business legislation."[10] Arnold championed the Chamber's agenda so strongly that after winning office, one of his early moves was to appoint the Chamber's vice president and chief lobbyist, Richard Costigan, as his legislative director. Talk about access! Now, instead of having to ask for meetings with staff in the governor's office as it had done in past administrations, the Chamber had its man on the inside who could not only feed them information, but could actively craft policy that would benefit the Chamber's members. Just hours after he was sworn in, Arnold sat down to a private lunch with big shots from the Chamber.

Most of us think of the Chamber of Commerce much like we think of the PTA—a local organization that represents homegrown businesses in our hometowns. What's good for the Chamber surely must be good for the rest of us.

But a closer look reveals that the California Chamber of Commerce primarily serves a handful of the most powerful multinational corporations in the world. Its board of directors includes representatives of oil companies BP, Chevron, and Shell; telecom giant AT&T; financial institutions like Ameriquest, US Bank, Bank America, Citibank, and Wells Fargo; Allstate, Pacific Life, and State Farm insurance companies; and mega-landowners like the Tejon Ranch and the Irvine Company of Orange County.

So, for instance, after the legislature enacted a law requiring California businesses to cover 80 percent of the health care coverage costs for their employees, the Chamber led efforts to repeal that law through a ballot referendum, Proposition 72 on the November 2004 ballot. The law exempted the mom and pop businesses of California that had fewer than 50 employees and was primarily aimed at powerful corporations like McDonalds and Wal-Mart, which offer many employees no benefits and count on taxpayers to make up the difference through programs like Medicare and Medicaid. Proponents of the health care plan spent $14 million to support the idea, but big business players including the Chamber spent $16 million against it, causing the measure to narrowly go down in defeat with 51 percent voting against it. Schwarzenegger had sided with the business interests. One month before the election, a poll found 45 percent of voters supporting the measure and 29 percent against. As is often the case with initiatives, a well-funded opposition campaign convinced most of the undecided voters to vote no.

Once they had their main man, Richard Costigan, leading

Schwarzenegger's legislative team, the Chamber lost no time wining and dining him and his staff to express their wish list of legislative favors. The Chamber gave Costigan a parting gift of a miniature model of the capitol building worth $589. Isn't that symbolism nice? They literally bought him California's capitol. The Chamber reported giving a total of 102 gifts to public officials in a 12-month period.[11]

Of course, the Chamber wasn't alone in giving gifts, which are currently limited to $340 in California. The Chamber got around this limit to give Costigan his capitol trinket by partnering with two other givers. Often corporations evade the $340 limit by leaving tickets for a public official's family at the "will call" box at the Kings arena, arguing that since neither the lobbyist nor public official physically gave the tickets to the family members it didn't count as a "gift."

Costigan accepted 24 gifts over 12 months. Oil behemoth BP gave Costigan's staff free tickets worth $246 to watch the Kings game in its corporate skybox. BP gave $3,580 in free tickets and other gifts to Schwarzenegger's administration in just six months. Phone company giant SBC gave out $324 worth of tickets to Disney on Ice. All told, Costigan's staff accepted more than $5,000 worth of gifts over a ten-month period. SBC alone would give nearly $4,000 in free tickets to various officials in the Schwarzenegger administration.[12]

Gray Davis, for all his ties to big campaign donors, had drawn a fairly bright line when it came to gifts. He had a written order that banned his appointees from accepting any gifts from interest groups that were lobbying them. "Over time, you'll feel the need to reciprocate," Davis explained. "The way to avoid any misimpression on the part of either party is to say 'I'd prefer to pay my own way.'"[13]

Schwarzenegger had relaxed Davis's standard back to the $340 legal limit. He even appeared to promote the idea of wining and dining on the lobbyist's tab. Schwarzenegger spokeswoman Margita Thompson said that gifts such as Kings tickets were actually part of Arnold's master plan because they could bring

Democratic and Republican legislators together to have a good time over dinner and drinks. "One of the things that has to happen to change the culture and create a more bipartisan atmosphere is that people have to talk to each other," she said. Thompson, who had personally received a free trip to Disneyland including meals, admission, and discounted hotel rates worth move than $300, also argued that sometimes feuding politicians' kids became friends at a sporting event and that helped the grownups get along better. The fact that corporate lobbyists were there just helped grease the skids of bipartisan cooperation all the more—so long as they were cooperating with what powerful business interests wanted.

Now, corporations aren't exactly known for their generosity. In fact, if their shareholders felt that they were giving away company money just for grins, you'd have a CEO fired faster than Donald Trump cuts loose a would-be apprentice. Corporations are required by law to maximize profits for their shareholders, not hand out charity or gifts that don't bolster the corporate bottom line.

Jack Coffey, a lobbyist for Chevron/Texaco, explained the gifts like this: "There's a lot of people who clamor for attention from various government officials, and having a relationship allows you to be higher on their calendar."[14] So, the next time you want to sit down and schedule a meeting with a member of the legislature, not even necessarily the one from your district, maybe you should bring along some NBA skybox tickets.

In the summer of 2006, right before his re-election, Schwarzenegger put an end to the practice of his staff accepting gifts from business interests. He did however, decide to pay several staffers (including Richard Costigan) salary bonuses from campaign accounts that were filled with contributions from the business community.

The Governor's Home Away from Home

While Arnold's staff enjoyed their share of the high life, the biggest gifts of all were reserved for Arnold himself. As a Hollywood big shot, Arnold had grown accustomed to an expensive lifestyle. Who wouldn't? Fun cars like the Hummer, lavish meals, fancy digs in the best hotels—we'd all enjoy them if we could. It's hard to fault a man for living the good life, so long as he's doing it on his own nickel.

Gray Davis had lived in a simple two-bedroom condo in Los Angeles and when in Sacramento had stayed in a suburban ranch-style house that served as a temporary governor's residence. California has not had a functional governor's mansion since the 1960s, when Nancy Reagan insisted that her family move out of the white gingerbread Victorian house on 16th and H streets, claiming that it was a fire trap. Periodically, someone takes up the call to build a permanent governor's mansion, but in the meantime governors have to make do with their own housing, just like the rest of us.

Schwarzenegger didn't want to live in the temporary governor's ranch house, so he had the state sell it. But, he knew better than to ask California taxpayers to foot the bill for his $7,000-a-month luxury suites in the Sacramento Hyatt—that's what some people pay all year for rent. But, contrary to his claims in the primary about being so rich that he didn't need other people's money, Arnold didn't want to pay for his housing himself. Instead, he set up a nonprofit group, the Governor's Residence Foundation, to raise giant sums of money.

Because these funds go for Arnold's personal care and feeding, not his campaigning, they are exempt from any disclosure laws in California. Initially, Arnold's lawyer Tom Hiltachk did say that Schwarzenegger would urge the directors of the foundation to disclose the sources, if not the amounts, of its donations. But the foundation was reluctant to reveal its donors. After stonewalling reporters for months, the foundation told the *Los Angeles Times* in August 2005 it had received funding from Lewis Investments, the Western Growers Association, and the Tejon Ranch developer. But the foundation did not make this information publicly available anywhere.[15]

Travel Perks

Arnold has used a similar trick to finance fancy tours to Asia and Tel Aviv, where he drums up business for California companies. The companies that pay for Arnold's trips get to send representatives along on the trade mission, and of course have the best shot at landing new deals. While it's great that we have a governor who can use his fame to attract business for California companies, I'll bet most Californians would want their governor working on behalf of *all* our companies, not just those paying his airfare.

The California Commission on Jobs and Economic Growth, the nonprofit group fronting much of Arnold's travel, has received funding from a Catholic Health Care West. That chain of more than 40 hospitals has a keen interest in reducing their nursing staffing levels. Other donors included energy firms Southern Cal Edison and PG&E, from whom Arnold had said he would not accept money in order to avoid a conflict of interest in his decisions about energy policy.

The so-called charity has also paid for travel within California, including to events that arguably had a political agenda. In July 2004, the nonprofit paid for Arnold to visit a shopping mall in California where he lobbed one of his famous insults, calling his Democratic opponents in the legislature "girlie men."

The other places where political gifts flow faster than gas going through the fuel-injectors of a NASCAR engine are the party conventions. Arnold was a keynote speaker at the 2004 Republican Convention in New York. Despite his reformist rhetoric, he was more than happy to indulge in the corporate-sponsored parties and bashes that have taken over what were once serious political events. Corporations and special interests spent more than $300,000 to fête Schwarzenegger and his staff at the convention.[16]

Arnold brought more than two-dozen aides to enjoy the festivities. They were given the royal treatment by special interests. The Chamber of Commerce threw a party at the Central Park Boat House worth $122 per attendee. Chevron/Texaco and other companies put out $177 for each politician who attended their bash. Some staffers got personal perks. SBC treated Schwarzenegger spokesman Rob Stutzman and his family to a Broadway show for $199. The drug maker Pfizer took the head of California's Department of Consumer Affairs to the Rainbow Room for $326. These are but a few examples of the many ways that lobbyists still conduct business as usual, despite the recall's promise to shake things up.

The Chamber's Victory on Workers' Comp

One of the things that the business community wanted most from California government was improvements in the system that compensates employees who are injured on the job. Gray Davis had signed two bills to reform the system, but premiums were not dropping much by early 2004.

Schwarzenegger put workers' comp reform high on his agenda. During his State of the State address on January 6, he told the legislature:

> [W]e must fix the state's business climate. And we must start with workers' compensation reform. Our workers' comp costs are the highest in the nation—nearly twice the national average. California employers are bleeding red ink from the workers' comp system. Our high costs are driving away jobs and businesses. My proposal brings California's workers' comp standards and costs in line with the rest of the country. To heal injured workers, it emphasizes the importance of health care and doctors rather than lawyers and judges. It requires nationally recognized guidelines for permanent disability. And it provides for innovative approaches. I call on the legislators to deliver real workers' comp reform to my desk by March 1st. Modest reform is not enough. If modest reform is all that lands on my desk, I am prepared to take my workers' comp solution directly to the people and I will put it on the ballot in November.[17]

Schwarzenegger vetoed two bills that contained minor reforms to the workers' comp system. He said that he would only accept comprehensive reform. The Chamber of Commerce and other business interests backed efforts to put a workers' comp initiative on the November 2004 ballot. Joel Fox, head of the Small Business Action Committee, played a leading role in putting together the initiative. The Consumer Federation of California and many labor groups opposed the changes, but after Arnold's success with the bond measures in March, legislators felt that his backing of an initiative in the fall could well mean it would pass. Legislators rolled up their sleeves and worked out a compromise with Schwarzenegger and business interests, passing a comprehensive bill on April 16. The bill sailed through the Assembly 77 to 3 and passed the Senate by a vote of 33 to 3. Schwarzenegger signed it three days later and had yet another victory under his belt.

Honeymoon Ends, Moneymoon Continues

In the lead up to the 2004 election, the honeymoon with Democratic legislators came to an end. Democrats began blocking Arnold's proposals in the legislature, and he began vetoing many of the bills they passed. But the moneymoon with big donors kept right on going. All told, special interests spent $212 million to lobby California government in 2004—that's $50 million more than Texas, which ranked a distant second. All too often, it was an investment that paid off.

In September 2004, Arnold vetoed a series of health care bills that consumer and health groups had pushed. The most prominent of these would have allowed Californians to re-import prescription drugs from Canada. We've all heard the stories about how the same pill sells for three or four times less in Canada than it does here in the U.S. Why not let California consumers pay the Canadian prices?

As you might imagine, the Pharmaceutical Research and

Manufacturers of America (known as PhRMA), thought this was a terrible idea. Drug companies' big profits had come from not only accepting government subsidies for researching new drugs but from charging high prices to customers. In other countries where consumers had less money to pay, the drug companies lowered their prices and still made money because the actual production cost of the pill is just pennies on the dollar of the selling price.

For whatever reason, Arnold saw things the way PhRMA did and not the way that the health groups did. He vetoed the re-importation bill, as well as three others dealing with prescription drugs.

PhRMA hadn't previously been a big contributor to California politics. After the Schwarzenegger vetoes, the drug companies kicked in about $360,000, most of it going to Republican candidates for whom Arnold was campaigning.

It's tempting to draw the conclusion that Arnold vetoed the health care bills in exchange for the campaign contributions. But such a conclusion is at minimum an oversimplification and at worst simply a wrong assumption that masks the more profound problem.

We should give Arnold the benefit of the doubt that he looked at these issues on the merits and simply concluded it was a bad idea for California consumers to get Canadian drugs at cheaper prices. Likewise, let's assume that PhRMA made no deal with the governor that they would help his team in the upcoming elections if he did what they wanted him to do and vetoed the bill. Merrill Jacobs, the lobbyist for PhRMA, says that the drug companies started giving out money because "there was something like 30 pieces of legislation dropped on our heads," and that consumer groups were trying to "put them out of business."[18]

Even if there is no *quid pro quo* deal to provide favors in exchange for campaign funds, money from the pharmaceutical industry helped candidates who favored that industry's position over those who favored the consumers' position. While that advantage isn't always enough to elect politicians who will always side with big business, it's enough to elect many of them, and in some cases makes a difference between a pro-consumer politician and a pro-industry politician winning office.

As one example, Cindy Montañez recently ran against Alex Padilla in a Democratic primary election for the California State Senate. While in the California Assembly, Montañez had championed a car buyers' bill of rights. It gave consumers who bought a used car two days to return it if they thought they had been swindled. As you might imagine, this angered car dealers to no end. As payback, car dealers spent at least $122,000 on an independent campaign to promote Padilla, who won the race.[19]

Knowing that campaign contributions can and often do make a difference in determining election outcomes, many politicians do the smart thing and take positions that make powerful interests happy. Who wants to be the next legislator to take on the car dealers after watching what they did to Cindy Montañez? On high profile issues like abortion and gun control, politicians will usually follow their own hearts and usually reflect the wishes of their constituents too. But on the hundreds of day-to-day decisions that lobbyists are pushing and politicians are trying hard to keep track of, it's often all too easy to just side with big money and hope that the rest of us won't notice.

All too often, we don't.

But when it all adds up, we have a sinking feeling in our stomachs that our elected officials aren't always looking out for our best interests but are instead feathering the beds of those big donors who helped get them elected.

Big Money Meets Its Match in Rigged Districts

Despite all the money from PhRMA and others, Arnold was unsuccessful in defeating Democratic incumbents in the legislature. Not a single one lost their seat. The biggest reason was that California's political districts are drawn to heavily favor one party or another.

Big money can help a pro-business Democrat win in a Democratic primary or a pro-business Republican defeat a

Christian conservative in a Republican primary, but big money usually can not help a Republican defeat a Democrat in a general election when two-thirds of the voters in that district are Democrats. In the Montañez–Padilla race mentioned previously, the Republicans didn't even bother to field a candidate in that district because it was so heavily tilted toward the Democrats. Whoever wins the primary goes on to win the general election in a cakewalk. Big money matters in primary races in these heavily partisan districts. In so-called swing districts that have nearly equal numbers of Republican and Democratic voters, campaign dollars have a huge impact in the general election, which is why candidates in those races can typically raise a lot more money than candidates in safer seats.

While Arnold was learning first hand the problems with political districts, others were trying to do something about it. Back in February 2004, Nancy Jewell Cross had filed a ballot question to take the process of drawing legislative boundaries away from politicians in the legislature and put it instead in the hands of a panel of retired judges that would also examine issues of the size of districts. Recall proponent Ted Costa had filed a similar proposal.

Gambling Jackpots

One issue that Arnold had gotten fully up to speed on was Indian gambling. In the recall, he had railed against Gray Davis for being too friendly to Indian tribes and attacked Cruz Bustamante for skirting campaign finance laws to take huge contributions from the tribes. Along with labor unions, Indian tribes were the group that Arnold most frequently had labeled as "special interests."

Yet by June of 2004, Arnold was meeting privately with these "special interest" Indians and cutting deals with them. At an awkward-looking press conference, Arnold announced that he had negotiated an agreement where the tribes would voluntarily pay taxes from their gambling operations, and in return Schwarzenegger would oppose an upcoming ballot measure to expand gambling to racetracks and other competitors to the tribes.

Prop 68 would have allowed for expanded gambling operations at horseracing tracks and card rooms to compete with the tribes while Prop 70 would have allowed some tribes to expand the number of slot machines in their casinos.

What a team they made! The tribes poured in $40 million to defeat Proposition 68 alone and Arnold happily lent his name and face to ads against the initiatives. The combination proved deadly, as the questions went down to defeat with 84 percent of voters opposing Prop 68 and 76 percent voting no on Prop 70.

Arnold went out of his way to criticize legislators (mostly from his own party) who opposed him on Proposition 70, and who received contributions from the tribes. "The legislators should not take money from the Indians, from the Indian gaming tribes, and then endorse Proposition 70. They should not," he lectured.

But, just as Schwarzenegger claimed his donors did not influence him, the legislators swore that the money from the tribes did not influence their endorsement of Prop 70, saying that they independently supported it on its merits. "If the governor was suggesting that our support of Proposition 70 was a matter of money, then he is just flat wrong," said Senator Bill Morrow.[20]

Both Morrow and Schwarzenegger miss the point. It doesn't matter if the politicians agree with the special interests; it just makes the problem more profound. When deep-pocketed interests like Indian casinos can use money to help put people who side with them in office, the rest of us lose. Morrow and the other legislators might have truly believed in Prop 70, but the tribe money they took still distorted the political process.

Ballot Questions are the Name of the Game

Arnold's interest in ballot questions was greater than even his interest in his own campaign for re-election. All during the fall of 2004, Arnold turned down money for his own campaign committee, but raised huge amounts of cash for his California Recovery Team. It became apparent that he viewed his initiative fights as a crucial component of his re-election strategy.

Beyond the gambling initiatives, another big money ballot question of 2004 was Prop 71, which provided $3 *billion* in taxpayer funds for stem cell research. By combining liberals who wanted to send a message to President George Bush, who had curtailed stem cell research at the federal level, and high-tech firms who stood to make a mint, Prop 71 sailed to easy passage—59 percent to 41 percent. The venture capital firms who backed it spent $21 million while its opponents spent about $275,000. Spending $21 million on something that gets you $3 billion represents about a 14,000 percent return on investment—not bad. Arnold supported it.

Companies like Phillip Morris and Chevron/Texaco pushed Prop 64 to make it harder for consumers to sue them after being hurt by their products or actions. Corporate interests gave $14 million. Trial lawyers spent one-tenth that ($1.7 million) in opposition. Arnold supported it. As you might guess, it passed.

Prop 72 would have required medium and large-sized businesses to provide health care for their employees. Companies like Wal-Mart, McDonalds, and others spent $14 million to defeat it. Arnold joined them.

Perhaps Arnold's most surprising victory was the defeat of an initiative to reform California's "three-strikes" law that sends someone to prison for life if they are convicted of three felonies. The measure was leading in the polls until Arnold weighed in against it. His last-minute opposition torpedoed the initiative.

The 2004 Election, California Style

Beyond ballot initiatives, the fall of 2004 had other reminders of big money's role in our political process. Bill Jones was running against Barbara Boxer for the U.S. Senate. Because Boxer was favored as a shoe-in, Jones had been able to raise only about $7 million compared to Boxer's $16 million. He wasn't able to run a single TV ad and, perhaps more important, the press covered him little because the race was seen as a non-event. Despite having an advantage in both polling and resources, Boxer did agree to debate

Jones.

Californians heard stories about big money in the presidential race in states like Ohio and Florida with nebulous-sounding "527 groups" like Swift Boat Veterans for Truth and Americans Coming Together. These groups got their name from an obscure section of tax code, but to most people they looked like old-fashioned mudslingers. But like other so-called safe states, neither presidential candidate spent much time in the Golden State and no outside groups spent their money to influence our votes. Under the current system, there is no reason for presidential candidates to care about California or two-thirds of the other states that are a lock for one party or the other. In fact, candidates spend three-quarters of their time and money in just five decisive states.

Nonetheless, most Californians managed to figure out who they wanted to choose as president just fine. It just goes to show that free speech and democracy can function quite successfully without huge amounts of campaign cash being thrown around.

Arnold wrapped up the year walking on air. His clear-cut victories on the bond ballot measures in the spring and the Indian gaming and three-strikes measure in the fall had given him a track record of winning. His stellar performance as a keynote speaker at the Republican National Convention had turned him into a rising national star in his party. California no longer looked foolish for electing a bodybuilder turned actor to its highest office.

Calls for the Arnold Amendment got a renewed push when Lissa Morgenthaler-Jones spent $20,000 on ads promoting the idea after the November 2004 elections, and news outlets like the *Los Angeles Times* and even *USA Today* picked up the story. The ads said, "You cannot choose the land of your birth. You can choose the land you love. Twelve million people have chosen America, now America wants to choose them. Help us amend the Constitution. . . . Help us Amend for Arnold."[21]

Arnold was feeling his oats, enjoying a 65 percent approval rating. He went into 2005 itching for a political fight.

That's exactly what he got.

CHAPTER 4

REINVENTING THE CRUZ LOOPHOLE

Arnold Adopts the Hybrid Model; Combining Ballot and Candidate Campaigns

Before telling the story of Arnold's mishaps in 2005, we must jump back in time to follow an evolving set of rules dealing with the financing of both candidate campaigns and ballot campaigns. These were once seen as separate types of campaigns, with different rules for each. But in 2005, Arnold would seamlessly mix the two, following in the footsteps of Cruz Bustamante.

On June 25, 2004, the California Fair Political Practices Commission adopted two new rules to close a loophole that donors and politicians were using to bypass California's law that limited contributions to candidates. Those rules applied limits on contributions to ballot committees that were controlled by candidates. The commission passed them largely in response to Lieutenant Governor Cruz Bustamante's fundraising during the 2003 recall campaign, but the rules would significantly hamstring Governor Arnold Schwarzenegger in the upcoming 2005 special election.

These new rules were important because they represented the latest attempt to prevent candidates from cheating the system by finding ways to get around restrictions on the amount of money they could raise from any single donor. At the federal level, this evasion had emerged in the 1990s when candidates raised so-called "soft money" into political parties who then spent it in ways that benefited the candidates who raised it. Congress reacted by banning soft money and placing limits on the funds that federal candidates could raise for any political committee or party. In the 2004 presidential race, large donors bypassed the new rules by giving to electioneering groups that operated independently from candidates. This has led many reformers, and President Bush, to a call for new limits on these independent electioneering groups. The struggle to prevent donors from getting around limits on contributions to candidates has become one of the central challenges in making campaign finance rules work.

In California's recall election, candidates began using ballot committees instead of political parties as vehicles for raising cash that they could not legally accept themselves. In using initiative campaigns to promote their own political careers, Cruz Bustamante and later Arnold Schwarzenegger were using a loophole that had existed in California law for nearly a century. Back in 1990, for example, John Van de Kamp had built his campaign for governor around his effort to pass a sweeping environmental initiative known as Big Green. Jerry Brown successfully used his campaign to pass the California Political Reform Act in 1974 to win election as governor the same year. But prior to 2002, California candidates faced no limits on contributions they could raise for their own candidate committees. As a result, they had little need to use ballot initiative campaigns as a means of avoiding contribution limits.

Citizens of other states that have the initiative process as well as limits on candidate fundraising will likely see similar charades in the near future.

To understand the new California rules and the ramifications for Schwarzenegger and the future of ballot initiative politics, we must first backtrack to follow California's difficult history with campaign finance regulations for candidates.

Previous Efforts to Reform CA Campaigns

Californians enacted the Political Reform Act by a vote of the people in 1974. The initial act set upper limits on the total amount candidates could spend on their campaigns and established rules for how contributions to candidates would be reported. It did not set any restrictions on how much candidates could raise from any given donor.

In 1976, the United States Supreme Court struck down a federal law that set mandatory limits on campaign spending in one of its most controversial and misguided rulings, *Buckley v. Valeo*. Like more than 30 other states that had enacted similar spending limits, California repealed them in the wake of the Supreme Court decision.

It is difficult to pass any sort of political reform because incumbent politicians do not like to change the rules that got them elected. They have already learned to win under the current system, why change it to make it easier for others to challenge them? In the 24 states that have the voters initiative process, including California, reformers often overcome this institutional resistance to reform by bypassing the legislature and taking reform legislation to the voters through ballot questions.

In 1984 and 1988, California citizen groups tried to overcome the *Buckley* decision by proposing initiatives that would entice candidates to voluntarily accept spending limits in exchange for public financing for their campaigns. The courts had approved this approach of voluntary spending limits. Voters defeated the '84 effort. The 1988 measure passed, but another measure qualified for the ballot by three legislators, including Ross Johnson, received more votes and trumped the public financing initiative. It also amended the Political Reform Act to prohibit any future use of public financing for political campaigns.

In 1996, reformers took a different approach. They decided to get a handle on out-of-control political fundraising by limiting the amount that a candidate could receive from a single donor. The Supreme Court had upheld contribution limits of this nature and most other states had adopted some form of contribution limits.

A group of reformers, led by Common Cause, qualified a reform initiative for the 1996 ballot. It called for contribution limits, which ranged from $250 to $1,000, and a voluntary spending limits system that did not include public financing as an alternative. That measure, Prop 208, received support from 61 percent of the voters.

Almost immediately, both the California Democratic and Republican parties challenged Prop 208 in court. The law was temporarily suspended pending a long trial and appeal process.

In 2000, the United States Supreme Court re-affirmed its support for contribution limits, even relatively low ones, in the case *Nixon v. Shrink Missouri Government PAC*. It became clear that the courts would uphold the Prop 208 contribution limits. Fearing that, politicians of both parties conspired to get rid of it. Because the Political Reform Act was passed by a vote of the people, the voters must approve significant changes to it. To undo Prop 208, the legislature would therefore need to place its own ballot measure before the people.

In March 2000, Gray Davis organized big money interests to defeat Prop 25, the campaign finance measure backed by Silicon Valley millionaire Ron Unz. But, given the favorable Supreme Court ruling from Missouri, the politicians knew it was only a matter of time before some sort of campaign limits were put in place for California. They decided to write their own rules to head off real reform at the pass.

In the summer of 2000, Republican and Democratic legislators voted to refer Proposition 34 to the ballot. Prop 34 gutted most of Proposition 208 and replaced it with contribution limits that ranged as high as $20,000 for candidates for governor. Like Prop 208, Prop 34 had voluntary spending limits, but there were few incentives for candidates to agree to them and no penalty for candidates who opted not to. Further, the law had many built-in loopholes, like one that allowed big donors to bypass the limits by giving unlimited contributions to political parties to spend on behalf of candidates if they did so independently. The limits were laughable to serious reformers. Common Cause, the League of Women Voters, and most editorial boards in the state joined together to oppose this cynical ruse.

Since Prop 34 was a legislative referral to the ballot, the legislature, not the attorney general, controlled which people were allowed to make statements of opposition to Prop 34 in the voters' guide. Rather than choosing any of the citizen reform groups, the legislature chose a Republican politician who opposed any contribution limits at all as the lead opponent for the voters' guide. Voters were thus presented with a false choice: no limits or the legislature's proposal. Not surprisingly, the voters passed Prop 34; unaware of the fact that they were repealing the much tougher contribution limits they had passed four years earlier in Prop 208.

It is important to know this history because it reminds us that California's campaign finance laws at the turn of the 21st century were far weaker than reform proponents had called for in the 1990s. Candidates who could not live within these very porous rules were running campaigns that were very different from those envisioned by populist reformers, relying heavily on big donors to fund never-ending TV ads rather than reaching out to thousands of small contributors to fund grassroots-style campaigns.

Nevertheless, Prop 34 was now the law of the land. Its limits were set to go into effect for the 2002 elections, except the limits on candidates for governor. When the measure was being drafted in the legislature, Gray Davis had insisted that those limits not kick in until after he was re-elected in 2002. That meant that while donations to support or oppose the recall itself were unlimited, the campaign for replacement candidates would be the first gubernatorial election held in California where limits on contributions to candidates would apply. Since Gray Davis's prolific fundraising was a major reason behind the recall effort, that seemed fitting.

Side-Stepping an Already Weak Prop 34

Given that politicians drafted the rules, it was no surprise that the contribution limits of Prop 34 quickly began to unravel. However, even under the Prop 208 rules, there would have been problems during the recall campaign. Gray Davis was exempt from the limits because he technically was not a candidate but rather just opposing the recall. The recall question itself was not a candidate election but rather a ballot question asking if the current governor should be recalled.

Because there are no limits on contributions to ballot campaigns, contributions to efforts in favor of, or opposed to, the recall were not limited. Congressman Darrell Issa used this provision to spend huge sums of money to qualify the recall petition in the first place. Schwarzenegger set up a cleverly named Total Recall Committee, based on one of his movie titles, to accept unlimited contributions that could be used to go after Davis and his record. Nearly every major candidate running to replace Davis established two committees, one to promote their own candidacy that was subject to contribution limits, and one to support or oppose the recall, which could accept unlimited contributions.

Contributions to candidate committees were limited to $21,200 under Proposition 34; an amount much higher than previous reform proposals had called for and well beyond the means of regular citizens to give. Although Prop 34 established a $20,000 limit, this amount had automatically been increased to take inflation into account. Any TV ads that featured a recall candidate promoting his or her election were subject to this limit.

Glossary

Candidate Committee: This is a political committee established and controlled by a candidate. Its primary purpose is to promote the election of that candidate but it can also use its funds to support ballot questions, pay for officeholder expenses, and make contributions to other candidates and political parties. Contributions to candidate committees were limited to $21,200 for candidates for governor during the recall.

Recall Committee: A recall committee is formed to support or oppose recall questions. Political candidates can control them, but recall committees cannot advocate the election of any candidate, only a yes or no vote on the recall question. There are no limits on contributions to recall committees.

Ballot Measure Committee: Political committees set up to support or oppose a single ballot issue are called ballot measure committees. They can accept unlimited contributions and must report them on a quarterly basis. Candidates can establish and control ballot measure committees, though the FPPC attempted to apply contribution limits to these candidate-controlled committees in 2004.

The Cruz Loophole

Cruz Bustamante, with the help of campaign consultant Richie Ross, quickly found a way around even these very high contribution limits. Bustamante had an old political committee that he used for his 2002 re-election campaign for lieutenant governor. That campaign was run under the old rules before Proposition 34 took effect, which meant that there were no limits on the size of contributions it could accept. The FPPC had ruled in 2001, against the warnings of reformers, that politicians could continue to raise funds for these pre–Prop 34 committees even after Prop 34 had gone into effect.

Bustamante began raising huge contributions into his old, pre–Prop 34, candidate committee. In response, the FPPC issued a statement on August 28, 2003, that attempted to clarify its past ruling, saying:

> Since implementing Proposition 34 in 2001, the commission has advised that state candidates may not solicit contributions into a pre-Proposition 34 committee for the purpose of using those funds in a post-Proposition 34 election.[1]

Yet this is precisely what Bustamante was doing. When his opponents objected, the FPPC did nothing. Liane Randolph, whom Davis had appointed as FPPC chair, said, "Anyone who files a complaint with this agency will tell you that it takes a long time." She added, "Every single election we get complaints right before the election, and the complainant always says, 'We want you to take action before the election.' Sometimes that is not always feasible. In fact, it is rarely feasible."[2]

Paul Ryan, an election law expert now working at the Washington, D.C.–based Campaign Legal Center criticized the agency, stating, "We have the FPPC that seems to have staked out a position but is in no hurry to enforce its position . . . and a candidate who has chosen to ignore the FPPC . . . and proceed with fundraising that would appear on its face to be in violation of the law."[3]

Senator Johnson Sues Cruz Bustamante

State Senator Ross Johnson was furious. "If [the FPPC is] not prepared to exercise their authority to go into court and seek injunctive relief on this, then I'm prepared to do it," he fumed.[4] California law allows private citizens to enforce campaign finance law if the FPPC is not taking action. Johnson did indeed go to court.

Without skipping a beat, Bustamante tried to dodge the lawsuit by cleverly announcing that he would not use these funds for his campaign to succeed Davis in the recall election. Rather, he would transfer the funds to a new ballot committee that he established to defeat Proposition 54, an anti-affirmative action initiative filed by Ward Connerly. This committee would run TV ads that featured, you guessed it, Cruz Bustamante talking about why Prop 54 was a terrible idea. Bustamante campaign director Richie Ross said that Bustamante would appear in the ads to demonstrate his leadership credentials. "Cruz feels that the [Proposition 54] campaign, in addition to being about issues, also gives voters an opportunity to size up how someone will deal under pressure with controversy," said Ross.[5]

Bustamante did legitimately hope to see Prop 54 defeated. But, by using his separate ballot committee, he was able to funnel huge contributions, in excess of the candidate contribution limits, and use them to put himself on TV. All told, Cruz raised some $3.8 million in amounts over the $21,200 limit from 16 donors, including Indian tribes and labor unions, for his ballot campaigns. One tribe alone gave $478,000. Jerry Perenchio, one of the biggest donors in California, kicked in $100,000 all by himself.

Ross Johnson was not amused by Bustamante's trick. "It stinks to high heaven," he said. "If the commercials feature the lieutenant governor, then the money is being used to support Bustamante for governor."[6]

Sean Walsh, who was spinning press for Schwarzenegger, sharply criticized Bustamante's move. He claimed the Prop 54 ads were simply a "mask to put himself up on television," and that "clearly there is a great deal of controversy and concern that he's not only violating the spirit, but the actual letter of the campaign finance law."[7]

Arnold was in a position to know a thing or two about the value of appearing in TV ads about ballot campaigns. Schwarzenegger had used a similar tactic back in 2002 to pave the way for an eventual run for governor. Schwarzenegger had received more than a million bucks from Jerry Perenchio to back Proposition 49, in addition to hundreds of thousands of dollars from corporations, developers, and Indian tribes. Prop 49 established an after-school program for kids, just the sort of thing that everyone loved. It was designed to make Arnold look like a leader and in many respects it succeeded.

Senator Ross Johnson won his lawsuit against Lieutenant Governor Bustamante, but it was a hollow victory. On September 22, about two weeks before the recall election, Sacramento Superior Court Judge Loren McMaster ruled that Cruz Bustamante had indeed violated the "plain and unambiguous language" of the law by accepting contributions well beyond those allowed by current California law. The judge ordered Bustamante to immediately stop using any contributions that he had received above the $21,200 limit. Too bad, his consultant Richie Ross chuckled. The campaign had already spent the money.

Bustamante wound up returning a paltry $177,000 of the $3.8 million he had illegally raised and spent—a small price to pay for breaking the law.

During the recall, the news media were highly critical of Bustamante's charade. It smacked of just the sort of thing Gray Davis would have done. His apparent lack of regard for campaign finance laws was a major reason for Bustamante's low approval ratings with voters. Indeed, it helped cement the desire for change among voters, creating a thirst for someone who seemed above the craven politics of fundraising in Sacramento.

That someone, of course, was Arnold Schwarzenegger.

Progressive independent candidate Arianna Huffington derided Bustamante for making a "mockery of campaign finance laws by using a ludicrous loophole." Conservative Republican candidate Tom McClintock told the press that he thought Bustamante's move was illegal, or at best "on the shady side of the law." Bob Stern of the Center for Governmental Studies said, "What [Bustamante's] saying is that Proposition 34 doesn't apply to statewide candidates. That's just nutty."[8]

Arnold's attorney Tom Hiltachk lashed out at the FPPC as a toothless tiger. "If they see a person with a gun pointed at someone, they will wait until they are shot and dead before they do anything. If the agency is not going to do something to stop this, then the taxpayers of this state have to ask why are they funding that agency."[9]

Days before the October 7, 2003, recall, Senator Johnson pleaded with the FPPC to take action against Bustamante. "You are a political watchdog. A watchdog can't just sit back and watch. From time to time you need to at least bark, and sometimes bite."[10]

Justice Delayed

The FPPC did eventually go after Bustamante by filing a civil lawsuit against him on January 7, 2004—three months after the election was over.

He finally settled the case on April 14, 2004, and agreed to pay a $263,000 fine—the largest fine ever paid by a candidate for violating California's campaign finance laws.[11] Still, the lieutenant governor was getting off easy. He could have faced fines of up to $9 million for his violation. Bustamante was allowed to pay the fine out of campaign funds he raised from others. Since the penalty did not come from his own pocket, it's doubtful he considered it more than a slap on the wrist.

Better Late Than Never

The week after it filed the lawsuit, the FPPC moved even further and reversed its 2001 decision that allowed candidates to continue raising funds into committees that existed prior to Proposition 34. Jim Knox, the director of California Common Cause at the time, told the commission that more than 50 candidates had used the loophole of pre–Prop 34 committees to raise millions of dollars in amounts higher than the law now allowed. In light of the ruling by Judge McMaster in response to the Ross Johnson lawsuit against Lt. Governor Bustamante, the commission concluded that it should revise its rules.

In this instance, it was fortunate for voters that Bustamante's use of huge campaign contributions backfired and cost him popularity during the recall campaign. Suppose, however, that it had worked out differently. Imagine the pickle that California would have been in had Bustamante won the recall through the use of millions of dollars of illegal campaign contributions. Would the legislature have had the stomach to launch impeachment proceedings? Would voters have had to launch another recall campaign? Would he have gotten off with a slap on the wrist and a fine?

Cruz Bustamante claimed he was the victim of a misunderstanding, that the FPPC rules were unclear. "It was never my intention to violate the law," he said in a prepared statement. "Unfortunately, the FPPC's regulations weren't as clear as they could have been. We believed that we were using a process the FPPC had allowed in the past and that our actions were consistent with the law."[12]

Several months later, the FPPC would take steps to clarify the rules.

First Beat 'em, Then Join 'em

In the meantime, newly elected Governor Arnold Schwarzenegger proved adept at learning the big money game. He stole a page from the Bustamante playbook and used his California Recovery Team ballot committee to support Propositions 57 and 58 on the March 2004 ballot. These measures authorized huge bond sales to finance the budget crisis Schwarzenegger had inherited from the Davis administration. Their passage was critical to Arnold's success as governor. He told voters that if they did not approve these bonds, he might be forced to raise taxes—something he had promised to avoid during his campaign. As the first President Bush learned, backing off from a promise like that can cost you your re-election.

Just as Bustamante had used huge contributions from tribes to fund his ads against Prop 54, Schwarzenegger's California Recovery Team raked in six-figure contributions from corporations like Anheuser Busch, Dole Foods, and the Kaiser Foundation Health Plan. Jerry Perenchio kicked in a quarter of a million dollars, as did developers Alex Spanos and William Lyon. In the first six weeks of 2004, Schwarzenegger raised $5.2 million—a pace of fundraising that far exceeded anything Gray Davis had done.

Arnold's New York fundraiser for the California Recovery Team was seen by many as a way to evade limits on contributions to his candidate committee. With ticket prices as high as

$500,000 each, from Wall Street brokerages who would stand to gain from marketing the $15 billion in bonds that the governor was pushing voters to approve, the event raised eyebrows. The Municipal Securities Regulatory Board had a rule prohibiting bond dealers from contributing to candidates. But that rule did not prohibit contributions to ballot measure campaigns, including bond questions. Schwarzenegger's staff said that he would reject contributions directly from bond brokers, but Wall Street in general saw its self-interest in getting these bonds approved and was happy to open its coffers.

Elizabeth Garrett, a law professor at the University of Southern California who specializes in campaign finance law, said that these huge contributions to Schwarzenegger's ballot committee were just as troubling as any other large contribution. "It is absurd to think that a $500,000 contribution to his issue campaign would not produce the same level of gratitude as would a $500,000 donation to his candidate committee. This is a . . . way to evade the contribution limits."[13]

On April 8, 2004, just four days before it would settle its lawsuit against Cruz Bustamante and 37 days after the March primary where voters had approved Arnold's bond measures, the FPPC discussed further regulations on candidate-controlled ballot committees as a way of preventing further end-runs around California's campaign finance laws. But it still wasn't prepared to act.

Closing the Cruz Loophole

On June 25, 2004, the FPPC was finally ready to take a stand. At a fateful meeting that hot summer day, the commissioners debated new regulations to implement the contribution limits enacted in Proposition 34. The first proposed rule, section 85309.5, said that if a candidate controlled a ballot committee, then contributions to that committee were subject to the same limits that the candidate was. The second rule, section 85310, set contribution limits of $25,000 for any ballot committee that spent more than $50,000 on ads that featured a candidate within 45 days of an election where the candidate was on the ballot if those ads were made at the candidate's "behest." This would prevent even supposedly independent committees from coordinating with candidates to do a complete end run around the candidate contribution limits.

Schwarzenegger weighed in heavily against the new rules. Days prior to the commission meeting, his lawyer, Thomas Hiltachk, wrote that the regulations would "prevent the governor from controlling a committee to oppose these two measures that are a direct assault on his constitutional power, unless he were to agree to oppose the well-funded campaigns for the initiatives using limited contributions."[14]

That prescient quote demonstrated that Schwarzenegger knew exactly what these new rules would prevent him from doing, yet he later chose to go ahead and do it anyhow. Hiltachk had previously served as the lawyer to the Institute of Governmental Advocates, a trade association for lobbyists. He knew campaign finance laws inside and out, and knew how to look out for what's good for lobbyists and their powerful clients.

In another insightful prediction, Schwarzenegger's lawyer said that the new rule would "force a candidate to disassociate from participating in campaign strategy and spending decisions regarding important policy matters facing our state. The commission would be inundated with pre-election complaints alleging that a non-controlled committee was in fact controlled, so as to impose contribution limits on the committee."

Schwarzenegger promised to work with Assemblymember Lois Wolk on a legislative solution to the problem of money in candidate-controlled ballot committees, but begged the FPPC not to take its own action.

At the hearing on the new rules, another Schwarzenegger lawyer, Chuck Bell, told the commission that he didn't believe the Political Reform Act authorized the FPPC to pass these rules. But in any case, its regulations were so full of holes that they were useless.

The day of the FPPC hearing, TheRestofUs.org issued a

news release pointing out two problems with large contributions, especially from corporations, to ballot committees controlled by candidates:

> First, wealthy interests can easily drown out the voices of the rest of us in public debate about ballot measures, creating an un-level playing field for public policy decisions. It is particularly troubling when corporations or tribes use state-conferred advantages that allow them to accumulate massive amounts of money to distort the political process.
>
> Second, many donors who give to ballot committees that are controlled by candidates, future candidates, and officeholders, have business pending before the state of California or other private interests at stake dealing with state action or regulation. They could easily gain privileged access and favorable treatment by public officials by giving such huge amounts to ballot campaigns either controlled by or prominently featuring those elected officials. (See full release in appendix A.)

Election lawyer Paul Ryan sent the commission a letter on behalf of the Center for Governmental Studies urging adoption of the rules. Ryan also testified at a public hearing on the matter. He told commissioners that a candidate builds political power by raising and spending funds—regardless of whether the candidate deposits the funds in a campaign account or a ballot measure account. Ryan reasoned that threat of corruption associated with large political contributions, long recognized by the U.S. Supreme Court, depends entirely on a candidate's receipt of large contributions, not on how a candidate chooses to spend such contributions. He described how his non-lawyer friends who voted to approve the Proposition 34 contribution limits could not imagine for a moment that somehow a contribution raised by a candidate would not have been limited by the law just because the candidate deposited the money in a ballot campaign account instead of a candidate campaign account.

Legislative leaders Fabian Núñez and Don Perata also weighed in supporting the rules. They asked the commission to put them into effect immediately and apply the same contribution limits to ballot committees controlled by all candidates. This would have avoided the inequity of a legislator who wanted to run a ballot committee opposing a governor only being able to accept $3,200 when the governor's committee could accept $21,200. While this made some sense, the FPPC didn't feel it had the authority to enact new uniform limits on candidate-controlled ballot committees, only extend the existing unequal contribution limits to candidates to the ballot committees that they set up. If the legislators wanted uniform limits, the commissioners told them that they should enact those in the legislature.

Ross Johnson, the Republican state senator who started the dispute with his lawsuit against Cruz Bustamante's ballot question fundraising, sent a letter to the commission supporting its rule, but urging it to combine contributions to candidate ballot committees and their own campaigns. Otherwise, a candidate could easily double dip and accept one maximum contribution for his or her own campaign, and then others for multiple ballot committees—in effect circumventing the contribution limits. Like Núñez and Perata, he urged that the commission put rules in place before the November 2004 election.

During the discussion, Commissioner Phil Blair specifically raised the possibility that a candidate could get a like-minded person to control a ballot committee for them, rather than controlling it themselves. Schwarzenegger's lawyers listened closely as Chairman Randolph agreed that this would be possible. But Commissioner Downey went out of his way to point out that this could not be done as a subterfuge to evade the law.

The commission adopted the first regulation by a vote of 4 to 1. That rule applied the same limits to a candidate's ballot committee that were already in place for their candidate committee. But, in a nod to Schwarzenegger and against Ross Johnson, they decided not to implement the rules until after the November election. That left Schwarzenegger free to use his California Recovery Team to raise huge contributions to help the Indian tribes defeat gambling Propositions 68 and 70 on the November ballot. The commission adopted the second rule unanimously to apply a $25,000 contribution limit to all ballot committees that aired ads featuring candidates near election time, if those ads were run at the request of a candidate.

Paul Ryan was pleased. "This vote terminates the reform governor's ability to raise money as he has into ballot measure committees," he said.[15] Perhaps Paul should have known from the movies that Arnold wasn't easily terminated and that his big money would quickly tell California, "I'll be back."

Schwarzenegger's lawyers were quick to take the wind out of Ryan's sails. They publicly explained that there were still plenty of loopholes that would allow the governor to raise unlimited sums for ballot campaigns. Chuck Bell sneered cryptically, "When you look at a piece of Swiss cheese, it does have holes in it."[16] Months later, he would prove just how right that was.

By the time the new regulations were passed by the FPPC, Schwarzenegger had raised a stunning $12.6 million, the majority of which came in amounts above the limit, now raised to $22,300 from $21,200 in the last election to take inflation into account. By the end of the year, that number would grow to $18 million.

State Treasurer Phil Angelides, who was planning to run against Schwarzenegger in 2006, took advantage of the loophole as well. Just four weeks before the rule kicked in, he set up the Standing Up for California ballot committee and raked in $730,000 in unlimited contributions. He doled out $200,000 of this to other ballot committees working on stem-cell research and health care initiatives, and pocketed the remaining half-million bucks to use later.

When the dust had settled after the November election, Schwarzenegger spokesman Marty Wilson told the *Sacramento Bee* that while the governor had opposed the new campaign finance rules when they were enacted, he was now prepared to live with them and would not appeal them. "We don't have the pressure to raise the kind of money in 2005 that we did in 2004. We can have a very fine and viable organization under these limits."[17]

But three months later, the governor would change his mind. Rather than abiding by the new rules, Arnold would try to get rid of them.

CHAPTER 5

SAVING CALIFORNIA'S CORPORATE CITIZENS

Arnold Creates a Front Group

By late 2004, Arnold and his advisors had abandoned the previous year's approach of working with Democratic lawmakers and instead decided upon all-out war against their political adversaries. During his State of the State Address on January 5, the Governator declared 2005 to be the "year of reform" and laid out what he thought that meant. The agenda was something the legislature was unlikely to support, setting the stage for Arnold to call a special election that would allow Arnold to bypass the legislature and take his ideas straight to the voters. A high-profile victory in 2005 would then put Arnold on track to win re-election in 2006. Arnold was creating a new model for success in California politics that merged candidate campaigns and ballot campaigns into one seamless re-election effort.

In his State of the State speech, Arnold told the legislature that if they did not reform California government, "the people will rise up and reform it themselves. And I will join them. And I will fight with them."[1] The California governor has the power to call a special election at any time to consider urgent ballot measures. While some of Arnold's advisors relished the idea of taking his partisan fight to the voters through qualifying initiatives for a special election in the fall, others hoped that his tough talk would force the legislature to the negotiating table and allow him to win more modest policy victories at a lower political risk. But even accomplishing that meant striking a tough initial bargaining position.

Arnold's advisors crafted a "reform" agenda to drive a dagger through the heart of several Democratic constituencies. By showing that he could take on Democratic interests like teacher unions and win, Arnold hoped to permanently weaken his opponents' political stature and strength. Here's the list of policies that Arnold took into battle:

1) Legislative redistricting. Arnold had campaigned for Republicans in the 2004 legislative races and hadn't gotten very far. In fact, the Republicans failed to pick up a single legislative seat in either the congressional or state legislative races. Ditto for the Democrats. Out of 153 races, not a single seat changed party hands. One big reason was that most incumbents, both Democrat and Republican, represented districts that were rigged from the get-go for one party to win.

Through a process called gerrymandering, California legislators had drawn their own political districts so that a majority of voters in any given district favored one party or the other. The term was coined after a Massachusetts politician, Eldridge Gerry, who drew a political district that looked like a salamander back in 1812 to foil his opponents. Although this is a terminally wonky subject matter, the impact of drawing district lines gained national attention when Tom DeLay orchestrated a 2003 redrawing of Texas's political map that resulted in Republicans picking up six seats in the following congressional election.

Arnold's plan was more equitable than DeLay's. Rather than taking a map that unfairly favored Democrats and redrawing it to unfairly favor Republicans, as DeLay had done, Arnold proposed permanently taking the process for drawing legislative districts out of the hands of politicians and having an independent panel take control. Rather than waiting for 2011, after the next census was done, Arnold wanted to do it now. This meant that every legislator's district would be redrawn before the next election, something they loathed because many would have to get to know a new set of voters. Some previously secure seats would suddenly be competitive. So, here was a reform that should seem fair to most people but would be violently opposed by the Democrats in the legislature—just what Arnold was looking for to allow him to pick a fight that would make his opponents look bad.

2) A state spending cap. In an annual well-worn ritual that creates California's budget, Democrats promote government programs that people like while Republicans promote tax cuts, which people also like. When both sides get their way, we take on more than we can afford, and wind up with the kind of $36 billion budget deficit that Arnold inherited when he took office. Arnold's solution was to set a cap on overall state spending. It meant that the governor could make whatever budget cuts he wanted to in the middle of each budget cycle if expenses were more than projected, or income was less than planned for, and if the legislature failed to correct the imbalance. For business interests that were concerned about the overall rate of taxation in California, a spending cap had great appeal.

The idea was modeled after a so-called Taxpayer Bill of Rights that had passed in Colorado in 1992. That measure had so crippled Colorado's budget that Republican Governor Bill Owens supported a successful ballot measure to roll it back in 2005.

3) Government pensions. It used to be that if you worked your whole life for a company, they'd take care of you in retirement through their pension plan. Then, corporate America told its workers it could no longer afford traditional pensions. Gradually, many corporate pensions that paid a guaranteed amount each month upon retirement replaced that pension plan with so-called fixed contribution plans where both the worker and the company would put in a set amount during the worker's career, but the payments depended on how much the nest egg was worth after the ups and downs of the stock market. For folks who lost their life savings in the Enron scandal, it didn't seem like such a good deal, but others had done okay. While a lot of the private sector had switched over to the non-guaranteed benefit plan, California government had not.

Spiraling costs of worker pensions were one of the things that were driving up the budget in California, causing real headaches for Arnold's plan to balance the budget without raising taxes. Schwarzenegger's "reform" was to take away the guaranteed pensions for public workers, including firemen and police. Wall Street liked the idea because it meant millions of dollars administering the new flexible benefit plans for employees. The government workers who stood to lose the guarantee of the pensions of course opposed such a move, just as Arnold anticipated. While ordinary voters weren't exactly clamoring for pension reform, something that lowered government workers' pensions to the same system that many of them were on probably wouldn't seem too bad, or so Arnold could have reasoned.

4) Teacher pay. No matter what election cycle it is, the one thing that all of us seem to agree upon is that our schools could use some help. While there are many reasons for it ranging from dysfunctional families to old textbooks, Arnold decided to focus the debate on teachers. His idea was to give "combat pay" to teachers who were doing a great job in some of the toughest schools in the state and to generally move toward paying teachers based on merit rather than years of experience.

5) The secret weapon—taking workers' money out of politics. You don't need to be a political expert to know that labor unions in California usually back Democratic politicians over Republicans. This hasn't always been the case, but as Republican politicians have increasingly catered to big business interests, labor unions have increasingly backed Democrats in response. Most of us, who neither belong to a labor union nor serve on a corporate board, take the whole thing with a grain of salt. But, in 2005, the business side of the equation decided to go for the jugular and take out the very thing that makes unions unions: their ability to act collectively.

We all know the old adage of "united we stand, divided we fall." Well, workers figured out a long time ago that they'd be better off if they hung together as a group—like the way oil producing countries do in OPEC when they all agree to sell oil at a fixed price. This means that sometimes the whole group of workers will take actions that not every member agrees with, like going on strike or agreeing to a cut in benefits. But, all workers vote on it as a whole, and they all agree to be bound by the majority's decision—sounds a lot like democracy, right? Well, workers have long been applying this all for one and one for all approach to politics as well as employer negotiations. It's helped them win policies that are arguably good for most of us, like the five-day workweek and the minimum wage.

Corporate America finally figured out a way to prevent workers from acting collectively in politics. Rather than letting workers pay their normal dues and then voting on how to use them politically as a whole, the Chamber of Commerce and other "friends" of the blue-collar man want to have workers act individually by each year deciding whether they want to use their dues for the unions' political activities. It sounds great, like if you could decide each year whether you wanted to pay taxes based on who won the last election. The corporations call the scheme "paycheck protection" even though unions are arguably the single biggest innovation in the history of the industrial revolution to protect the workers' paycheck and it would take the heart out of workers' ability to stand united in politics. Under federal law, workers who disagree with their union's political agenda can have the portion of their dues that supports politics refunded to them. Even though the initiative only dealt with public employee unions, Arnold and his allies knew that every union in the state would come out adamantly opposed and would have to spend most of their resources to defeat this measure if it were to appear on the ballot.

Schwarzenegger's team adopted a good-cop bad-cop strategy on this union funding initiative. Arnold played the good cop, and negotiated with the Democrats in the legislature on the rest of his reforms, all the while acting like he hadn't decided whether to back the paycheck protection measure. Meanwhile, the Small Business Political Action Committee did the work to get paycheck protection on the ballot. But, everyone knew that if he didn't get what he wanted, Arnold would put his muscle into this measure too, vying to permanently weaken the other side for the foreseeable future.

These reforms were hardly at the top of the list of concerns of most Californians. Rather, they were intentionally chosen so that Arnold could pick a fight. There were several reasons why it made sense for Schwarzenegger to stop working with his opponents and instead try to bulldoze them. He needed to show the business community that had invested heavily in his campaigns that he could deliver results for them, rather than just boost his popularity through compromise.

Arnold also desperately needed to maintain his macho tough-guy image and show he wouldn't back down from a fight. He began hurling insults at legislators when just months earlier he had been shaking their hands and working out bipartisan compromises. The political operatives in Arnold's corps of advisors salivated at the idea of permanently weakening the Democratic base. Perhaps a final reason for Arnold to go on the warpath in 2005 was to create room for him to move back toward the center in 2006 after pleasing his Republican base with their red meat agenda in 2005.

The ballot initiative process was the ideal arena for Arnold to go to battle. By going directly to the people, he could make use of his fame and personal charm, which was unrivaled in California politics. He could frame the issues in the light most favorable to his side. And, most important, he could play in electoral politics without being burdened by limits on campaign contributions. This meant that he could appear in TV ads all year long without having them count as ads for his re-election campaign. It was as cunning a move as when political consultant Dick Morris blew open the federal soft money loophole in 1996 by putting Bill Clinton on TV across the country during the presidential primary season by cleverly having the ads stop short of the magic words "vote for Bill Clinton." By avoiding these words, Clinton could raise six-figure contributions instead of being limited to raising contributions of $1,000 for his official candidate campaign.

In a move equally devastating for democracy, Schwarzenegger's consultant Mike Murphy had found a way for Arnold to raise unlimited sums of money, which he could not legally accept for his campaign, by having Arnold appear in ads for ballot questions that stopped short of saying, "re-elect Arnold," but accomplished the same thing. For his services, Murphy and his firms would eventually earn more than $950,000 from Schwarzenegger's campaigns.

As one advisor told *The New York Times,* off the record, "by shunning the legislature and going directly to voters with a package of 'reforms,' Schwarzenegger could go a long way toward cementing his populist, anti-establishment reputation. . . . Success in the off year would pretty much catapult him to a second term."[2] To ensure success, fundraiser Marty Wilson announced a plan to raise $50 million for Arnold's ballot initiatives plus another $50 million for his re-election campaign.[3]

There was one catch.

To raise previously unheard of sums of money to promote his agenda, Schwarzenegger had to raise it for a ballot committee that he did not technically control. The new Fair Political Practices Commission ruling put limits on contributions to candidate-controlled ballot committees as of November 2004. Not one to be stopped by technicalities—remember the illegal "loans" he gave his campaign during the recall—Arnold and his gang devised a fairly simple scheme that would let them do everything that they wanted. They set up a front group.

Selfless Corporate Citizens

Just days after Arnold's State of the State speech where he announced his "year of reform," several of Arnold's closest corporate allies and advisors formed a new organization, Citizens to Save California. These citizens would raise and spend the unlimited sums of money that Arnold couldn't legally control himself.

The people who set up Citizens to Save California were veterans of California politics, who had a history of working hand in hand with the same corporate interests that Arnold was partnering with. Many had helped put Schwarzenegger in office, or helped with his previous ballot campaigns. Here's a quick look at these citizens:

Allan Zaremberg, president of the California Chamber of Commerce. The Chamber's agenda was Arnold's agenda and Zaremberg was the man with a plan to make it happen. Remember, during the 2003 recall campaign, Arnold was the first candidate for governor that the Chamber had ever endorsed in its entire history. Arnold had gone to bat for them on workers' compensation reform, after they had helped gather signatures for an initiative if need be. The Chamber was determined to both help Arnold pass their mutual agenda and make sure he stayed in office for another term. The Ohio Chamber of Commerce had previously seen great success starting a front group called Citizens for a Strong Ohio, and Zaremberg was happy to borrow a page from the playbook of his buddies in Ohio.

R. William Hauck, president of the California Business Roundtable. In 2004, Arnold tapped Bill Hauck to co-chair a panel that reviewed a massive proposal for overhauling state government, the "California Performance Review." The Roundtable's members had welcomed the governor's vetoes of minimum-wage bills, measures to cut prescription-drug costs, and bills to make it harder for corporations to outsource jobs overseas.

Joel Fox, the former chief policy consultant to Arnold Schwarzenegger's 2003 gubernatorial campaign and president of the Small Business Action Committee. Fox worked for Schwarzenegger in the recall campaign, and sponsored a workers' compensation reform initiative that the governor had championed in 2004. The Small Business Action Committee took the lead role in sponsoring the "paycheck protection" scheme aimed at taking the wind out of labor's sails.

Jon Coupal, president of the Howard Jarvis Taxpayers Association. Along with Ted Costa of People's Advocate, Coupal carries on the legacy of California's Proposition 13, which capped increases in property taxes back in 1976. Its passage has reduced the growth of property tax revenue for local government and education while protecting many elderly people and others on fixed incomes from being priced out of their own homes as property assessments skyrocketed in their neighborhoods. Prop 13 also created some perverse incentives for local government to raise funds by building giant auto malls and other big sales tax sources. Coupal's interest and expertise was clearly the state spending cap initiative. Coupal had helped Arnold win his election by endorsing him and appearing in radio ads with Schwarzenegger.

Rick Claussen, political consultant. Claussen ran Arnold's campaigns for Propositions 57 and 58 in March 2004. From that experience, he knew exactly how the governor and his team put together campaigns and was in a perfect position to run the CSC campaigns in the same way, while pretending to be completely independent of Arnold.

It is clear from the beginning that Schwarzenegger knew he could not legally control Citizens to Save California. But to raise big campaign contributions, they needed to assure donors that helping CSC was the same thing as helping Schwarzenegger. That way, donors would invest in CSC, even if they didn't care too much about the immediate CSC agenda, because they wanted to see Arnold re-elected. For instance, Jack Coffee, the head lobbyist for Chevron/Texaco, said businesses might be reluctant to write checks for reforms that didn't seem to touch their own bottom lines, like the teacher tenure and redistricting reform. "Good government is a great thing to be for, but it's unlikely that you'll raise [as] much money for good government as something that hits your pocketbook," he explained.[4]

To send this signal, CSC representatives walked a fine line in the press.

Arnold isn't allowed to exert "legal control" over CSC, said Joel Fox, but "we can certainly talk to the governor's office. We can get a feel of where the governor is going to go. He's the big king on the chessboard. Wherever he moves, a lot of things move with him."[5]

Rick Claussen explained, "The governor laid out an agenda in the State of the State speech" last week. Our desire is to help him achieve that agenda."[6] In other words, giving CSC your money is just as good as giving it to Arnold.

Marty Wilson, who was in charge of raising both $50 million for the governor's re-election campaign and another $50 million for the probable special election, nonchalantly told the press that "it is my guess that [CSC] will be a very important ally."[7]

Jon Coupal echoed the point that the CSC will take guidance about what the governor wants through signals he has sent in the legislature and in his speeches.[8]

Arnold pledged that he personally would help with fundraising and promotion of CSC. "I will help them to endorse it and to do TV campaigns, because it is according to my agenda," he crowed.[9]

To further cement the public connection between Arnold and CSC, the fundraising effort began with a series of joint events between Arnold's re-election committee and CSC. Joint invitations to swank luncheons and dinners around the state were sent out on Schwarzenegger campaign stationery. Speakers included not only Arnold himself, but chief legislative aid Richard Costigan and Allan Zaremberg representing CSC.[10]

As Ned Wigglesworth, my colleague at the time, pointed out in the *Los Angeles Times*, "What Schwarzenegger is doing by having Joel Fox and people that he's close to create this committee is using the disingenuous distinction that it's not under his legal control. That seems to me to be a slap in the face both of the campaign contribution limits that exist for candidates and also for the FPPC regulations."[11] Politicians had previously used big money to get their way, but Arnold had told us he would be different. Plus, Gray Davis and other politicians had used huge campaign war chests when it was perfectly legal to do so. Voters had stepped up to change the rules through supporting numerous campaign finance reform initiatives, but Arnold was still trying to play by the old system of unlimited contributions.

Rebecca Avila, the state chair of California Common Cause,

said, "This is disheartening. The governor seems to be relying upon the legal distinction between committees he controls and those he does not. In the voters' minds, however, this distinction doesn't exist. In the public's view, big money and elected officials equals influence."[12]

The Misdemeanor Offense—Selling Access

What's wrong with shaking hands at a few fundraising dinners? After all, there was no proof that any favors were directly exchanged for contributions at the CSC events.

The press was quick to pounce on one problem that was the most obvious, if not the most troubling, aspect of Arnold's escapades—the sale of access to the governor in exchange for contributions to Citizens to Save California.

As has become customary in the waltz between fat cats and politicians, the invitations to Arnold's CSC events carried steeper price tags for higher levels of interaction with the governor. For $100,000, a "Dinner Chair" donor and three other guests could sit at the head table at a fundraising dinner with Arnold himself and have four pictures taken with him (but only two guests per photo—let's not get carried away!) "Co-Chairs," for $50,000, got two seats at the head table and three photos. The cheap seats were for $10,000, which only bought you two seats at a table in the back and a single picture with the Governator—probably just a quick handshake.[13]

Arnold apparently knew enough to try to keep these access-selling fundraisers out of the press. One attendee reportedly said that as he went around the room shaking hands, Schwarzenegger said, "I'd like for this meeting to stay out of the *L.A. Times*."

It didn't.

While few believe that the governor or any other politician actually sells favors at these meet-and-greet events, they do offer some real benefits to the donors that attend at the expense of the rest of us. The donors get pictures to hang on their walls, showing clients and business partners that they have access to the governor and implying that they can trade on that access. More importantly, donors can follow up on the event with phone calls and meetings with staff members to discuss state affairs that impact their bottom lines. Politicians routinely have staff keep lists of who their donors are and instruct them to be sure to find time to take their phone calls and meeting requests.

Offering access for sale to the highest bidder also gradually causes elected officials to lose touch with regular folks. Even if there is nothing insidious discussed during these over-priced chicken dinners, the conversation is much more likely to be about the latest price of stocks on Wall Street than food prices at the supermarket. Imagine how different government would be if the governor of each state ate dinner each night with working-class families who were scratching their heads figuring out how to pay for their health care plans or save for their kids' college tuitions. When politicians are constantly exposed to the cares and priorities of the superrich and their lieutenants, it's easy to forget about what matters to everyone else.

The Real Crime—Buying Democracy

Of course the real crime wasn't that Arnold shared a meal for money, like a dime-a-dance girl selling companionship. The real crime was that Arnold, like Gray Davis before him, was consorting hand-in-hand with powerful groups to help them pass their agendas instead of looking out for what's best for all Californians. The fact that he had part and parcel adopted the Chamber of Commerce's agenda as his own gave little comfort to those citizens who did not share the Chamber's profit-maximizing strategies. We all want businesses to make a profit, but not at the expense of public safety, reasonable protections for workers and consumers, or rules to ensure a fair marketplace.

Our high-school textbooks say that democracy means rule of the people. Each person has one vote, and we send representatives to the capitol to pass laws on our behalf because it wouldn't be practical for us all to show up in the state legislature each day.

When the legislature fails to act on something that the people demand, such as reforming car insurance rates, citizens can take matters into their own hands by placing questions on the ballot. If a majority of people vote yes, the idea becomes law.

☆ ☆ ☆

DEMOCRACY: Government by the people, exercised either directly or through elected representatives. *American Heritage Dictionary*.

☆ ☆ ☆

Through expanding the role of big money in the California initiative process, Arnold and others were standing the idea of direct democracy on its head. It would have been one thing had Arnold gone out to the shopping malls and state fairs of California and asked regular folks to get behind his plan. Instead, he took corporate jets to hotel ballrooms outside of California and asked the folks who really run things, the fat cats, to get on board. From Columbus to Manhattan to Tallahassee, Arnold traveled the country with hand outstretched to private and powerful interests.

The Roadshow

Arnold went out of his way to make his corporate agenda for California a national project. Rather than go back to the same rich Californians who had funded his previous campaigns, Schwarzenegger said he wanted to solicit well-heeled businesspeople across the country. Arnold described his fundraising plan for Citizens to Save California by saying, "I feel it's wise not to just rely on the same people that we normally go to, and let other people participate a little bit."

The Governator described likely donors as people who've been ". . . successful in the real estate market or successful in the restaurant business." Maybe Arnold doubted that the regular people of California saw the upsides of his agenda, so asking them to send in small contributions to help get it passed would be about as fruitful as squeezing water from a rock. He suggested that his supporters could ". . . contribute $10,000 or $20,000 or $50,000, or be in charge of raising $500,000 from smaller donors."[14] Given that the average contribution to Citizens to Save California clocked in at $23,723, you have to wonder what Arnold's idea of a "smaller donor" is.

Perhaps nothing better demonstrated the hypocrisy of big-donor fundraising than Florida Governor Jeb Bush's role in helping raise corporate cash for Arnold's agenda. As a Republican governor of a state with a Republican legislature, Jeb Bush thinks that the citizen initiative process is a bad idea. It gives voters a chance to pass legislation that would never see the light of day in the legislature because Jeb's buddies bury them six feet under once they enter their first committee.

So Jeb Bush and his friends at, you guessed it, the Florida Chamber of Commerce, are working to make it much harder for citizens to qualify ballot questions. In 2004, the legislature referred a constitutional amendment to the ballot that dramatically shortened the number of days that initiative proponents had to circulate petitions. The previous deadline to turn in signatures to qualify ballot initiatives was 91 days before an election; Governor Bush and his team rolled back to eight months. When you consider that it takes more than 611,000 signatures to qualify a question for the Florida ballot, shortening the circulation period by five months can mean the difference between success and failure. Jeb was hoping for failure.

One citizen initiative that Jeb Bush particularly hated was an idea to take the responsibility for drawing congressional and legislative districts from the legislature and place it in the hands of an independent commission. You see, the party who controls the legislature (in this case Republicans) can rig district lines to ensure that they have a big advantage. We all know, from the razor-thin Florida margins of victory for president in 2000, that the state is basically split evenly between Democrats and Republicans. In fact, there are actually more registered Democrats in Florida than there are registered Republicans. But, 15 of 22 members of Congress from Florida are Republicans. Likewise, about two thirds of both houses of the state legislature are controlled by Republicans.

How is that possible, you might ask? By cramming Democratic voters into districts that are overwhelmingly Democrat, Republicans rig the majority of the districts to have slightly more Republican voters than Democrats. This means that many Democratic legislators are elected by landslide margins, but many of those votes are effectively wasted. Putting the process in the hands of nonpartisan commissions would make it harder for either party to rig things in their own favor.

If this independent commission idea sounds familiar, that's because it's the *exact same thing* that Arnold was promoting in California. As a Republican governor in a state run by Democrats, Arnold was eager to get this process out of the hands of the legislature and into a more independent group of people. Arnold had the audacity to walk into Florida and ask Republican donors to help him pass in California the very thing they were opposing in Florida and to do it with the initiative process that they were also trying to cripple.

Jeb Bush later told big-business interests in his state, "Democracy is imperiled a little bit when big donors that can't get their way through the traditional way of creating policy through the Florida legislature, [and] secret donors who do not disclose who they are, come into our state from out of state to advance in many cases a left-wing political agenda, to put things on the ballot that sound good but create long-term challenges for us."[15]

Proving that politicians are never ones to let intellectual consistency get in the way of outright powerplays, Jeb Bush didn't bat an eye at Arnold's plan to take money from outside of California to advance things that sounded good on the California ballot. He was more than happy to help his friend Arnold pass whatever he wanted in California. "There is nothing ironic about my support for Arnold Schwarzenegger," stammered Jeb. "I know he has very difficult challenges in a state that is critical to our country. If

California does not get out of its morass, it makes it difficult for our country."[16]

Damien Filer, who had worked to support an initiative in Florida to reduce school class size that Jeb Bush had opposed, saw it differently. "The irony here almost makes your head spin," he said. "Irony isn't the word. Hypocrisy is the word."[17]

When asked why what's good for California wouldn't also be good for Florida, Bush stammered, "The context in which we operate here in Florida is very different from the context in California."[18] Perhaps by that he meant that his state's legislature was controlled by his party while California's was not.

When pressed, Bush admitted that he didn't really know what any of Arnold's ballot measures were about and was just helping raise money for them because he supported Arnold. Jeb's admission offers one of the few instances where politicians actually pull back the curtain and expose the wizard pulling the strings behind American politics. The big lie that politicians, donors, and even judges use to justify the massive exchange of cash between fat cats and candidates is that this is simply an expression of the donor's freedom of speech. What could be more American and apple pie than that? By giving funds to a candidate who shares their ideas, donors are simply providing a megaphone for those ideas to reach other citizens.

Of course, when the ideas of a candidate are the polar opposite of the ideas expressed by the donor, this freedom of speech argument falls apart like a house of cards. It becomes clear that what's really going on is that big-business players are using big bucks to get what they want from the government, leaving the rest of us hanging high and dry.

$ $ $

DONOR PROFILE: WAL-MART. Christy Walton, one of the heirs to the Wal-Mart fortune, contributed $250,000 to the California Recovery Team and $250,000 to the California Republican Party in October 2005. Her brother S. Robson Walton gave $250,000 to support Schwarzenegger's redistricting initiative, Prop 77. John Walton, now deceased, gave $200,000 to the CRT, $100,000 to Prop 77, and another $100,000 to the Small Business Action Committee, which promoted several of Arnold's initiatives. Wal-Mart as a corporation gave $100,000 to Citizens to Save California and another $100,000 to support Prop 77. All told, since 1999 the Waltons have personally given more than $6.75 million to California political committees and Wal-Mart has given another $6.6. While the Walton's individual donations tend to be ideological, many of the company's contributions go to local officials, who have control over siting new Wal-Mart stores, and to ballot committees with names like "Contra Costa Consumers for Choice," "Citizens for a Better Glendora," and the more accurately named "Committee to Welcome Wal-Mart to Inglewood." The Walton siblings are tied for 6th on the Forbes 400 list, with an estimated net worth of $15 billion each.

$ $ $

Escalating the Arms Race

Arnold's first response to criticism about his national money-grubbing tour was, "People don't see it as a negative. Maybe the press does, but the people don't. I have never seen anyone come up to me and say 'Governor, please stop the fundraising.' "[19]

A slightly more credible response would have been that he needed to compete against the huge sums of money that his opponents would spend against his special election ballot initiatives. Fair enough. We shouldn't ask him to stop fighting for what he believes in or to show up at a gunfight carrying only a knife.

There was nothing in California law that prevented anyone,

even out-of-state corporations, from contributing unlimited and ungodly sums of money to try to influence the way Californians voted in the special election. But Arnold wanted more than that. He wanted to raise this money himself, and he wanted it spent by people that would make sure it not only helped pass the ballot measures but also helped position him for re-election in 2006. To accomplish this, Arnold blew a Hummer-sized hole in California's campaign finance rules that will perhaps be his most enduring legacy.

CHAPTER 6

The Lawsuit

Arnold Asks Activist Judges to Gut Campaign Finance Rules

On February 5, 2005, the *Los Angeles Times* published an eye-opening story by reporters Robert Salladay and Peter Nicholas. The article described a series of fundraising luncheons that Governor Arnold Schwarzenegger was headlining to raise money for the ballot committee Citizens to Save California (CSC). Accompanying Schwarzenegger to many events were Allan Zaremberg, executive director of the California Chamber of Commerce, board member of CSC, and Schwarzenegger's legislative aide Richard Costigan, who had been the legislative director for the Chamber prior to going to work for Arnold. The invitations were printed on Schwarzenegger's official stationery, giving the impression that this was an event of the governor's, not just CSC's. The invitation suggested three levels of contributions for the event: $25,000, $50,000 and $100,000.

Schwarzenegger spokesperson Marty Wilson described the events as a prelude to the governor's upcoming fundraising drive for his own re-election. Arnold would offer his vision for California and give a briefing of the state's current financial situation.

There was nothing new about a California politician raising money for ballot campaigns. But since the Fair Political Practices Commission had closed the loophole exploited by Cruz Bustamante during the recall campaign, there were new rules in place. Candidates could no longer raise unlimited amounts of money for ballot committees that they controlled. If a ballot committee wanted to accept unlimited chunks of cash from powerful donors, they had to remain independent of any candidate.

Phony Independence

CSC claimed that it was independent of Schwarzenegger because he was not on their board of directors and therefore did not have legal control over the committee. However, when the group formed and began raising money, they told donors it was to help Schwarzenegger achieve his agenda. Initially CSC did not endorse any particular ballot measure on its own. How were donors to know whether they supported CSC's agenda? The only way to

REFORMER PROFILE: Bob Stern joined the Center for Governmental Studies in 1983. For more than 20 years, CGS has been a leading authority in the fields of campaign finance reform and community engagement, developing an impressive record of program development and publication in this area as well as other areas of governance and public policy. CGS identifies governance, social and economic problems, conducts in-depth studies, and proposes solutions. CGS then works with government agencies and community organizations to implement solutions through new laws, regulations, improved procedures, and technological systems.

Before joining CGS, Stern served as general counsel of the California Fair Political Practices Commission for nine years. He has co-authored a number of statewide initiatives, enacted by California voters, including the Political Reform Act of 1974.

know was to trust CSC's word that they would follow Arnold's lead. This is precisely what suggested that CSC was indeed not acting independently of Schwarzenegger, but rather was following the course of action he wanted them to take.

In the *Times* story, Bob Stern of the Center for Governmental Studies said that Schwarzenegger was clearly ". . . not abiding by the spirit" of the new regulations. As a three-decade veteran of good government policies in California, Stern is known for his no-nonsense, polite analysis. He's not a bomb-thrower by any stretch of the imagination, so when Bob says you're crossing the line, you should think twice about what you're doing.

The following day, Schwarzenegger responded to Stern's comment when talking to a reporter at the *San Jose Mercury News*. Arnold claimed that he was abiding by the letter of the law, but whether he was honoring the spirit of the law was ". . . a matter of opinion."[1] Rather than sounding like someone who had come to town to kick out the special interests, Arnold was beginning to sound like a politician who operated in an ethically grey area and debated what the meaning of "is" is, as Bill Clinton famously remarked.

☆ ☆ ☆

THE LETTER OF THE LAW: A "controlled committee" is defined by Government Code section 82016 as one that is "*controlled directly or indirectly by a candidate* or state measure proponent *or that acts jointly with a candidate, controlled committee*, or state measure proponent in making expenditures. *A candidate . . . controls a committee if he or she, his or her agent, or any other committee he or she controls has a significant influence on the actions or decisions of the committee.*" (emphasis added.)

☆ ☆ ☆

Karen Getman, a former head of the Fair Political Practices Commission went further than Bob Stern, saying in the *Times* story that the governor was "clearly coordinating with Citizens to Save California."

Back in the offices of TheRestofUs.org, we read that line over and over. We had been watching Arnold's charade play out and were asking that very question. If Arnold was *clearly coordinating* with this ballot committee, then it meant that the committee was no longer independent. The committee was raising contributions greater than $22,300, based on its own printed invitations. It looked like Arnold was breaking the law.

And nobody was doing anything about it.

I telephoned Karen Getman to ask if I was interpreting her remarks correctly.

I was.

I asked what I could do about it. She told me that any citizen could bring a complaint to the Fair Political Practices Commission and ask them to investigate. Given that nobody else was stepping up to challenge Arnold's brazen circumvention of the law, we decided the time had come for TheRestofUs.org to move from observing money in politics to trying to stop it.

TheRestofUs.org Files a Complaint

TheRestofUs.org compiled the information we had about Schwarzenegger's coordination with Citizens to Save California and wrote up a complaint to the FPPC (see appendix B).

We weren't sure what would happen next.

The FPPC didn't exactly have a reputation for speedy investigations—remember that it took four months before it ruled on Cruz Bustamante's violations during the recall campaign. But, perhaps Arnold would comply with the rules now that someone had blown the whistle. Maybe Citizens to Save California would fess up to being in cahoots with Arnold and would abide by the still very generous contribution limits of $22,300.

Maybe Arnold really was fighting to stand up for the regular guy and was simply not paying close attention as his consultants planned out fundraising details that skirted the law. Maybe once the issue was brought to his personal attention, Arnold would put an end to it.

Or maybe not.

Arnold Sues to Repeal Reform

Rather than comply with the new law as Marty Wilson had said he would three months earlier, Arnold moved to kill it in the courts. The man who had run for office on pledges to clean up California politics was now actively working to dismantle the most recent campaign finance rule in the state.

On February 14, 2005, Arnold Schwarzenegger sent his lawyers to ask a judge to overturn FPPC regulation 18530.9, the rule that closed the Bustamante loophole. Citizens to Save California had initially filed the lawsuit on February 8, the day following our complaint about their fundraising with the FPPC. Schwarzenegger evidently felt the need to work closely with CSC on this lawsuit as well as on the ballot initiatives so he joined the case as a co-plaintiff. Assemblymember Keith Richman was also part of the suit.

The Citizens to Save California lawsuit said that their committee would like to consult with Governor Schwarzenegger and Assemblymember Richman on strategic decisions regarding the ballot initiatives that both CSC and the governor were supporting. But, they correctly pointed out, FPPC regulation 18530.9 prevented this. Therefore, they wanted the regulation declared unconstitutional.

It was curious *to say the least* that neither the governor nor Citizens to Save California challenged this regulation until TheRestofUs.org asked the FPPC to investigate whether they were breaking it. Indeed, CSC referenced our complaint in their lawsuit and said that they were worried that the agency will launch an investigation ". . . premised on the incorrect belief that the regulation is legal and enforceable."

We viewed the lawsuit as a clear admission by Citizens to Save California that they had stepped over the line of coordinating with Arnold Schwarzenegger. Why else would they have waited to file their challenge to the law?

Arnold and his allies based their complaint on the fact that the U.S. Supreme Court had thrown out an ordinance in Berkeley, California, in the 1981 case *Citizens Against Rent Control v. Berkeley*. That ordinance set a $500 limit on how much anyone could give to a local ballot measure campaign. While this might seem like a good idea to many, the Supreme Court thought otherwise and ruled that since there were no candidates involved in those ballot measures who could have been personally corrupted by large contributions, there was no basis for upholding the limits using the court precedents at that time.

Citizens to Save California and Arnold also argued that the FPPC regulation was unfair. Committees that coordinated with members of the Assembly faced contribution limits of $3,300, while those that coordinated only with candidates for governor faced limits of $22,300. Meanwhile, committees that coordinated with no candidates at all faced no limits at all.

The different treatment of different ballot committees was indeed unfair. It would have been better to apply contribution limits to all ballot committees. But that is not what the FPPC had done, in part because of the *Citizens Against Rent Control* ruling and in part because the California Political Reform Act clearly set contribution limits for candidates, but not ballot committees. It made sense that all contributions to candidates be covered, including those that candidates used to promote their own pet ballot campaigns. But, beyond the expected court challenges, extending contribution limits to all ballot campaigns would have required an additional change in the Political Reform Act by either the legislature or the people through a ballot initiative aimed at reforming ballot initiative financing.

There was good legal precedent for limiting all contributions raised by candidates, regardless of how they used them. In 2003, the U.S. Supreme Court upheld the Bipartisan Campaign Reform Act, sponsored by Senators John McCain and Russ Feingold and signed by President Bush in 2002. That law prohibited federal candidates from raising money in amounts greater than the federal contribution limits that applied to candidates.

Loyola Law School professor Rick Hasen studied the 2003 Court rulings and concluded that the justices might now be ready to accept more stringent regulations on ballot measure campaigns. Professor Hasen moderates an election law listserv that most of the leading election law experts in the country participate in. He is considered the top in his field. In January 2005, Hasen presented a paper at a symposium sponsored by the University of California at Irvine suggesting that limits on candidate-controlled ballot committees could now be found constitutional. Going even further, he suggested that contribution limits to all ballot measure campaigns and laws that banned corporate contributions to ballot measures ". . . have a surprisingly good chance of standing muster today."[2]

The lawsuit brought by CSC and Governor Schwarzenegger provided the first chance to test Hasen's theory that the courts now recognized at least some of the problems with big money in ballot measure campaigns. Beyond the immediate ramifications for Arnold and his ballot initiatives, there was an important policy precedent at stake.

Public Interest Groups Weigh In

Because of the long-term ramifications of the outcome of this case, the nonpartisan California Public Interest Research Group (CALPIRG) sought to intervene in the case to help defend the FPPC regulation. Maintaining limits on candidate-controlled ballot committees not only helped prevent large donors from evading contribution limits to candidate campaigns, it also could set the stage for contribution limits on all ballot campaigns that would significantly reduce the role of corporations and other special interests in defeating citizen-initiated ballot measures.

CALPIRG had a long history of working on campaign finance laws in California, and its sister organization in Montana had pioneered a law in 1996 to ban corporate contributions to all ballot campaigns in that state. As a veteran of many ballot initiative efforts that were heavily outspent by corporate interests, CALPIRG saw what was at stake in this case.

Arnold and his allies had no desire to let a public interest group defend California's election law. Perhaps fearing that an independent group would pursue the case more vigorously than the government, Arnold and CSC filed a motion opposing CALPIRG's involvement. On March 4, 2005, a Sacramento County judge sided with the governor. Even though Schwarzenegger was allowed to intervene on behalf of CSC, the judge ruled that CALPIRG could not join in support of the Fair Political Practices Commission because he felt that the FPPC would do just fine defending itself and didn't need any help.

Undeterred, CALPIRG filed a so-called friend of the court brief in the case, as a way of making the public interest heard. The Campaign Legal Center likewise filed a friend of the court brief, authored by Paul Ryan, the election lawyer who had originally urged the FPPC to issue the challenged regulation when he was employed by the Center for Governmental Studies in Los Angeles.

More Phony Independence

Meanwhile, Arnold and CSC continued the charade of independence. On March 17, CSC rejected a ballot question calling for a strict state spending limit and instead backed the milder version supported by Schwarzenegger. They dropped their earlier neutrality on the Schwarzenegger-backed redistricting decision, coming out in favor of it. Finally, CSC endorsed Schwarzenegger's proposal to base teacher pay on job performance rather than experience after previously backing the idea of extending teacher tenure requirements.[3] Schwarzenegger issued a statement saying, "I want to congratulate the Citizens to Save California for doing a great job in completing their agenda for reform." Of course he did.

As the *San Diego Union Tribune* reported, ". . . the committee that had once been split on a spending-control measure and seemed to be going its own way on some issues is now in virtual alignment with Schwarzenegger."[4]

What a coincidence.

When Richard Claussen's staff saw focus groups indicating that Schwarzenegger's original idea of merit pay for teachers had weak public support, it shifted gears to the idea of reducing teacher tenure from five years to two. Arnold followed their lead.

Marty Wilson sliced the baloney even thinner: "As I understand it," said Wilson, "this becomes a controlled committee if the governor or his agents exercise substantial control over its spending decisions. He will not. [Rather, he will] make appearances and appeals for [CSC] and offer opinions on how Citizens to Save California should spend their money."[5]

The Judge Sides with Arnold

Judge Shelleyanne Chang presided over the case. CALPIRG told Judge Chang that the FPPC was authorized to adopt reasonable regulations to carry out the provisions of the Political Reform Act—California's bedrock campaign finance law that voters had amended in 2000 with the contribution limits of Proposition 34. Based on Bustamante's use of ballot committees in the 2003 recall and Schwarzenegger's use of the California Recovery Team in supporting 2004 ballot measures, CALPIRG concluded that Proposition 34's contribution limits would be rendered meaningless unless the Fair Political Practices Commission applied them to all funds raised by candidates.

CALPIRG's position was that if the court accepted Schwarzenegger's argument, it would "essentially gut the contribution limits by allowing any and all candidates to open controlled ballot measure committees that would allow completely unregulated fundraising.[6] The experience of 2003 and 2004 leads to the unavoidable conclusion that the *only* reasonable interpretation [of Proposition 34] is that reflected in Regulation 18530.9," wrote

CALPIRG.

The Campaign Legal Center's brief addressed the constitutionality of the FPPC's new rule, concluding that:

> applying the U.S. Supreme Court holdings detailed in this brief to the facts of this case leads to one inescapable conclusion: if the candidate contribution limits of Cal. Govt. Code 85301 and 85302 are a reasonable and constitutional means of preventing real and apparent corruption of candidates, then the FPPC regulation applying these limits to candidate-controlled ballot-measure committees is likewise constitutional.[7]

REFORMER PROFILE: Paul Ryan is an expert on election law who has worked at the Center for Governmental Studies in Los Angeles and more recently at the Campaign Legal Center in Washington, D.C. Ryan regularly represents the Campaign Legal Center before the Federal Election Commission (FEC). He also litigates campaign finance issues before federal and state courts throughout the United States. Mr. Ryan has testified as an expert on election law before numerous legislative bodies and ethics agencies, including the FEC, the California State Legislature, the California Fair Political Practices Commission, the New York City Council, the Los Angeles City Council and the Los Angeles City Ethics Commission. He has appeared as a campaign finance law expert on news programs on *CNN*, *NBC* and other media outlets and has been quoted by *The New York Times*, *Los Angeles Times*, *The Washington Post*, *Roll Call* and other news publications.

In other words, unless Judge Chang was prepared to throw out the contribution limits to candidate campaigns, it made no sense to throw out the FPPC's extension of those limits to ballot committees controlled by the candidate.

The Campaign Legal Center reminded Judge Chang that the Federal Election Commission had recently issued a very similar ruling to its counterpart agency in California. That ruling found that members of Congress could not raise money in excess of federal contribution limits for ballot campaigns that they controlled. This makes sense. It does not matter what kind of committee a candidate controls. A candidate would feel beholden to any donors who gave them huge chunks of cash for any committee. "The fact that a candidate uses contributions to support ballot measures in no way reduces the threat of corruption," according to the Center's brief.

California Superior Judge Shelleyanne Chang didn't see it that way.

On March 23, 2005, Arnold and his allies won a major victory. Judge Chang issued a tentative ruling that the Fair Political Practices Commission was not authorized by California law to issue the regulation that limited contributions to candidate-controlled ballot committees. She finalized that ruling two days later. This meant two things: 1) ballot committees such as Citizens to Save California were now free to coordinate with candidates such as Arnold Schwarzenegger, and 2) candidate-controlled ballot committees such as the California Recovery Team could once again accept unlimited contributions.

California law states: "Unless clearly unreasonable, the court cannot substitute its own judgment for the agency's within the agency's authorized area of expertise."[8] And yet, this is exactly what Chang did. Chang decided that in her opinion, contrary to the FPPC's, it did matter whether candidates used a contribution for their own re-election committee rather than for a ballot campaign they supported. More significantly, Judge Chang decided that she would substitute her own opinion for the Fair Political Practices Commission's opinion and would strike down the agency's attempt to make the contribution limits of Proposition 34 meaningful.

No wonder people are getting fed up with activist judges who have decided that when they don't like the laws, they will simply rewrite them. It is hard enough to get any sort of campaign finance reform enacted in the first place because politicians all have a self-interest in preserving the rules that got them where they are. When judges undo what few campaign finance laws we have, it deepens citizen frustration with our government and undermines the very legitimacy of the judiciary.

Sweeping Special Interests from Sacramento?

Californians now had a self-declared reform governor, who embraced the people's use of ballot initiatives, winning a court battle to weaken a previously passed ballot initiative that set up campaign finance rules—Proposition 34. As I told the *San Francisco Chronicle*, there's a

> level of irony that he's ignoring the expressed will of the voters as put forth in an initiative, in an effort to forward his own initiative. There's also the irony that he ran for office on the platform of getting special interest money out of politics, and he's just blown a hole in our campaign finance laws that will bring more special interest money into politics.

Doug Woods, a lawyer in the attorney general's office who represented the FPPC, expressed dismay. "Candidates will now be in an arms race to join ballot measure committees. It's important to keep candidate-controlled ballot measure committees consistent with candidate committees to head off this artificial rush," he stressed.[9]

Bob Stern of the Center for Governmental Studies said the ruling would start a "donnybrook," and predicted that legislative leaders would soon begin using ballot committees to forward their political careers as well. I had to look the word up in the dictionary, but when I did I had to agree with Bob.

Donnybrook: n. An uproar; a free-for-all. [After Donnybrook fair, held in Donnybrook, a suburb of Dublin, Ireland, and noted for its brawls.] *American Heritage College Dictionary.*

Fortunately, Judge Chang's ruling did not find that it was inherently unconstitutional for California to set limits on candidate-controlled ballot committees, only that the FPPC did not have the authority to do so in this case. Chang found that the Political Reform Act appeared contradictory in parts, so it was unclear whether the FPPC could indeed set limits to some ballot committees but not others.

Loyola law professor Rick Hasen did not think the ruling invalidated his core argument that such limits are indeed constitutional. He noted, "The big constitutional question was not really answered in this opinion. . . . I think there's a strong case to be made for the constitutionality of a well-drafted statute."[10]

While the ruling was a huge win for Arnold in the short term, it left the door open in the long term that California could enact a new law that applied contribution limits to candidate-controlled ballot campaigns, or potentially go even further.

But until the legislature, or the people through a ballot initiative, repair the damage done by Arnold and Judge Chang, California candidates are now free to use ballot committees to circumvent campaign finance law.

And have they ever.

CHAPTER 7

Recovering from Reform

The California Recovery Team Spends Big Bucks, The Rest of Us Say, "Stop!"

With the FPPC rule putting limits on contributions to candidate-controlled ballot committees suspended, Arnold was free to use his California Recovery Team as the primary vehicle for pursuing his ballot agenda, just as he had done in 2004. Unlike Citizens to Save California, Arnold didn't need to pretend that he didn't control the Recovery Team. As Arnold revved up the CRT to act more like a political slush fund to advance his own re-election than a committee devoted only to ballot questions, he crossed another line that may have violated the law.

The ability to *directly* control the money he was raising for his ballot agenda gave Schwarzenegger a boost. Arnold's campaign director Mike Murphy boasted in the *Sacramento Bee,* "Any advantage the Democrats thought they'd have because of the bifurcated nature of the campaign has evaporated. Now they're going to face everything we've got."[1]

Marty Wilson, who had told the press just months ago that Arnold was prepared to live with the FPPC regulation and would be able to run a perfectly viable organization under the new rules was now saying that "clearly [the ruling] is going to make our life a lot easier. . . . What this does is put the governor's own committee back in the driver's seat."[2]

Arnold's spin-men may have just been trying to scare his opponents, but even neutral observers saw Judge Chang's ruling as a real advantage for Schwarzenegger. Jaime Regalado, of the nonpartisan Pat Brown Institute of Public Affairs, observed, "This gives the governor just what he wants at the right moment. It should open up the coffers beyond what he's already receiving. It's going to be even tougher for the other side to compete now because it will be easier for people to give with Arnold now directly related to it. There's no having to hide under the guise that this was being operated by some independent expenditure committee."

Both Murphy's and Regalado's comments are a reminder that even when campaign finance laws don't work perfectly, they do have an impact. Arnold was bypassing the FPPC regulation on candidate-controlled ballot committees with a loophole worthy of Cruz Bustamante. But, as with Cruz, that loophole came with a price. It not only made Arnold look like he was trying to game the system, it meant that the money he raised was less effective because he controlled it only indirectly via signals he sent in his speeches. Consultants like Murphy who were on Arnold's payroll could not explicitly instruct CSC in what to do. While fat cats often use so-called independent expenditures to get around campaign finance laws, we need only remember that neither politicians nor donors set these things up unless they are forced to. As soon as they don't need to use a loophole, they go back to having the cash run straight into a candidate's account.

With Arnold's need for Citizens to Save California gone, the committee fell into inactivity—arguably demonstrating its connection to the governor all along. From January 1 to April 15, Citizens to Save California raised $9.2 million while the California Recovery Team raised only $770,000. Once the Recovery Team was allowed to take unlimited contributions, it raised $9.3 million from April 15 to July 30 while CSC raised only $737,000.

A similar dynamic occurred with Schwarzenegger's official candidate committee. In the first three-and-a-half months of 2005, Californians for Schwarzenegger raised $1.8 million, much of it through joint fundraisers with CSC. In the following three-and-a-half months, Arnold only raised $47,300 for his re-election committee, and even transferred a million dollars from his candidate committee to his California Recovery Team. This suggests that Schwarzenegger's candidate fundraising was done to advance his reform initiative with spending directly under his control. Once he could do that through the CRT, not only did the CSC wind down, but Schwarzenegger also stopped raising money into the committee for his candidacy in an election nearly 20 months away. The model of politics that Arnold was creating combined candidate and ballot committees into one function, and raising money into the CRT meant he didn't have to deal with the contribution limits that applied to his candidate committee.

$ $ $

DONOR PROFILE: William Armstead Robinson owned most of DHL, the international cargo delivery company until he sold it recently to Astar Air Cargo. In 2003, Robinson gave $1 million to help found Chimp Haven in his native Shreveport, Louisiana. He contributed $21,200 (the legal limit at the time) to Schwarzenegger's 2003 candidate campaign and another $200,000 toward Schwarzenegger's Total Recall Committee. In 2004, Robinson kicked in $450,000 to Schwarzenegger's California Recovery Team. The next year, he gave $1 million to Citizens to Save California, another $2.3 million to the California Recovery Team and a half-million to the California Republican Party. In 1992, the IRS sought $18 million in back taxes from Robinson. He had deducted some $185,000 for his horse breeding and tennis activities. In 1998, a judge ordered DHL to pay $550 million in delinquent back taxes, but the company reduced the amount on appeal. Robinson is one of America's foremost breeders of Lusitano show horses. He spends most of his time in his two homes in Idaho, but also owns three houses in California and one in Mexico.

$ $ $

PR Stunts

Using the Recovery Team, Schwarzenegger staged a series of campaign events that had at least as much to do with promoting Arnold as a political figure as they did with any ballot question. The CRT paid for a steady stream of media stunts, such as Arnold appearing with a huge prop of red ink and claiming to turn it off on the people's behalf. Arnold the movie star knew how to film hero-spots, and it seemed nothing could deter him from doing a new stunt each week.

One stunt involved Arnold going into a San Jose neighborhood to fix a pothole and announce that he was seeking $1.3 billion to fully fund Proposition 42, which voters passed in 2002. Ten public employees were given brand new orange vests to act as "seconds" for the governor's little PR shoot. Schwarzenegger strutted up with the music "Taking It to the Streets" by the Doobie Brothers blasting in the background. "I'm here to let everyone know that we're going to improve transportation all across our state," crowed Arnold.[3]

Neighbors were a bit annoyed at having their street shut off for what looked more like a commercial than a real repair. "For paving the streets, it's a lot of lighting," said Nick Porrovecchio, commenting on the Hollywood-style floodlights that had been set up to light the governor.

The icing on the cake was that there had been no pothole in the first place. Work crews took a backhoe and dug a new hole in the middle of the street that morning so Arnold would have something to fill up with asphalt.

Nurses and teachers angry about Schwarzenegger's policies had been dogging him at events around the state, so the whole thing was kept under wraps to prevent protesters from showing up. Just the day before, some 10,000 protesters had rallied in Sacramento and Los Angeles. Reporters and TV cameramen were told to meet in a parking lot where they would then be personally handed directions to the secret event location.

Rob Stutzman, spokesman for Arnold, knew that this event

California nurses protest Arnold's fundraising.

was political and that it would be wrong for Arnold to be paying for such a stunt with taxpayer dollars. Never fear, he assured reporters, the California Recovery Team was paying for this event. But what fixing potholes had to do with Arnold's initiatives on budget caps, teacher tenure, or legislative redistricting was anyone's guess.

Perhaps the cheekiest campaign moment was when Schwarzenegger drove out of the Capitol aboard a military-style Humvee with license plates that read "REFORM 1." Arnold had actually removed his real license plates because they were from Indiana, the only state that allows street registration of a real military Hummer. With camera crews riding on a film truck ahead of him, Arnold drove five miles away to an Applebee's restaurant to talk to diners about his reform agenda. His aides moved aside the restaurant's potted plants so the cameras could get a good shot as Arnold went from table to table, asking folks to sign petitions to put his initiatives on the ballot. This event, also paid for by

Arnold's California Recovery Team, at least did have something to do with his ballot agenda even if it also served to bolster Arnold's re-election chances.

The thing is, had Arnold really spent his time touring California's restaurants and talking with real people about their lives, he might have succeeded in not only passing his ballot agenda but boosting his popularity as well. Instead, he did cheap photo ops aimed at promoting himself more than any idea or initiative.

Hiram Johnson Rolls in His Grave

The fundraising continued whole hog. The duplicity of a governor who ran for office decrying a system where "money comes in and favors go out," raising record sums of money from among the most special of interests in the country disappointed true reformers. Paul Ryan of the Campaign Legal Center expressed his frustration by noting, "the fundraising activity of Arnold Schwarzenegger since taking office I think speaks volumes to his lack of commitment to political reform."[4]

Yet Arnold clung to the image of a reformer. He compared himself to Hiram Johnson, the California governor who pioneered the initiative and recall process at the turn of the 20th century so that citizens could fight back against the power of the railroads and other corporate interests. Arnold was now using that same process to advance the agenda of those corporations. Amazingly, Union Pacific Railroad—the same company that Hiram Johnson battled—kicked in $25,000 to Arnold's ballot campaigns. Other checks poured in from Fortune 500 firms like Citigroup ($100,000) and Chevron/Texaco ($50,000).

My colleague Ned Wigglesworth came to a similar conclusion as Paul Ryan. "From the beginning, it was hard to accept the governor's statements that he was interested in reform, when he's pulling in money from the same old cast of characters that's been spending money to dominate the California political process for years," Ned told the *San Francisco Chronicle*. "I think most Californians think it's ridiculous that he would even claim the title

☆ ☆ ☆

Hiram Johnson: "The first duty that is mine to perform is to eliminate every private interest from the government, and to make the public service of the state responsive solely to the people. . . . Where under our political system, therefore, there exists any appointee of the governor who is representing a political machine or a corporation that has been devoting itself in part to our politics, that appointee will be replaced by an official who will devote himself exclusively and solely to the service of the state. In this fashion, so far as it can be accomplished by the executive, the government of California shall be made a government for the people. . . .

"And finally when we reach, if we do, some representative, not only of the former political master of this state, the Southern Pacific Company, but an apostle of "big business" as well (that business that believes all government is a mere thing for exploitation and private gain), a storm of indignation will meet us from all of those who have been parties to or partisans of the political system that has obtained in the past; and particularly that portion of the public press which is responsive to private interest and believes that private interest should control our government, will, in mock indignation and pretended horror, cry out against the desecration of the public service and the awful politics which would permit the people to rule. . .

"In the consummation of our design at last to have the people rule, we shall go forward, without malice or hatred, not in animosity or personal hostility, but calmly, coolly, pertinaciously, unswervingly and with absolute determination, until the public service reflects only the public good and represents alone the people."

—Inaugural Address, January 3, 1911.

☆ ☆ ☆

of reformer, or claim the legacy of Hiram Johnson, when he's taking sizable contributions of the kind and from the very contributor that Hiram Johnson started the initiative process to combat."[5]

A Limitless Slush Fund

Back in the office, Ned and I began taking a closer look at the California Recovery Team even before Judge Chang freed it up to rake in unlimited contributions on March 23. We observed that the CRT wasn't really acting like a ballot committee; it was acting more like a political slush fund aimed at re-electing Arnold Schwarzenegger as governor.

The California Republican Party was clearly ginning up for Arnold's re-election. It took the unusual move of endorsing him as its candidate in February 2005, about a year earlier than it normally would have. This freed up the party to begin raising unlimited funds to promote Schwarzenegger's re-election.

Indeed, it was simply impossible to separate Arnold's ballot agenda from his re-election agenda. When talking to the *Washington Post* about his ballot agenda and the behind-the-scenes negotiations with Democrats, Arnold gushed, "The whole thing is a big stage play. They are all very important characters in this play, in order to carry out this play. It's wonderful. . . . Since they are all part of the play, you have to appreciate all those pieces and all those characters."

When the reporter asked him what his role in the play was, Arnold replied with a smile, "Leading role. Above-the-title billing."[6]

It was no exaggeration.

Many of the events CRT staged, such the one where he filled the bogus pothole, didn't even mention any upcoming ballot questions. They simply appeared to be a way for Arnold to boost his popularity as part of the permanent campaign for re-election that begins the day any officeholder is sworn into office.

California politicians had become accustomed to using their campaign funds for events like this and other so-called officeholder expenses such as sending flowers to an important constituent's funeral or paying for their travel to a political event. But Proposition 34 had banned politicians from using an old campaign committee to raise additional funds to pay for ongoing expenses once they had taken office.[7] Most politicians got around this prohibition by simply setting up a new committee to run for re-election and rolling their funds over into that new committee as their slush fund. If a politician was prohibited from running for re-election due to term limits, they would set up a campaign to run for some other office, even if they had no intention of doing so. Former California Assembly Speaker Willie Brown notoriously set up a committee to run for insurance commissioner just to have someplace to transfer his war chest from his existing Assembly campaign committee.

But for Schwarzenegger there was no other office to file for, he'd already filed to run for governor again. The downside of using his Citizens for Schwarzenegger 2006 Committee to pay for general PR stunts and other so-called officeholder expenses was that he would have less money to spend on TV ads and other campaign items. Contributions to his re-election committee were limited to $22,300, so once that money was spent it was harder to replace. Rather than having his 2006 re-election committee pay his political expenses, Arnold was having the California Recovery Team pay these expenses because that committee could raise a separate and unlimited pool of money from the same donors. After the *CSC v. FPPC* ruling, there were not any limits on the size of the contributions the Recovery Team could raise.

As this sunk in, we concluded that what Arnold was doing with both the California Recovery Team and Citizens to Save California violated basic California campaign finance law that predated any of the FPPC regulations about candidate-controlled ballot committees. Any political committee was free to accept unlimited contributions so long as it limited its activities to promoting ballot measures. But, the minute a committee began helping candidates, too, it was no longer considered a ballot committee but a candidate political action committee (PAC), regardless of whether it was controlled by the candidate it was helping.

Proposition 34 had set a limit of $5,000 on contributions to PACs. The purpose, in part, was to prevent huge donors from getting around the contribution limits that applied to candidates by simply giving a huge sum to a PAC that then helped the candidate. In other words, if Jerry Perenchio can only give $3,200 to a legislative candidate named Ima Stooge, he can't then give $100,000 to a committee called the Stooge Recovery Team in order to help Ima Stooge get elected. At most, he can give the Stooge Recovery Team $5,000. This is true even if the Stooge Recovery Team also supports some ballot measures.

If in fact the California Recovery Team was acting to promote Arnold as a candidate, rather than only promoting ballot questions, it should have been governed as a candidate PAC, not a ballot committee. Candidates are allowed to control PACs, and PACs can certainly contribute to ballot campaigns. But, PACs were subject to a contribution limit of $5,600 under the California Political Reform Act, an amount indexed for inflation from the original $5,000 limit.

The FPPC had advised politicians in the past that they were allowed to establish and control ballot campaign committees that were separate from their own re-election campaigns, even if those ballot campaigns happened to help their candidacy. But, those letters originated before there were any contribution limits in place for candidates, so there was no reason for candidates to use ballot committees to evade limits to their own campaigns. Further, that FPPC advice had not been tested in court and, as we had seen with Ross Johnson's lawsuit against Cruz Bustamante, courts sometimes reverse FPPC findings.

There was a section of the Political Reform Act dating back to 1974 that said that all contributions raised to benefit a candidate must be deposited into one bank account. Allowing candidates to establish a separate account for ballot questions seemed to violate that. Indeed, this was precisely what Ross Johnson had complained about to the FPPC regarding Cruz Bustamante, and why he had argued that contributions to a candidate's ballot committee should count toward the limit that they can accept for all their committees, including their re-election campaigns. But, in any case, it was clear that the FPPC advice only addressed ballot committees that limited themselves to spending money only on ballot questions, not committees that also promoted a candidate's re-election.

The bottom line was this: in promoting Schwarzenegger's qualifications for office, albeit in a ham-handed fashion, the CRT was either 1) violating the single bank account rule by acting as a separate Schwarzenegger candidate committee, or 2) making in-kind contributions to Schwarzenegger's candidacy which would subject it to the $5,600 contribution limit.

TheRestofUs.org Stands up to the CRT

Based on this understanding of the law, and how Arnold appeared to be breaking it, TheRestofUs.org considered filing another complaint at the Fair Political Practices Commission. If candidates were free to use ballot committees as slush funds to promote their own candidacy, then they would simply set up multiple ballot committees as easy ways to get around the rules on fundraising for their candidate committees. Arnold was blazing a trail that others would surely follow, thereby rendering any limits on campaign contributions meaningless.

However, the commission hadn't appeared to do anything in response to our past complaint. Indeed, the commission seemed to have a track record of weak-kneed enforcement from an overworked staff. The FPPC had around 60 staff people, 20 fewer than they had in 1999 even though its case load had doubled. It had a backlog of cases 737 long.

Somehow, the politicians hadn't seen fit to fully fund the agency that policed their campaign behavior.

In 2004, Schwarzenegger had proposed cutting the agency's $6 million budget by $1 million. In 2005, the legislature and Arnold had actually cut $500,000 from the FPPC's budget. On average, it was taking about two years for the commission to deal with complaints—almost always after an election was over. This timeline meant that it was unlikely our complaint would actually stop Arnold from illegally raising or spending any money. Like Bustamante in the recall, he'd spend the cash long before the courts told him not to. If we wanted something done before it was too late to matter, we would need another plan.

We amended our previous complaint at the FPPC about Schwarzenegger's control of Citizens to Save California to include our claim that both Citizens to Save California and the California Recovery Team were acting to promote Arnold's re-election and should therefore be subject to the $5,600 limit on contributions. But we knew that the FPPC was unlikely to act until the special election was over. So we asked a judge to intervene.

The Political Reform Act allows citizen groups to enforce campaign finance laws themselves by filing a request in civil court. You can't get a fine against the offender unless you go through a lengthy process of allowing the FPPC to first exhaust its options, but you can get a court to order a political campaign to stop its illegal activity. This was all we were looking for.

We found lawyers who were among the foremost experts in California campaign finance law. One of them had actually helped write parts of the law. Our lawyers agreed with our instincts that we had a strong case and advised us to move forward immediately. We filed our complaint on March 15, 2005, the week before Judge Chang threw out the FPPC regulation on candidate-controlled ballot committees. So, while we were disappointed in Judge Chang's ruling that tossed the new rules, we thought Arnold was breaking an older and more fundamental law. As PACs making contributions to Arnold's candidacy, both Citizens to Save California and the California Recovery Team should be subject to the even stricter PAC limits of $5,600 than the $22,300 limit that the FPPC ruling applied to candidate-controlled ballot committees.

Our lawsuit noted that Arnold appeared to be violating the California Political Reform Act, which said that "all contributions or loans made to the candidate, to a person on behalf of the candidate, or to the candidate's controlled committee" must be deposited into one single bank account. We contended that Arnold had several accounts: in addition to Arnold's official re-election committee Californians for Schwarzenegger '06, there was the California Recovery Team and Citizens to Save California, all of which were working together to further Arnold's re-election.

The Evidence

Going to court is not a quick and easy process. I had expected that for an important case like this, we would have to go through a lengthy trial before a judge would even consider applying campaign finance law to a ballot committee in the middle of a ballot campaign. In the normal course of litigation, both sides go through a process called discovery where they can examine documents and ask witnesses to testify under oath or by affidavit as part of collecting evidence for the trial. Because a trial could take a long time, perhaps dragging on past the special election Arnold was likely to call, we hoped the judge would order an immediate halt to both the California Recovery Team and Citizens to Save California from raising amounts greater than $5,600 until the trial was over—a process called a preliminary injunction.

In this case, the governor's team steadfastly refused to provide any documents, affidavits or testimony that could confirm or deny the public statements of Citizens to Save California's board members that it was in fact looking to public statements of Arnold Schwarzenegger to guide its decisions. Nor did they provide any information on whether or not these committees were spending money in ways that helped Arnold directly, not just his ballot questions. We had numerous statements of Arnold's staff and consultants saying precisely this in the newspapers, but to be admitted in court we needed to get these same statements said under oath.

The Smoking Gun

But as we looked closer, we found irrefutable evidence that

the California Recovery Team was promoting Arnold as a candidate simply by going to Arnold's campaign website, www.JoinArnold.com. It was filled with pages that had nothing to do with ballot questions but everything to do with how great Arnold Schwarzenegger was. The website carried a disclaimer saying that instead of being paid for by his re-election campaign, it was ***paid for by the California Recovery Team***. We couldn't believe what we were seeing. If the Recovery Team was paying for Arnold's re-election web page, then surely it was acting to promote his re-election, not just promote ballot questions.

The homepage clearly said, "Contribute!—Please Join Our Efforts To **Support** Arnold Schwarzenegger." Supporting Arnold Schwarzenegger is clearly a different thing than supporting a ballot question. Using the word support next to a candidate's name is one of the classic examples that courts have found to fit the definition of electioneering in favor of that candidate. The page also carried a quote from Arnold saying, "I will work honestly, without fear or favor, to do what is right for California," which again has more to do with his qualifications for office than any ballot question. In short, the JoinArnold.com website, paid for by the Recovery Team, was simply a giant pro-Arnold piece of propaganda.

The Law

California law says that if a candidate asks or suggests that a political committee make any payment whatsoever, technically called a payment "at the behest of a candidate," that the payment counts as a contribution to that candidate unless "it is clear from the surrounding circumstances that the payment was made for purposes unrelated to his or her candidacy for elective office."[8] In other words, if candidate Ima Stooge asked a ballot committee called the Stooge Recovery Team to pay for a 100,000-piece mailing that had a picture of candidate Ima Stooge on it, and talked about why Ima Stooge is fantastic, that would count as a contribution to Ima Stooge. In this case, it was crystal clear that the California Recovery Team was acting on the "behest" of Schwarzenegger because they outright admitted that Schwarzenegger controlled the committee.

The law also says that any payment for "election-related activities" counts as a contribution to a candidate's campaign. The law gives eight types of examples of what could count as an "election-related" activity, including: 1) soliciting contributions to a candidate, 2) communications that contain a "reference to" the candidate's "qualifications for elective office," and 3) communications that contain express advocacy, which simply means telling people to support or oppose a candidate.

While any one of these activities was enough to mean a committee was making a contribution to a candidate, and was thus subject to the $5,600 limit, we thought that the California Recovery Team was doing all three and Citizens to Save California was doing at least one of them.

Raising Contributions for Arnold's Re-election

Taking the most clear cut example first, the home page of the JoinArnold.com website had a button that said, "Contribute! Please Join Our Efforts to Support Arnold Schwarzenegger." Elsewhere on the site, we found the following details:

> **Contributions**
> JoinArnold.com uses a secured server for online credit card and e-check donations.
>
> Contributions to *Californians for Schwarzenegger* (emphasis original) are not tax deductible. Foreign nationals are prohibited from making contributions to this committee, unless they have permanent residency status in the United States of America (a Green Card.)
>
> Contributions are limited to $22,300 from a single source. Spouses may each give $22,300 by separate checks, credit card transactions, or internet donations.

Further, there were the fundraisers where Arnold had raised money for both his re-election committee and "Governor Schwarzenegger's California Recovery Team." No explanation was given about the difference between the two committees, and unless a donor was very knowledgeable about campaign finance law they might assume they were both Schwarzenegger campaign committees. A fax that accompanied the invitation to one such fundraiser said that the event "is the only event scheduled so far this year in Los Angeles ***to benefit Governor Schwarzenegger."*** It was impossible to look at these invitations and say that it was clear that this fundraising had nothing to do with Arnold's political career.

Touting Arnold's Qualifications for Office

The JoinArnold.com website, paid for by the California Recovery Team, also contained numerous references to Schwarzenegger's qualifications for office and leadership qualities, including these webpages:

About Arnold—with the headline, "Through hard work, fierce competitiveness and an unmatched desire to succeed, Arnold Schwarzenegger embodies the American dream." The page tracks Arnold's life story of coming to America, his bodybuilding success, his movie career, and his commitment to kids.

Leadership—with the headline, "Schwarzenegger, the American Dream and Leadership." The page touts Arnold's leadership qualities and experience, talking again about Prop 49 but not about propositions on the 2004 ballot.

Endorsements—containing the endorsement of 120 politicians and political groups, 31 educators, 31 public safety officials and groups, 275 local politicians, and 21 veterans. The endorsements were clearly for Arnold as a candidate, not any particular ballot question.

These pages all said that they were paid for by Californians for Schwarzenegger and carried a 2003 copyright, even though the homepage now said it was paid for by the California Recovery Team. It appeared that the Recovery Team was simply paying to keep Arnold's old campaign materials on the Internet, not to mention soliciting funds for his 2006 candidacy.

Beyond the website, many of the events, like the pothole event, paid for by Arnold's California Recovery Team seemed like they had a lot more to do with Arnold's qualifications for office than any ballot question.

Expressly Advocating Support for Arnold

Deciding whether an ad, flyer, or webpage expressly advocates the election or defeat of a candidate has become perhaps the highest stakes issue in campaign finance law. The whole controversy stemmed from a footnote in the 1976 Supreme Court ruling in *Buckley v. Valeo* where the Court suggested that federal contribution limits only applied to communications that used so-called magic words like "vote for, support, or elect." California had adopted similar guidelines to determine whether something was for candidate support and subject to regulations that apply to candidate campaigns. California regulation 18225 specifically says that a communication "expressly advocates" the nomination or election of a candidate if it contains words of advocacy such as "support."

The JoinArnold.com website, paid for by Arnold's California Recovery Team, had numerous examples of what sounds a lot more like support for a candidate than support for a ballot question.

> Join Arnold—The web domain itself and every page on it urges citizens to "join Arnold," which sure sounds like advocating support. Arnold seemed to think so himself, as during the 2003 recall, "Join Arnold" was the slogan that his campaign used to build support for his election.

> Support Arnold—The contribute button on each page said,

> "Please join our efforts to Support Arnold Schwarzenegger," not support any ballot question.
>
> The Press Room page has a picture of Schwarzenegger at the top with a quote saying "I am running for governor to lead a movement for change and give California back its future." How much more explicit can you get?

A TV ad aired by the California Recovery Team titled "Cafeteria" began with an on-screen display of the "JoinArnold.com" website and featured Schwarzenegger himself for virtually the entire ad discussing "my reform agenda" and asking voters to "help me reform California."

A campaign expert testified, "Words like 'help me . . .' 'Join me . . .' or 'support me . . .'" are standard campaign phrases for candidates to use, and that good media consultants never tell people to "vote for" a candidate because that is less effective than asking for their help or support.[9] In fact, this "Cafeteria" ad was very similar to a TV ad run by Schwarzenegger's campaign in the 2003 recall.

Further, the law says that *any* expenditure at all by a political committee "shall be treated as a contribution" to a candidate for whose benefit the expenditure is made, if it is made 1) with the cooperation of or in consultation with the candidate, 2) in concert with, or at the request or *suggestion of*, the candidate; or under any arrangement, coordination, or direction with respect to the candidate.

This would mean that even if CRT paid for something that didn't raise money for Arnold's re-election, tout his qualifications for office, or expressly advocate his re-election, it was still a contribution to his campaign, unless it was limited to ballot question advocacy, because it was done at his request. The FPPC had advised that candidate-controlled ballot committees did not fall within this limitation if all they did was advocate for ballot measures, but the JoinArnold.com website had many things that had little or nothing to do with ballot measures.

More Arnold Propaganda, Paid for by the CRT

In spring of 2005, the "opinion" page of JoinArnold.com included columns such as one from *Sacramento Bee* Columnist Dan Weintraub saying, "Both Parties Should See McPherson is a Good Pick;" one called "California's Environmental Legacy," although the Recovery Team was not promoting any environmental ballot questions; one piece titled "Cut Newly Serious Schwarzenegger Some Slack," and 13 different articles published before Schwarzenegger was even elected with titles such as "Students Support Arnold," "Recall Davis, Elect Arnold," and "Davis Falls Flat, While Schwarzenegger Connects."

The JoinArnold.com website contained a downloadable 42-page color brochure called "Progress on the Road to Recovery," that was promoted on the home page and most other pages. The summary page says: "This book highlights many of the governor's accomplishments during the first year in office—a year of 'promises kept'" to recapture the promise of California. It carried the date November 2004, and notes that it was "paid for by Californians for Schwarzenegger—2006." The brochure lists an impressive set of accomplishments, including Arnold's past passage of Propositions 57 and 58, repeal of the car tax, renegotiation of state employee contracts, his victory on workers' compensation reform, the increase in California jobs, and Schwarzenegger's commitment to environmental causes like hydrogen fuel and solar homes. Nowhere does the brochure mention the California Recovery Team or any of the ballot measures it was supporting, but yet the Recovery Team was paying to promote this brochure on its website.

CSC Also Promoted Arnold as a Candidate

Arnold's other front group, Citizens to Save California, also crossed the line. The CSC website looked like a cheap rip-off of JoinArnold.com. Rather than saying "Join Arnold" and "Support

Arnold" it said, "Help Arnold." It had signs and banners that supporters could download saying "Help Arnold" but making no reference to any ballot question. Virtually every page of the CSC's website included a picture of Schwarzenegger and often a quote from him, like, "I get up every morning wanting to fix things here in Sacramento. And today I ask you: help me fix them." Its home page said that it exists to "support the reform agenda of Schwarzenegger and others," although no others are mentioned.

During March 2004, Citizens to Save California sponsored five Schwarzenegger campaign appearances and filmed footage of the governor for its future TV ads. By March 7, they were running ads that featured Schwarzenegger and said things such as, "Help the governor clean up the mess in California," and "Help Arnold Reform California Politics." Far from being clear that these ads were made "for purposes unrelated" to Schwarzenegger's candidacy, as the law required, they were being run precisely for that purpose.

The direct mail that CSC sent out with its petitions literally repeated the messages Schwarzenegger had used in his candidate campaign, saying "Join Arnold," and "Join me in reforming California." One included the official seal of the governor of the State of California, along with pictures of Arnold. The signs and Internet banners that CSC distributed did not mention any initiative at all, saying only "Help Arnold reform California politics." Their flyers likewise said nothing about any specific initiative, saying only, "2005 is the year of reform for California," and quoting Schwarzenegger saying, "I will not stop. I will not slow down. I will not give up until we have reached our fullest potential for our state. Together, we can keep California moving forward and restore the great promise of our state."

Another clear link between Schwarzenegger and the supposedly independent CSC was the fact that he constantly mentioned he was raising $50 million for "his" initiatives, not "CSC's" initiatives. Further, since CSC did not even announce its ballot question endorsements until March of 2005, the people who were giving CSC millions of dollars before that could not possibly have been giving to support CSC's ballot agenda because it had none. All that donors knew was that CSC would be supporting Arnold's "agenda" or "vision."

With regard to fundraising, Schwarzenegger was upfront about the fact that he was jointly raising money for CSC and his re-election campaign. His chief fundraiser, Marty Wilson, described a "dual-track financing strategy that includes a series of fundraising events for the governor's re-election committee," and for CSC.[10] All the spending that CSC did just to pull off these fundraisers had to be coordinated with Schwarzenegger, just to be sure that he'd be able to show up, if nothing else. This was clearly one area where Arnold had to be in the loop on the expenditure side of things, not just the fundraising side.

The Big Picture

A Schwarzenegger campaign advisor told Philip Matier and Andrew Ross of the *San Francisco Chronicle* that the whole special election is "going to be like having the 2006 election a year early, because if we're able to push through all this stuff—either through negotiations with the legislature or through the election outright—he's going to be golden."[11] Matier and Ross further wrote:

> No one wants to talk about this on the record, the advisor says, "But I don't think anyone is going to deny it, either."
>
> When asked about the play, gubernatorial spokesman Rob Stutzman stuck to the party line, but said; "We could do a safe agenda and probably still get re-elected. But this is a guy who thinks about what the history books are going to say."

Two months later, Schwarzenegger campaign advisor Mike Murphy boasted over lunch with a select group of reporters that, "we'll beat them (Democrats and unions) like a drum," and added "Winning this year is a big step toward winning re-election [in 2006]."[12]

Whether or not the Citizens to Save California ballot committee was controlled by Arnold (as we thought it clearly was), the committee was paying for flyers, signs, webpages, and even TV ads that said "Help Arnold." That sure didn't look like it was "clearly unrelated" to Arnold's candidacy—just the opposite, in fact. This was particularly true when Arnold's own people were saying that the special election agenda CSC was pushing was the key toward winning Arnold's re-election. It was unavoidable; Citizens to Save California was making contributions to Schwarzenegger. Instead of the million-dollar contributions the group was raising, it should have been limited to the $5,600 required by the law.

California law says that if a committee is engaged in raising funds for a candidate, or is coordinating with a candidate in touting that candidate's qualifications for office or advocating that candidate's election by using words like "support," it is in fact a PAC that is subject to $5,600 contribution limits. A quick glance at the Recovery Team's and Citizens to Save California's own websites told us that they were both indeed doing these things, and therefore should be subject to the limit. Yet, they were raising contributions as large as $1 million. Our lawyers felt that this evidence was strong enough to request a preliminary injunction from the court that would immediately put a stop to the illegal fundraising.

Based on this advice, TheRestofUs.org decided to take on the governor of California and the campaign organizations representing the biggest corporations in the world's sixth largest economy. We filed for a preliminary injunction—a request for the court to stop both CSC's and CRT's illegal fundraising in amounts greater than $5,600—pending a full trial.

CHAPTER 8

Arnold v. The Rest of Us

Slapping the Watchdog

Arnold responded to our lawsuit with a vengeance. He sued us back.

SLAPP

California law has something called an anti-SLAPP suit provision. SLAPP stands for Strategic Lawsuit Against Public Participation. California's anti-SLAPP suit laws were created in 1992 to prevent huge corporations from suing small citizen groups "primarily to chill the valid exercise of [their] constitutional rights of freedom of speech and petition."[1] Corporations had been suing local groups as a means of intimidating them and getting them to stop bothering the corporations, often around environmental issues. Even if the lawsuit had no merit, most small nonprofits couldn't afford the massive legal fees involved with a lawsuit, so they would back down from protesting the corporation. Underfunded groups could now file an anti-SLAPP suit as an inexpensive defense mechanism against attacks on their First Amendment rights.

Arnold turned that idea on its head.

Here, the most powerful man in California backed by tens of millions of dollars was suing a tiny grassroots political watchdog. The reason was clear. If he won his suit, a judge would dismiss ours.

Our lawyers had anticipated that the governor might lash back with an anti-SLAPP suit. We were prepared to defend ourselves using a provision passed by the California legislature in 2003 known as the public interest exclusion. This exclusion was enacted to prevent powerful interests from using the anti-SLAPP statute against public interest plaintiffs.

To qualify for the public interest exclusion, a lawsuit needs to meet four criteria:

1) The lawsuit must be brought in the public interest, not by a party that would see a financial gain by winning the suit. For instance, the courts had ruled that someone who owned a nice Victorian house in San Francisco did not qualify for the public interest exception when he sought to keep a neighboring Victorian house from being torn down because the action clearly affected his own property values. TheRestofUs.org was a nonprofit, nonpartisan citizen organization that promoted the public interest through advocating for a more vigorous democracy. Its mission, posted on its website, was to "stand up for the rest of us against special interests by promoting fairness and accountability in a government where the majority rules." Neither the staff or board members, nor the organization as a whole, stood to gain a dime from the lawsuit, so we felt we should easily meet this criteria.

2) The plaintiffs in the lawsuit must seek no more relief than what the general public would receive. In our situation, we were simply asking that a court stop Arnold's illegal fundraising of contributions greater than $5,600 for the California Recovery Team and Citizens to Save California. The public would benefit by having its campaign finance laws enforced to the same extent that TheRestofUs.org would.

3) The lawsuit must deal with an issue of important public significance. Petty lawsuits over trivial matters were still subject to anti-SLAPP provisions. We certainly thought the issue of unprecedented sums of money flooding into California politics in violation of basic campaign finance laws was important and hoped a judge would agree.

4) The lawsuit must deal with something where private enforcement is needed. If a local or state attorney general was already prosecuting an offense, a lawsuit by a citizens group regarding the same offense would not qualify for the public interest exception to the anti-SLAPP suit law. We had filed our complaint with the Fair Political Practices Commission but saw no reasonable hope that the commission would act until long after the special election was over.

Slinging Mud

To prevent us from qualifying as a public interest group, Arnold's lawyers launched a full-out attack on the credibility of TheRestofUs.org. In 15 years of working with nonpartisan advocacy groups, I had never seen anything like it. But it came as no surprise, and the mud didn't stick.

Further, Arnold's lawyers argued that private enforcement was not needed in this matter, because the FPPC would look into it. The irony was almost unbearable. The guy who had railed against the FPPC's sloth-like inaction against Cruz Bustamante during the recall was now arguing that the agency would thoroughly investigate this matter and, therefore, our lawsuit was not subject to the public interest exclusion to the anti-SLAPP suit.

If the judge agreed with Arnold, she could have immediately thrown out our lawsuit entirely. Adding insult to this injury, Arnold then wanted us to pay for his lawyers.

Beating the SLAPP Rap

After the initial trepidation that comes from being sued by the governor of California and a ballot committee worth millions of dollars, we calmed down and set about figuring out how to respond. Our lawyers asked me to prepare a statement for the court that outlined our activities, including times where we had been critical of Democrats. I dug up our Internet postings where we had called for the legislature to impeach Democrat Kevin Shelley for using laundered money to win his election to the secretary of state's office (see chapter 14). I recounted the time I had stood with Republican Secretary of State Bill Jones and called on the Davis administration to release conflict of interest records for Chris Fabiani and Mark Lehane, the energy consultants who had been on Southern California Edison's payroll.

We found examples where our blog, *Democracy's Daily Posts*, had been critical of Democrats, including Steve Westly. We pointed to our support of federal legislation to regulate the so-called 527 groups that liberals like George Soros had funded heavily in the 2000 presidential election. President Bush shared our position on 527 reform while many liberal groups opposed it. Finally, we reminded the court of our support for Arnold's own proposals to revamp the redistricting process in California to remove it from the hands of self-serving legislators.

Judge Shelleyanne Chang, the same local judge who had thrown out the FPPC rule applying limits to candidate-controlled ballot committees, heard our case. Fortunately, Judge Chang didn't buy any of Arnold's rhetoric, and she ruled with us. Our lawsuit was clearly brought "solely" in the public interest, ruled Chang, and the mere fact that the FPPC could take action did not preclude our lawsuit:

> There is no evidence that the commission intends to pursue the claims, must pursue the claim, or if such a prosecution would be immediate. The asserted violations are ongoing, and delay in adjudication could translate into significant public harm if the claims are sustained. Under such circumstances, the necessity of the private enforcement prong is sufficiently met.[2]

TheRestofUs.org and our lawsuit qualified for the public interest exclusion. We had won round one.

Round Two—the Exception to the Exclusion

But Schwarzenegger's lawyers had another trick up their sleeve. When the legislature created the public interest exclusion from anti-SLAPP suit laws in 2003, they had also created an "exception" to the "exclusion." My head spun with all the legal mumbo jumbo. This exception to the public interest exclusion covered:

> 1) Any person engaged in the dissemination of ideas or expression in any book or academic journal, while engaged in the gathering, receiving, or processing of information for communication to the public,
>
> 2) Any action against any person or entity based upon the creation, dissemination, exhibition, advertisement, or other similar promotion of any dramatic, literary, musical, political, or artistic work, including but not limited to a motion picture or television program, or an article published in a newspaper or magazine of general circulation.[3]

The legislative history on the passage of this exception suggested the legislature meant to protect things like George Orwell's novel *1984*, or movies like Michael Moore's *Fahrenheit 9/11* by excepting them from this public interest exclusion and making even public interest plaintiffs meet a high burden of proof before suing authors or newspapers.

Arnold's lawyers hadn't devoted much space in their arguments to this "exception" to the public interest exclusion and our lawyers didn't think it was that serious a challenge, more of something thrown in to distract us. We didn't expect the judge to equate a governor's TV ads with a book or movie, so we did not spend much time refuting it in our brief. That turned out to be a crucial error.

Judge Chang agreed with Arnold that his political fundraising and TV ads constituted "political works" and therefore any lawsuit that implicated these "works" could not qualify for the public interest exclusion to the anti-SLAPP suit laws. This was a relatively new issue in our case, but since then other judges have gone on to rule the same way. This will make it considerably harder for citizens to enforce campaign finance laws in the future.

Arnold's team had won this round, which meant that the judge would now consider their anti-SLAPP suit on its merits. This essentially led to a mini-trial of our allegations against Schwarzenegger, albeit one where we did not have the ability to put witnesses on the stand.

Arnold's Defense

Arnold's lawyers argued our lawsuit was unlikely to prevail and should be thrown out even before going to trial. Their defense had three main components:

1) **Neither CSC nor CRT could possibly be assisting Arnold's re-election campaign because Arnold was not a candidate for re-election.** Citizens to Save California, who supposedly had no knowledge of the governor's plans, said in its brief, "The evidence is clear that Governor Schwarzenegger is not now running for re-election."[4]

My jaw hit the floor. Arnold's advisors like Mike Murphy were all over the papers talking about how winning the special election would guarantee Arnold's re-election while at the same time his lawyers were in court arguing that he wasn't even running? Arnold's lawyers said that he hadn't decided for sure if he would seek re-election and even if he had, he certainly hadn't announced it on TV.

2) **Citizens to Save California was not controlled by Governor Schwarzenegger.** The CSC lawyers spent most of their time arguing that it didn't matter if the governor controlled them since the court had thrown out the FPPC regulation that set $22,300 contribution limits on candidate-controlled ballot committees. But, they also presented evidence that even though many of their consultants had worked for Arnold's recall campaign and/or ballot question campaigns, they were not taking any money from Arnold's committees

while they were working for Citizens to Save California. Plus, Arnold was not on their board of directors, and therefore he did not officially control them. They said nothing about the quotes of Joel Fox, John Coupal, or Marty Wilson that indicated that CSC would be taking suggestions from Arnold's public statements. CSC even admitted that Arnold was influencing its communication spending but said it didn't matter: "Even if some of CSC's communications are made 'in coordination' with Schwarzenegger, they are still not contributions 'to' him, because the purpose of all of CSC's communications is to support ballot measures."[5]

3) **Neither Citizens to Save California nor the California Recovery Team expressly advocated Arnold's re-election.** Arnold's lawyers argued that because neither of these ballot committees told citizens to "vote for" Arnold Schwarzenegger, they weren't supporting his candidacy and therefore were not subject to the $5,600 contribution limit that applies to PACs that support candidates. Allan Zaremberg of the Chamber of Commerce told the judge, "Citizens will not spend even one nickel supporting or opposing the election of the governor or any other candidate for public office."[6] Mr. Zaremberg evidently did not believe that spending millions telling people to "help Arnold" would in fact help Arnold. The California Recovery Team did admit to one "overlooked remnant" of the 2003 campaign: Arnold's statement that "I am running for governor . . ." on its website. CRT acknowledged it paid for all of the JoinArnold.com website, but it argued vehemently that this was not the official website of Arnold's re-election campaign. Marty Wilson testified in a written statement that Arnold's campaign had given the domain JoinArnold.com to the California Recovery Team "shortly after the election of Governor Schwarzenegger." Since then, the Recovery Team had been converting it over to support Arnold's ballot agenda, but it had simply forgotten to take down the remnant quote of Arnold saying he was running for governor because "no one had noticed" it. This was remarkable, given

that it was at the very top of the press page, and that the page had been updated at least 42 times since Arnold's election with new press releases and opinion articles. As soon as our lawsuit had brought it to his attention, Wilson said he had taken down Arnold's quote and fixed the disclaimer about contributions to Californians for Schwarzenegger to be about contributions to the California Recovery Team.[7] He had indeed done so on June 8, 2005, but that didn't mean that the past statements did not exist and were not contributions toward the Schwarzenegger re-election effort.

$ $ $

DONOR PROFILE: B. Wayne Hughes Sr. gave a cool $1 million to Schwarzenegger's California Recovery Team in 2005 and another $100,000 to the anti-union measure Prop 75. Hughes gave $50,000 to support the stem cell research initiative in 2004, which Arnold also backed. In 2000, Hughes gave $250,000 to the Republican Party, but other than that had not been a major political donor until Arnold tapped him. Hughes earned his money from Public Storage, the self-storage chain with more than 1,400 locations. He ranked #70 on the 2005 Forbes 400 list, with an estimated worth of $3.2 billion.

$ $ $

Our Response

The judge's anti-SLAPP suit ruling put us back on our heels. We would now need to prove that we were likely to win our case should it go to trial. We had to make our case before being allowed to put Arnold's consultants under oath or examine any of their documents. Their anti-SLAPP suit had frozen our evidence discovery process, meaning we could only rely upon publicly available documents. Fortunately, we had enough of those to refute Arnold's defense. Our response to their three points was:

1) **Of course Arnold was a candidate.** On January 15, 2005, Schwarzenegger had filed form 501 with the secretary of state's office declaring under penalty of perjury that he was a candidate for governor in 2006. He had opened a campaign committee and had raised $4,145,292 into his re-election campaign. California law says that anyone who receives a contribution or makes an expenditure with the view of bringing about his or her election is a "candidate" under the Political Reform Act.[8] If Schwarzenegger was not a candidate, then it would have been illegal for him to raise this $4 million. Arnold couldn't have it both ways.

As a clear-cut matter of law, Schwarzenegger was a candidate for governor. The California Republican Party had already endorsed Arnold for governor. The fact that he had not officially announced his candidacy on *The Tonight Show* meant nothing. Otherwise, candidates would be free to evade campaign finance laws entirely simply by not publicly declaring that they were running until days before the election, leaving them free to accept unlimited campaign funds up until then. Further, it was patently obvious to everyone who followed the news in California that Arnold was running for re-election, but like all politicians he was being coy about his intentions so he could wait until the ideal time to officially announce. His consultants talked regularly about his re-election in the news.

2) **Citizens to Save California was indeed controlled by Arnold Schwarzenegger.** We did not dispute that CSC's consultants were not working for Arnold at the same time that they were working for CSC, but nevertheless identified several overlapping consultants who had worked for both entities. Rich Claussen, the campaign manager for CSC, had been a paid consultant for Schwarzenegger's Balanced Budget Committee and California Recovery Team and as such was an "agent"

of Schwarzenegger within the definition of California law.[9] Wendy Cantor Hales was working as a fundraiser for CSC. She had previously raised money for Schwarzenegger during the recall and was also thus his "agent" under the law. Further, we submitted the public statements of CSC board members Joel Fox and Jon Coupal printed in California's most widely read newspapers indicating that they would follow Arnold's lead and that he was the king of the chessboard. In response, Arnold's lawyers trotted out some case law that essentially said that judges aren't allowed to read the newspaper. Even though every citizen in California could read it in the *Los Angeles Times*, Judge Chang was not allowed to consider these statements as official evidence because they weren't given under oath. Of course, Coupal, Fox, and Wilson all refused to answer any of our questions under oath. While they did not deny these statements, they simply told the judge she couldn't take them into account.

3) In addition to CSC and CRT expressly advocating support for Arnold, **these committees were spending money at Arnold's "behest" that aided his candidacy** through public relation stunts, TV advertisements, their web pages, and the entire special election agenda that was designed to ensure Arnold's re-election. Arnold's lawyers had not denied these facts, but merely argued that they were legal, based upon old advisory letters of the FPPC and the court's recent ruling in *CSC v. FPPC* that candidates can control ballot committees that have no contribution limits. We pointed out the distinction between supporting ballot questions and supporting Arnold, and noted that both of these committees were doing more of the latter than the former. Plus, there was a ton of evidence that the committees were clearly advocating Arnold's re-election, even beyond Schwarzenegger's quote about running for governor.

Moreover, the very premise of Arnold's lawsuit against us seemed to prove our point that donors were giving more to

On January 14, 2004, Arnold Schwarzenegger personally signed a statement officially making him a candidate for governor.

Candidate Intention Statement

Type or Print in Ink.

Date Stamp
RECEIVED AND [F]
In the office of the Secretary
of the State of Californ[ia]
JAN 15 2004
Hand Delivered, Sacra[mento]
KEVIN SHELLEY, Secretary

Check One: ☒ Initial ☐ Amendment (Explain) ______

1. Candidate Information:

NAME OF CANDIDATE (Last, First, Middle Initial)	DAYTIME TELEPHONE NUMBER	FAX NUMBER (optional)	E-M[AIL]
Schwarzenegger, Arnold	(310) 458-1405	(310) 260-2656	

STREET ADDRESS	CITY	STATE	ZIP
3110 Main Street,	Santa Monica	CA	90

OFFICE SOUGHT (POSITION TITLE)	AGENCY NAME	DISTRICT NUMBER, if applica[ble]
Governor	N/A	N/A

OFFICE JURISDICTION
☒ State (Complete Part 2.)
☐ City ☐ County ☐ Multi-County: ______ (Name of Jurisdiction) 2006 (Year of Election)

2. State Candidate Expenditure Limit Statement:

Candidates for statewide office are not required to complete Part 2 until 11/6/02. CalPERS candidates, judges, judicial candidates, and candidates for local offices are not required to complete Part 2.)

______ (Year of Election) *Primary/general election* ______ (Year of Election) *Special/runoff election*

(Check one box)

☐ I accept the voluntary expenditure ceiling for the election stated above.

☒ I do not accept the voluntary expenditure ceiling for the election stated above.

Amendment:

○ I did not exceed the expenditure ceiling in the primary or special election held on: ___/___/___ and I accept the voluntary expenditure ceiling for the general or special run-off election.

(Mark if applicable)

☐ On ___/___/___, I contributed personal funds in excess of the expenditure ceiling for the election stated above.

Voluntary Expenditure Ceilings:
(Gov. Code Section 85400)

Office

(Effective 1/1/01)
Assembly
Senate

(Effective 11/6/02)
Board of Equalization
Governor
Lieutenant Governor, Attorney General, Insurance Commissioner, Controller, Secretary of State, Supt. of Public Instruction Treasurer

3. Verification:

I certify under penalty of perjury under the laws of the State of California that the foregoing is true and correct.

Executed on 01/14/2004 (month, day, year) Signature ______ (Candidate)

Schwarzenegger declined to abide by voluntary campaign spending limits

Schwarzenegger than they were to ballot questions. He claimed he was hurt because donors could not support his agenda. But nothing in California law or in our lawsuit prevented any donor from giving any amount of money to a ballot committee working on any of the ballot questions that Arnold supported so long as that committee operated independently of the governor. The very fact that Schwarzenegger wanted to control and coordinate those committees indicates that he himself believed that donors would otherwise not contribute to those same measures without his involvement and benefit.

Round Three Goes to The Rest of Us

At the end of the day, Judge Chang ruled with us:

> For purposes of these motions, this evidence is sufficient to make a prima facie or minimal merit showing that ***Governor Schwarzenegger is a "candidate"*** both as an officeholder, a candidate for elective office in 2006, and a recipient of contributions as defined under Government Code section 82007.
>
> Likewise, Plaintiffs have presented sufficient circumstantial evidence to demonstrate a prima facie showing that ***Recovery Team and Citizens are controlled by Governor Schwarzenegger*** as that term is defined under Government Code section 82016.
>
> And, Plaintiffs have presented sufficient evidence that ***monies received by Citizens and Recovery Team have been used for election-related activities as defined under Government Code section 82105, including communications that may constitute "express advocacy," and thus constitute contributions.***[10]

This meant that we had defeated Arnold's anti-SLAPP suit

and that our lawsuit could go forward.

So far, so good.

After the judge issued her tentative ruling, Arnold's lawyer Chuck Bell made some last ditch attempts the next day to get the anti-SLAPP suit to stick. He told Judge Chang during oral arguments that in order for a political committee to be deemed a candidate PAC, it must make contributions to *candidates*. We had only presented evidence that CSC and CRT had made a contribution to one *candidate*—Arnold Schwarzenegger. His hair-splitting argument that somehow the difference between the plural *candidates* and the singular *candidate* should mean our lawsuit should be tossed reminded me why people have a bad attitude about lawyers.

Fortunately, the judge wasn't buying it.

Alternatively, Arnold's lawyers argued that there was no proof that the Recovery Team's spending on its website had exceeded the $22,300 contribution limit that a PAC could give a candidate for governor. Of course, that didn't matter. If in fact the Recovery Team had made any contribution, no matter how large, then it was acting like a candidate PAC and was subject itself to limits of $5,600 on contributions it could accept.

No Speedy Resolution

The judge's next step was to rule on our request for a preliminary injunction that would immediately stop Citizens to Save California and the California Recovery Team from accepting contributions greater than $5,600 pending the outcome of a trial. Our burden of proof was much higher for this request than it was for defeating Arnold's anti-SLAPP suit. We had to show not only that our lawsuit had a reasonable chance of winning, and therefore was not frivolous, but also that we had a strong likelihood of winning and therefore the judge should take action even before a full trial.

Judge Chang was not willing to go that far. Since we had not yet been able to cross-examine any of the other side's witnesses under oath, our evidence was not yet as strong as it would be at a trial. Further, she balanced the harm that would be done to Schwarzenegger's committees versus the harm that would be done to the voters of California in allowing Arnold to continue raising unlimited chunks of cash, and decided that she would not take the big step of issuing a preliminary injunction.

Nonetheless, we felt vindicated. Judge Chang had rejected Arnold's attempt to throw our lawsuit out and we could now proceed to the full trial that we had eagerly been waiting for.

Our lawyers, however, gave us some depressing news.

Unappealing Choices

Beating Arnold's countersuit wasn't good enough. Because of the way we had defeated the anti-SLAPP suit, Arnold's lawyers would be able to appeal it. Had we won on the basis of the public interest exclusion, that would have ended the matter and a trial would have come next. But, because we won on Judge Chang's ruling that we had shown a likelihood of prevailing, the other side could challenge that finding in the California Court of Appeal. It seemed like a technicality, but it had grave consequences.

It was already late June, and the other side's appeal process could take months. Even if we eventually won the appeal of the anti-SLAPP suit and then won the trial, a final decision would almost certainly come after the special election was over. Just as Bustamante managed to spend his illegally raised money during the recall before a judge told him to stop, Arnold would raise and spend millions on the special election well before we would see a ruling on our case.

The only reason to go on would be for the long-term precedent to prevent Arnold, or another governor, from doing this sort of thing again. This was important; arguably more so than the details of this particular special election. But, this was also something that the FPPC could do. That agency's glacial timeline would not prove to be any worse than the timeline that we would be able to accomplish on our own through the courts. Plus, there was always the chance that we could lose the appeal of the anti-SLAPP suit and then get stuck with paying for Arnold's high-priced lawyers. Our attorneys thought the appellate panel that would take our case might have judges who would not be friendly to campaign finance reform. With some regret, we decided to drop the lawsuit and focus instead on telling people what Arnold had done and letting them make up their own minds about whether it was right or wrong. Perhaps this was now a case best settled in the court of public opinion.

We did take some solace that our lawsuit had forced the California Recovery Team to clean up its act and remove many blatantly illegal pages of its website. More importantly, our vigilance over the first six months of 2004, beginning with our first complaint at the FPPC and ending with this lawsuit, had meant that Arnold could not call the shots on his ballot strategy to the full extent that he had wanted to. His aides had to walk a finer line in their public statements and in the signals that they could send to donors and to CSC. Perhaps most important, our actions had helped spur a growing media interest in Arnold's fundraising, which in many ways caused it to backfire. The more money he raised, the more Arnold's poll ratings dropped.

On July 14, 2005, we handed our case back to the Fair Political Practices Commission by updating our past letters of complaint. We pointed them toward the new evidence we had uncovered, particularly the pieces from the JoinArnold.com website and the California Recovery Team's payment for Arnold's public relation stunts like the pothole filling.

Later in the fall, the California Recovery Team would disclose that it paid $49,000 for "candidate travel" on July 7, 2005, and another $34,000 for the same thing on July 13. These filings would appear to contradict the CRT's lawyers' claims that it was not paying a dime to support any candidate.

On September 16, just weeks after we dropped our lawsuit, Arnold officially announced his re-election campaign in San Diego, a day before the Republican state convention in Anaheim. Insiders familiar with his ballot campaigns later told us that donors to those campaigns demanded Arnold announce he was running as a condition for their continued financial support.

KCRA news similarly reported:

> Political analyst Tony Quinn said the governor has been backed into a corner by the people and businesses giving money to his special election campaign.
>
> "And you can understand they're likely to say, 'Well, governor, we're not going to go way out on a limb for you in this special election without some guarantee that you're going to be around for the next four years,'" Quinn said.[11]

The fat cats weren't about to fund his special election agenda if in fact he was not going to run again—proof, of course, of our main point that the primary purpose of the special election was to bolster Arnold's re-election and that this was the reason that corporations emptied their wallets into his ballot committees. State Senator Abel Maldonado made the explicit link between the special election and Arnold's re-election, saying, "If he wins in November, he will be King Kong," Maldonado said. "If he loses, it's going to be an uphill battle."[12]

The stakes were high and the money flowed accordingly.

CHAPTER 9

Plutocracy Run Amok

Big Money Plays Games, Takes Hostages

With the courts throwing out the rule that put limits on candidate-controlled ballot committees and with the lawsuit from TheRestofUs.org behind him, Arnold had cleared two major legal hurdles on his road to the special election. Politically, however, things were going considerably worse. Arnold's attempt to work his agenda through the legislature provides a good example of how powerful interest groups spar with one another and dominate the political process to the point where concerns of regular citizens get left behind.

Arnold began 2005 with 62 percent of voters giving him favorable ratings according to the Public Policy Institute of California. Arnold taunted the legislature, saying that they were unhappy with him because his poll numbers were so high while theirs were not. "Poor little guys there—they're in the 30s" he jibed.[1]

By February 2005, Arnold's numbers had slipped to 55 percent. These were still solid numbers, but some commentators pointed out that Gray Davis had been at 62 percent popularity after being in office for 13 months. Arnold was behind Gray's pace. By May, Arnold had slipped down to 40 percent and by July he had reached 34 percent.

Poor guy.

At least three major factors contributed to Arnold's precipitous drop in the polls:

1) A costly public relations war with nurses, teachers, firefighters, and policemen.

2) A series of mishaps with Arnold's ballot initiative agenda.

3) A steady stream of negative stories about Arnold's fundraising.

Taking on Our Public Servants

It was one thing for Arnold to pick on Indian tribes and faceless union bosses during the recall campaign, but in deciding to go to war in 2005, Arnold had taken on nurses, teachers, firefighters, and law enforcement officials. These folks didn't look nearly as sinister to voters as Arnold tried to make them out to be.

Arnold's conflict with the nurses began with his decision to reverse a regulation that required every California hospital to maintain at least one nurse for every five patients. This ratio was created by the Department of Health Services to implement a law passed by the California legislature in 1999. The California Nurses Association (CNA) argued that this was the only way to ensure that patients got adequate care and that nurses weren't stretched too thin on the job. Hospitals and HMOs worried that it would drive up costs and reduce their profits.

During 2004, when Schwarzenegger was in the mode of cooperating with Democrats, liberal interests groups had gone along with the honeymoon and negotiated compromises. The teachers, for instance, agreed to forgo planned increases in school funding as part of Arnold's deficit reduction plan. Arnold was so popular that nobody wanted to take him on.

But when Schwarzenegger went after the hard-fought patient ratio victory that nurses had won, they weren't about to give in. Instead, they mounted protests everywhere Arnold went. When he staged a publicity stunt, they were there. When he held a high-priced fundraiser for Citizens to Save California, the nurses were there.

At first, Arnold seemed to relish the fight. He labeled the nurses as "special interests" and explained that of course the special interests were mad at him because he was "kicking their butts."[2] Arnold thumped his chest and proclaimed that when special interests push against him, he'll push back.

Somehow, the image of a huge muscle-bound man with boatloads of money, both personally and in his campaign coffers, threatening to kick the butts of overworked nurses didn't quite conjure up the hero mindset that Arnold seemed to think it would. Rather, he looked like a bully.

Things got so bad that the California Highway Patrol, which provided security for the governor, was ordered to keep anyone who looked like a nurse away from Schwarzenegger. When Arnold hosted a movie opening at the Crest Theatre in downtown Sacramento, nurse Kelly DiGiacomo thought she would attend. She was accosted by the state patrol and questioned for more than an hour because she had decided to come to the event wearing her nurse's uniform. The CHP explained that they were only looking out for the governor's safety. Rose Ann DeMoro, the executive director of the CNA, replied in the press, "It's appalling that the highest constitutional officer of our state feels a nurse's uniform is threatening."[3]

The teachers too had turned on Arnold. They saw his proposal for merit pay as an all out declaration of war against their philosophy that all teachers should be treated equally and they responded in force. Moreover, the budget he submitted contained $3 billion less than what teachers thought Arnold had promised them in the compromises they had worked out the year before. It was almost as if he was going out of his way to pick a fight. Teachers joined in protests with the nurses. At times, more than 10,000 people turned out to protest the governor and his policies.

TV cameras were eating it up.

The protests effectively turned one of Arnold's biggest assets, his ability to stage charming public appearances, into a liability. Every event he staged turned into more negative publicity for him, so Arnold began dodging the media instead of courting it.

In addition to their protests, the teachers dug into their pocketbooks. Some 800 elected delegates of the California Teachers Association voted overwhelmingly to assess all teachers an extra fee amounting to five bucks a month for three years to fight the governor's agenda. With 335,000 teachers chipping in, that added up to a war chest of $60 million. By the spring, they were taking out ads that trashed the governor and his special election agenda.

When policemen and firefighters joined the opposition, it was too much for Arnold to take. These public servants were upset by Arnold's pension reform plan that would have taken away their guaranteed benefits and replaced them with 401(k) style plans where the benefits would go up and down with the stock market.

Arnold Gets a Bad Rap With the Cops

The conflict with the cops was the result of one of many missteps that the governor's team made in their rush to qualify questions for a special election. After Citizens to Save California had turned in a hastily drafted ballot initiative on public employee pensions, the attorney general's office wrote a ballot summary that said that the initiative would cancel the death benefit for widows and widowers of firefighters and cops who died in the line of duty.

For voters who still had images of fallen firefighters who died while rescuing others in the September 11 attack on the World Trade Center, the notion of taking money away from firefighters' surviving families was hard to swallow.

Arnold disputed the ballot summary, saying that it was never his intent to repeal death benefits and that the attorney general's ballot summary was unfair. The glitch highlighted one of the major quirks in California's initiative process that gives enormous power to the attorney general to decide how any given ballot question will be described to the voters. Pollsters and politicians alike have learned that the way you ask a question has lots to do with how people will respond to it, so getting unfavorable ballot language from the attorney general can be the kiss of death to any initiative effort. Fairly or not, this gives enormous power to the attorney general's office in deciding the fate of many a ballot measure.

By April 5, Arnold folded his tents. He decided to drop the pension initiative from his special election agenda. That same day Schwarzenegger had tried to hold a 700-person fundraising event in San Francisco. The California Nurses Association turned out so many protesters that no more than 100 of Arnold's invitees were able to make their way into the hotel. Somehow, the police officers (whose pensions were in danger of being axed) weren't too interested in helping Arnold by breaking up a peaceful demonstration. It might have been a coincidence that Arnold dropped his pension reform plan that same day. It might not have been.

The supposedly independent Citizens to Save California came to the same conclusion as Arnold and dropped the pension initiative. The mishap over ballot language did demonstrate, however, that even pretending to be independent from CSC had created real problems for Schwarzenegger. While he had been able to raise money for them and send them signals about what initiatives to support, Arnold's lawyers and advisors had not been able to draft the initiative themselves. Had they not undertaken the charade that CSC was independent, they might have been able to avoid the drafting error that led to the unfavorable ballot language. Once again, a campaign finance rule had proven consequential, even if not foolproof.

Other Snafus

Arnold also ran into difficulties with his teacher pay proposal. Arnold's initial idea, laid out in his January State of the State address, was to pay teachers based on merit rather than years of experience and to provide "combat pay" for taking on tough assignments in schools that needed the most help. However, when Rick Claussen's team at Citizens to Save California conducted focus groups on this idea, it wasn't a big hit.

So, Citizens to Save California actually did act independently and decided to replace the merit pay idea with a proposal to postpone teacher tenure awards to five years after being hired instead of the current two. This would mean that teachers would not receive protection from being fired until they had proven themselves over a longer period of time. Arnold went ballistic. He wanted merit pay. Hadn't they read the signals he was sending them correctly? Quickly, CSC reconsidered. But in the end, CSC prevailed upon the governor to change his mind and back the teacher tenure initiative instead of merit pay. You have to wonder how they managed to convince each other and come to agreement while at the same time remaining completely independent and without being influential in each other's decision making. That simply does not seem possible.

Arnold and CSC also both coalesced around a modified, weaker version of a budget cap proposal that packed considerably less punch than the Colorado law it was modeled after. His bold reform agenda of the State of the State address was now pared to three points: a modified teacher tenure initiative, a modified spending cap, and the redistricting initiative that was already in the works by Ted Costa and the People's Advocate. Even to some of his supporters, it began looking like Arnold's game plan wasn't holding up too well, and it was a long way until Election Day.

Steady Drip of Fundraising Stories

Beyond the vocal opposition of nurses, teachers, firefighters and cops and the missteps made by his own team, a final factor in Arnold's drop in popularity was a steady stream of news stories about his prolific fundraising. These stories eroded Arnold's image as a populist maverick that he had successfully cultivated during the recall. He was starting to look like any other politician, and in particular Gray Davis, with a limitless appetite for campaign cash.

Most of Arnold's big fundraising events in California received heavy coverage by the media, sometimes front-page stories. Some papers beefed up their newsrooms just to cover the governor. Unlike in the past, it wasn't just the newspapers that covered political fundraising by the governor. After the recall election had rekindled interest in California politics, many TV stations from Los Angeles and San Francisco had opened bureaus in Sacramento. With Arnold putting a special election agenda front and center of the state's agenda, these stations began covering all his moves to make that happen, including his fundraising.

There were also specific stories about some of the people who had seen fit to give Arnold big wads of cash. One man, Emmanuel I. Bernabe, ran a chain of 11 nursing homes in California. He contributed $67,300 to Arnold and served as a dinner chairman at a March 16, 2005, fundraising dinner. When stories broke that his nursing homes had been fined $285,000 for more than 50 violations of state health code, some people had to wonder why a skinflint like Bernabe wanted Arnold to be governor. State regulators had been preventing Bernabe from purchasing more nursing homes based on the problems that had surfaced at his existing facilities.

"The record is very clear and speaks for itself," said a state official. "There is a clear indication that we believe they have serious compliance problems, problems providing care."[4] Things were so bad that the Department of Justice had prosecuted Bernabe's firm for 13 misdemeanor offenses in March, the same month that Bernabe chaired Arnold's fundraiser. Marty Wilson, who raises money for the governor, claimed that Bernabe had not yet asked Arnold to lift that ban on his expansion or for any other favors.

As noted earlier, the Hilmar Cheese Company had contributed $21,200 to Schwarzenegger during the recall campaign. In January 2005 the Central Valley Regional Water Quality Control Board fined the company $4 million for repeatedly discharging pollutants into fields that surrounded its plant in Merced County. A *Sacramento Bee* exposé had shown that the company had been dumping some 700,000 gallons of untreated water per day, often with high amounts of salt and dairy waste. Hilmar Cheese had been violating state water rules for more than 16 years. The same day the fine was announced, the company's co-owner Chuck Ahlem announced he would step down from his position as the state's undersecretary of agriculture after the Sierra Club and other environmentalists had called for Schwarzenegger to fire him.

Governor Pete Wilson had appointed Ahlem to the water board and Schwarzenegger had promoted him to the number two spot in the Department of Food and Agriculture three months after being elected. Thomas Pinkos, the head of the water board that issued the fine, resigned his position in June 2005 because of the controversy that the fine had created. You had to wonder if the company's contributions were aimed at keeping the state off their backs and allowing them to avoid $43 million in upgrades that would be needed to stop their illegal polluting. In March 2006, the water board cut the fine from $4 million to $3 million and allowed the company to keep dumping illegal amounts of salt and effluent for at least 18 months in a move that environmentalists sharply criticized.

Schwarzenegger had appointed six of the nine water board members at that point.

Thomas Noe, a rare coin dealer in Ohio, was another troubling donor to Schwarzenegger. By early summer of 2005, stories were breaking in Ohio newspapers that Noe had likely stolen at least four million dollars in state workers' compensation funds. He claimed that he had invested the funds in gold coins and that some of those coins had been "lost in the mail." The FBI raided his associate's house in Denver, Colorado, and found a safe full of rare wine and Cuban cigars. When they went back the next day, the loot was gone. Federal investigators then announced that they suspected Noe of illegally reimbursing his associates for contributions they made to President Bush's re-election campaign. Noe bundled those illegal contributions so he could reach Pioneer status by raising $100,000 for Bush. Ohio Governor Bob Taft admitted he had failed to disclose golf outings that Noe had paid for. Noe was Ohio's biggest scoundrel by far, eventually being convicted of 29 counts of corruption, theft, and forgery.

Tom Noe had given Arnold Schwarzenegger $10,000. Further records revealed that Noe had made the contribution on an Ohio state credit card. It looked as though Noe had used money that he stole from the people of Ohio to make a contribution to Arnold.

Talk about robbing Peter to pay Paul.

TheRestofUs.org called on all politicians who had accepted money from Noe, including Schwarzenegger, to give it up. While other politicians wisely gave the money to charities or gave it back to the Ohio Bureau of Workers Compensation, Arnold initially resisted. When he did give it up in June 2005, he gave it back to Noe himself. When shocked reporters asked why he would give what was probably stolen cash back to the guy who stole it, all his spokesman Marty Wilson could say was " had we known about the other options, we may have made a different choice, but that's hindsight. The fact is the money has gone out."

Ohio state senator Mark Dunn was furious. Noe had given Schwarzenegger "money that clearly wasn't his money to begin with and Governor Schwarzenegger knew it," charged Dunn. "If he wanted to contribute to Tom Noe's defense fund, that's up to him," but the people of Ohio wanted their money back. [5]

Arnold's blind spot to the backlash against this fundraising may have come from his advisor Mike Murphy. Political advisors make their money off of campaign ads, often receiving a cut of each ad that is placed. The more ads run, the more money they make. Murphy's firm was paid more than $950,000 by the California Recovery Team. But beyond the money, most campaign hacks believe in what they do. They earnestly think that they are doing voters a service by manipulating them with selective information and half-truths packaged in 30-second attack ads and junk mail from committees you've never heard of.

Consultants seem to think that is what democracy is all about.

When asked about Arnold's record-shattering sums of money, Mike Murphy told a reporter at the *San Francisco Chronicle*, "I've never found fundraising a cutting issue."[6] That's his way of saying that the negative fundraising publicity just didn't matter.

While consultants aren't dumb enough to think that nobody cares at all about political fundraising, their polls tell them that voters are so cynical about it that they think all politicians are equally bad when it comes to money in politics. Indeed, there is some truth to this. To be seen as credible in today's political system, a candidate has to raise huge sums of money. This means that all candidates that are not seen as on the fringe tend to look equally tainted by their fundraising. Until we change the system, voters get to choose between Republican candidates backed by corporations and CEOs and Democratic candidates backed by trial lawyers, labor unions and Hollywood liberals. Seeing no real distinction in fundraising, voters often then make their decisions based upon other issues, like jobs, crime, health care, abortion, etc. As a result, consultants tell politicians that it doesn't matter how bad they look when it comes to money in politics—voters will support you anyhow at the end of the day.

This time, Murphy was wrong.

The steady stream of stories was taking a toll. After a couple of appearances on Los Angeles TV, TheRestofUs.org received a phone call from a viewer who had clearly changed her mind about Schwarzenegger based upon a news story that we were featured in. This woman was more than 80 years old. She had voted for Nixon, Reagan, and George W. Bush in addition to President Clinton—a classic independent voter with a knack for picking winners. She had voted for the recall and for Schwarzenegger to replace Gray Davis. But she said she wouldn't be voting for him again because she was disgusted with all the fundraising.

It wasn't just an isolated incident. We were hearing from independent voters across the state, as were the pollsters. The *New Republic* magazine wrote:

> As Schwarzenegger began touring nationally to raise money from wealthy donors for his initiatives, erstwhile supporters like Derek Cressman expressed their disillusionment. 'He told us that he would not need to take money from special interests,' Cressman wrote on his organization's website last February, 'Yet now he's become the Donald Trump of campaign cash—he just can't get enough.' Schwarzenegger's following among independents fell accordingly. In a mid-June Field Poll, only 36 percent of moderates and 35 percent

> of independents said they would vote for his re-election.[7]

Whatever the reason, the more money he raised, the more Arnold's poll numbers fell. Perhaps it was because there was no opposing candidate that looked equally bad as Arnold. Perhaps it was because he had set an expectation that he would be different and would not take money from private interests, but instead would sweep them from Sacramento. Perhaps California voters really had meant to shake things up in the recall election and that the old conventional wisdom that endless money-grubbing would not come without a political price was no longer true.

A Cornucopia of Initiatives

Beyond the war with the nurses and other public servants, the negative publicity about his fundraising, and the problems controlling his own team's initiative efforts, Arnold had to contend with a host of other forces that his State of the State speech unleashed.

Other players soon realized that if there was going to be a special election, they had an opportunity to take their own ideas to the ballot as well. Beyond Arnold's original ideas for ballot questions, there were initiatives filed dealing with teenage abortion, limiting fees by trial lawyers, urban casinos, prescription drug plans, electricity deregulation, and car dealer restrictions. Many initiative proponents filed multiple versions of the same idea, looking to see what sort of ballot summary the attorney general would provide for each one. There were nine different measures filed dealing with teacher pay and education reform, nine different redistricting reform measures, three measures aimed at crippling unions political fundraising, five versions of Arnold's deficit reduction plan, and three different versions of initiatives to increase the minimum wage.

All told, various proponents filed a total of 79 initiatives, with 71 being filed just in the month after Arnold's State of the State speech. The previous record for initiative filings had been in 1997 when 82 questions were filed in the entire year. The attorney general added 20 new staff people to deal with the influx of filings. Just as the recall had led to a huge number of candidates for governor, Arnold's special election had led to a boom in initiatives.

Predictably, there were soon calls to restrict the ballot process, to make it harder for citizens to use the tool that Hiram Johnson had brought forth nearly a century before. What had once been a process for citizens to check the role of powerful interests was now being used by those interests to get their way.

"We have to limit the number of initiatives on the ballot. At some point, the door closes," said former assembly majority leader Robert Hertzberg at a San Francisco event sponsored by the Commonwealth Club.[8]

What these elites failed to realize is that voters have their own way of controlling ballot measures. When they think the process is getting out of control, and that too many crazy ideas are getting on the ballot, they vote no. When this happens enough, ballot proponents realize that it is getting harder to get their way through the initiative process and they decide against doing future initiatives.

Taking Hostages

Many of the ballot initiatives filed with the attorney general's office in January were bluffs—threats by their proponents intended to be used as leverage to gain something else. This does not mean that the proponents did not sincerely believe in the policy that they had filed. Rather, various interests groups had multiple objectives and they may have been willing to bargain one compromise or defeat in exchange for a victory elsewhere. Many political elites find this negotiation by initiative distasteful, but it's really no different from the logrolling and compromise that goes on in the legislature every day. The fact that initiative politics sometimes take on aspects of legislative politics should come as no surprise. Certainly that reality should not serve as a reason to restrict the initiative process any more than it serves as a reason to restrict the legislative process.

The teacher merit pay and tenure reduction measures were likely bargaining chips. By threatening the teachers with the fight of their lives, Arnold created a situation where he could be a peacemaker by offering to drop the teacher pay initiatives if Democrats compromised on Arnold's priorities. Likewise, the pension reform plans threatened other public service workers, most of whom were unionized and who typically backed Democrats. This too could serve as a useful bargaining chip.

But the central negotiating chit in Arnold's arsenal was the so-called "paycheck protection" initiative filed by Lewis Uhler. Its clear purpose was to make it much harder for workers to pool their money collectively to work on a common political agenda. Corporate and libertarian interests had been pushing the idea for years, dating back to the Newt Gingrich–era in Congress. In fact, Governor Pete Wilson, national anti-tax activist Grover Norquist, and others had qualified a similar anti-union measure in California back in 1998, Prop 226. Voters had defeated it, but only after labor groups spent more than $17 million in opposition.

Uhler's 2005 effort was narrower in scope than the 1998 measure. It dealt only with public sector unions. This potentially would reduce the opposition from the private sector unions and perhaps give it a greater chance of passage. The conventional wisdom was that labor could defeat this measure again, but doing so would require them to spend at least another $20 million. This would leave them with less money to spend fighting Schwarzenegger's other ballot measures and less left in their coffers to spend against him in his 2006 re-election bid.

As appealing as it was, there were some in Arnold's camp, perhaps even the governor himself, who would have been happy to negotiate a truce on the paycheck protection measure if Democrats would accept some of the reforms Arnold wanted—namely the redistricting reform and the state budget spending cap. By holding a gun to the head of the Democrats' biggest backers, labor groups, Arnold figured he could force Democrats into accepting compromises that they otherwise would never have gone for.

This initiative blackmail was so sensitive a game that for months Arnold distanced himself from the Uhler anti-labor measure. While some of the board members of Citizens to Save California championed Uhler's initiative, others did not and CSC initially remained neutral on the measure. Arnold said he was sympathetic to its aims, but declined to endorse the measure early on so as not to poison the well with Democrats. Uhler kept the funders of his measure secret by having the money flow through front groups like the Small Business Action Committee. Since the SBAC was a multi-issue ballot committee, it would not have to report who its donors were until July, after negotiations would be over. Many Democrats figured the SBAC was essentially the same people funding Arnold's other initiatives. Senate leader Don Perata publicly said that he believed that Schwarzenegger "could stop it if he wanted to."[9] But the secrecy gave Arnold some plausible deniability for several months.

Ameriquest Money

Perhaps the most important donor behind qualifying Arnold's initiatives for the special election was Roland Arnall and his company Ameriquest. Mortgage giant Ameriquest, along with its owners Roland and Dawn Arnall, contributed more than $2.3 million to California candidates and political committees in the first six months of 2005. The bulk of that sum was funneled through a series of committees to support Schwarzenegger's ballot agenda. Ameriquest's $1.7 million in ballot initiative contributions, largely filtered through intermediaries, accounted for just over half of the $3.4 million donated to the official ballot committees for four initiatives during that time.

Like Arnold, Ameriquest tried to distance itself from the anti-worker initiative. To head off a worker protest in June 2005, the company told its employees that it would not endorse paycheck protection. "Ameriquest has never supported that measure and we did issue a statement to the union to clarify that," confirmed company representative Alan Maltun.[10] Although Ameriquest may not technically have endorsed the measure, it turned out to be largely Ameriquest money that put the paycheck protection initiative, Prop 75, on the ballot. Lewis Uhler was avoiding disclosing this fact both to protect Arnold and Ameriquest.

Ameriquest was the single largest contributor to the California Business PAC, run by the Chamber of Commerce, giving $250,000. Ameriquest was also the biggest donor to the New Majority PAC with $268,000 and the second largest donor to the California Business Properties PAC at $200,000. These contributions provided the bulk of the funding for Prop 75.

The accompanying chart shows not only the extent that a single company was responsible for such a significant amount of funding for Arnold's agenda; it also shows the lengths that Arnold's team went to disguise this fact.

$ $ $

DONOR PROFILE: Roland Arnall, head of the sub-prime home loan company Ameriquest, is among America's biggest political donors. Arnall, his wife, and business have contributed more than $8 million to California candidates since 2000. Arnall helped raise $250,000 for Gray Davis in his first run to become governor in 1998, leading Davis advisor Garry South to say, "Roland was responsible for Gray becoming governor."[11] Governor Gray Davis presided over Arnall's wedding to his second wife, Dawn. Arnall kicked in $100,000 to help Davis oppose the recall, but also gave $100,000 to Schwarzenegger's Total Recall Committee. Both Davis and Arnold attended Arnall's 2004 holiday party. The Arnalls and Ameriquest have contributed more than $1 million over the years to both the California Republican and Democratic Parties, and to Schwarzenegger's California Recovery Team.

After Arnall served as a Pioneer Fundraiser for George W. Bush and raised more money than anyone for Bush after 2002, the president appointed Arnall to be ambassador to the Netherlands in 2005. The Arnalls reportedly raised more than $12 million to help Bush's various efforts.[12] The Arnalls personally made more than $2 million in contributions to federal candidates and parties from 1999 to 2004. Roland's wife, Dawn, gave $5 million to the national electioneering group Progress for America in 2004. The Arnalls, Ameriquest, and its subsidiaries kicked in another $1 million for the Bush 2004 inaugural.

Arnall is ranked number 106 on the Forbes 400 list.

In 1996, the U.S. Justice Department accused Arnall's company of charging more for loans to minorities and people over 55 than it did for others. Regulators in more than 30 states have investigated Ameriquest for predatory lending practices. Predatory lending practices sometimes result in people losing their homes and life savings. Lawsuits allege that Ameriquest's agents dupe people into loans with higher than expected fees and interest rates. In January 2006, Ameriquest agreed to a $325 million settlement with 49 states to resolve the claims against it. This was one of the largest consumer protection settlements in history. Ameriquest has a definite, and special, interest in actions taken by California government. It has spent more than $1.6 million lobbying the governor and legislature on issues relating to consumer privacy, predatory lending, and its own court settlements.

$ $ $

Ameriquest's Deceptive Web of Donations

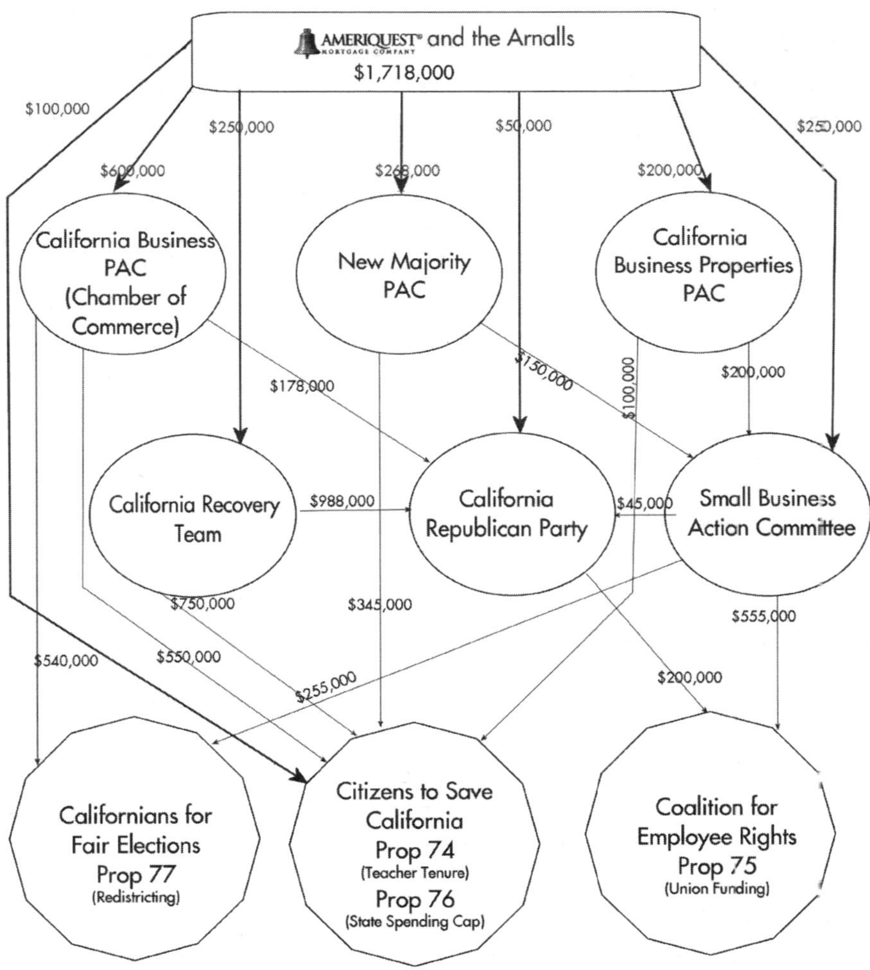

The three ballot committees that backed Arnold's initiatives received more than half of their funding from Ameriquest and its intermediaries in the first half of 2005.

Labor's Chits

Labor groups joined the fray, filing initiatives that they knew might not win at the ballot box, but which could frighten their opponents into either dropping the special election altogether or scaling back their agenda. Labor's first bullet was an initiative to require corporations to get the votes of their shareholders every time they wanted to make a political contribution. It was the mirror image of Uhler's paycheck-protection approach. Labor never fired this bullet. Rather, after they gathered enough signatures to qualify it, they held on to them instead of turning them in. The implicit threat was that if the Chamber of Commerce and other corporate interests dumped tons of money into passing Uhler's paycheck-protection measure, then labor would turn in its anti-corporate initiative and the corporations would have to deal with that in the next election.

Labor groups also backed initiatives to create a drug prescription plan that would require pharmaceutical companies to offer more reasonable prices to all Californians if they wanted to keep doing business with the state's Medi-Cal plan. This had been on labor's agenda already, and the special election provided an opportunity to go forward.

Pharmaceutical companies saw labor's move as an immediate threat to their bottom line. In response they filed their own paycheck-protection measure aimed at labor's political funding.

Just as labor groups hoped that their prescription drug initiatives would drive turnout on their side, Republican interests backed an initiative to require parental notification when their underage daughters were having an abortion. They were betting that religious Californians, many of whom are conservative, would turn out to support this measure and at the same time would back the rest of Arnold's agenda.

A final tit-for-tat measure was an initiative aimed at rolling back much of the deregulation established under Governor Wilson that had allowed Enron and other companies to manipulate California's energy market.

The Negotiation Phase

The stage was set with loaded guns pointed at various hostages' heads. Arnold and his allies were holding a gun to labor's head with the paycheck-protection and teacher-pay measures, asking the Democrats to offer up a ransom by passing redistricting reform and a state spending cap. Labor in turn held a gun to the head of the pharmaceutical and energy industries, hoping to reduce their enthusiasm for Arnold's confrontational approach or at least make them spend a lot of money that might otherwise go to Arnold. Arnold's final card to play was whether to carry through his threat to call the special election. He had until early summer to decide. With tensions high, Arnold entered into negotiations with the legislature.

By outside appearances, there were some good faith efforts by both sides to work things out. On March 1, Democrats in the legislature offered a compromise on redistricting that would have taken the power to draw lines out of the legislature's hands, but only at the end of the decade when lines are typically redrawn. Arnold spurned the idea, saying he would go ahead with his plans for a mid-decade redistricting.

By April fifth, Arnold's hand was beginning to weaken. He withdrew his pension reform initiative in the face of opposition from firefighters and policeman. Democrats were beginning to get bolder as Arnold's ratings dropped due to the nurses' protests and the bad press about his fundraising. Some were beginning to think they could defeat Arnold's measures at the ballot, so why bother negotiating?

On April 26, the pharmaceutical lobby announced it was dropping its paycheck-protection measure in the hopes that they could reach some compromise with labor groups on the prescription drug issue. This might have worked but for the fact that Lewis Uhler was going ahead with his initiative, so labor was still going to have to fight it on Election Day anyhow.

Two days later, Arnold started trimming his sails. He mentioned nonchalantly at a town hall event in Silicon Valley that he would be fine if redistricting didn't happen until the end of the decade. "The key thing," said Arnold, "is not the year that we change the system but that it will be changed."[13]

The next day, Arnold faced sharp criticism from Bill Mundell, a Los Angeles businessman who had sunk more than a million bucks of his own money into helping qualify the redistricting measure. Mundell released a statement saying, "we believed the governor when he told us that the timeline was non-negotiable. The people want redistricting reform now. The people have spoken. The question now is: Is the governor listening?"[14]

Unlike CSC, Mundell truly was independent of the governor. He had heard Arnold's State of the State speech and decided that he would get involved helping with redistricting reform. Mundell had his own agenda as well. He was looking to build some name recognition and political experience to pave the way for a possible campaign against Senator Diane Feinstein in 2006. Again we were seeing the hybrid model of politics, where initiative campaigns were used to pave the way for candidate campaigns. But there was no doubt that Mundell had also become a true believer in the cause of redistricting reform and he wasn't happy when it looked like Arnold was going to back away from the goal of fixing things sooner rather than later.

In May, both sides' positions began to harden. Uhler's Coalition for Employee Rights turned in its signatures for the paycheck-protection measure on May 3, with its funders still unknown. By the May 10 deadline, eight initiative proponents had turned in enough signatures to qualify for the next election. These included two of Arnold's original five reform platform planks: redistricting reform and a state spending cap. A third measure to shorten teacher tenure replaced Arnold's original merit pay idea. The paycheck-protection measure was a fourth, unofficial, measure in Arnold's arsenal. The teenage abortion measure qualified as well. Labor groups qualified two initiatives: one to lower prescription drugs and one to re-regulate energy markets. Pharmaceutical companies responded by filing their own voluntary prescription drug plan that was not only part of their strategy to defeat the labor proposal but had the added benefit of making future drug reform more difficult by requiring any changes to go back to the voters.

Arnold Pulls the Trigger

Anticipation mounted as Arnold had not yet announced if he would indeed call a special election. If he didn't, these measures would simply have appeared on the June, 2006, ballot. That still left some wiggle room for Arnold to work out a deal with the legislature. On May 17, Arnold's campaign advisor announced to the media that Schwarzenegger would almost certainly call for a special election.[15] Yet Arnold's team still dropped hints that if the legislature would cut a deal, he might not call a special election. The initiatives would appear on the next regularly scheduled election, but if a deal was worked out proponents could tell voters that there was no need to enact them.

The stakes were high, and everyone knew it. San Jose State University professor Larry Gerston summed it up, saying:

> If the governor prevails on most, if not all, of his proposals, this will give him a resurgence of momentum and likely break the back of the Democratic opposition. If he loses, after putting all of his prestige on the line, this will cut the legs out from under him. We're really looking at a crossroads here.[16]

Mike Murphy beat the drums in an effort to rally his troops, scare the other side, and dismiss Arnold's slide in the polls. "Arnold has not touched the legislature with a feather yet compared to what the real campaign will be. It's a referendum on the governor versus the legislature, and he will win," he boldly predicted.[17]

Murphy's remarks may have been aimed at getting Democrats to cut a deal, with the not so subtle threat that he would come out swinging in favor of Lewis Uhler's paycheck-protection initiative. Murphy claimed that the governor had distanced himself from it up to that point "to create some goodwill for negotiations, because

Democrats go bonkers when you mention it." But, he implied that Schwarzenegger was prepared to endorse it if the Democrats didn't budge in other negotiations. "The fate of the paycheck protection measure is in the governor's hands now," said Murphy, after noting that polls indicated it could not pass without Arnold's support.[18] He even went so far as to say that the governor had instructed him to look into what it would take to pass the measure. "We're ready and prepared to win that campaign if he decides to give it a push," he threatened.[19] The gun was cocked, but the Democrats apparently weren't prepared to negotiate with hostage takers. Nobody wanted to cut a deal.

On June 13, Arnold announced that he was indeed calling for a special election to be held in November. Nonetheless, his team dangled an olive branch by saying that negotiations could continue and that his team could always tell voters to reject their initiatives if the legislature passed a compromise measure before ballot pamphlets were printed.

County clerks immediately began grumbling about the cost of the special election. The *Los Angeles Times* printed one estimate that the election would cost $70 million to hold. Secretary of State Bruce McPherson estimated $45 million. Either way, it was going be expensive. Yolo County Clerk-Recorder Freddie Oakley threatened to boycott the election and simply not hold it in her county unless the state agreed to pick up the costs. The state did eventually agree to reimburse counties for election expenses.

Whether people, the legislature, or the county clerks wanted it or not, the special election was on.

CHAPTER 10

Arnold's Second Job

The Muscle Mag Editor's Conflict of Interest

As the spring of 2005 turned to summer, Schwarzenegger confronted a completely different story about money in politics that would further distract from his special election agenda. This time, the story was about Schwarzenegger's personal finances, as opposed to those of his campaigns or ballot committees.

Arnold the Editor

On July 14, 2005, a publishing company called American Media Incorporated (AMI) filed some routine paperwork with the federal Securities and Exchange Commission. AMI is the king of the tabloids, publishing many of the gossip rags you see as you stand in the checkout line at the supermarket including the *National Enquirer*, the *Globe*, and *Star*. In 2002, AMI purchased two bodybuilding magazines, *Muscle & Fitness* and *Flex*, from Joe Weider—a long-time friend of Arnold Schwarzenegger who had helped bring Arnold from Austria to America in 1968.

AMI's filings indicated that it had a special contract with a "Mr. S," who had agreed to write columns under the title of executive editor. The *Los Angeles Times* and *Sacramento Bee* lost no time in discovering that this "Mr. S." was Arnold Schwarzenegger.

The fact that Arnold had a business deal with bodybuilding magazines was not news. He had disclosed this arrangement more than a year prior to this SEC filing. But the filing revealed that the terms of the contract were far more lucrative than Schwarzenegger had led us to believe.

In return for writing a monthly column, Schwarzenegger received a one percent cut on all advertising revenue in these magazines, with a minimum guarantee of one million dollars a year. AMI estimated that the total royalties over the five-year duration of the contract would come to about eight million bucks.

Nice work if you can get it.

Beyond the columns, the magazines had other features promoting Schwarzenegger. The January, 2005, edition of *Muscle & Fitness*, for instance, was called the "Arnold Training" special edition It featured a 12-page spread detailing his fitness routines plus a huge foldout poster declaring him the "greatest body-builder of all time." Both magazines were heavily involved in promoting Arnold's annual bodybuilding event in Ohio, the Arnold Classic.

The business arrangement was quite profitable to the magazines. *Muscle & Fitness* profits went up 17 percent the year after Schwarzenegger signed the deal and they ran ten percent more ads.

In March of 2004, when a Schwarzenegger spokesman disclosed the fact there was a deal between the governor and the publisher, he described the compensation that Arnold would receive as "petty compared to the movies."[1] On January 16, 2005, the *San Francisco Chronicle* quoted AMI spokesman Stuart Zakim as saying that his company had agreed to compensate Schwarzenegger by giving $1.25 million over five years to the Governor's Council on Physical Fitness, a nonprofit group that Arnold had created in 2004. Zakim said that this payment was "not a salary" and that the governor receives no other paychecks for the work. Arnold's office did nothing to correct this statement.

Back in October of 2003, on the very day after he was elected as California's next governor, Arnold held a press conference and promised the people of California "I will work as the governor. I will work as much as I can, even if it is around the clock. There will be no time for movies ***or anything else***. I will pay full attention to this job." Somehow, finding spare time to write columns for magazines didn't seem to square with this promise. Ned Wigglesworth, of

TheRestofUs.org, said in the *San Francisco Chronicle*, "serving as a state legislator or governor is not a paper route or lemonade stand. It deserves and demands an official's full attention."[2]

But the real problem with Arnold's contract was not the time it took away from attending to the business of California. Both Schwarzenegger and the publisher said that Arnold just spoke on the phone with the magazines about once a month and their writers would then convert that conversation into a column. Other governors probably wasted an hour a month on personal affairs of their own, so if that was the only issue there might not have been much of a problem.

The first truly troubling aspect about Arnold's deal with American Media was the lengths Schwarzenegger went to keep the details secret. Arnold signed the contract just two days before being sworn in as governor and just weeks after his promise to work full time for the people of California. Yet, he said nothing about his second job until four months later. Even then, his spokespeople gave scant details about the arrangement and described it in terms that were downright misleading.

The second problem with the American Media contract is that it created a clear conflict of interest between Arnold's personal bottom line and the business of the state of California. Larry Noble, head of the Center for Responsive Politics, described the arrangement as "one of the most egregious conflicts of interest that I have ever seen."[3]

The Supplement Veto

Arnold's conflict wasn't just a hypothetical problem. He had taken a stand on public policy that not only directly affected the bottom line of these magazines, but his compensation as well. As governor, Schwarzenegger vetoed legislation that would have required the California Department of Health Services to create a list of "Performance Enhancing Dietary Supplements," or PEDS, and banned high-school students from participating in official school sporting events if they used these supplements. The basic idea was not unlike Major League Baseball prohibiting its players from using steroids. Indeed, the year before there had been a major flap over a California company called BALCO providing steroids to major league baseball players. Jose Canseco admitted to using steroids and many suggested that BALCO client Barry Bonds was also using them.

There is considerable controversy over just how safe these so-called dietary supplements are. We're not talking about basic vitamins and minerals; the bill explicitly exempted these. But nor are we talking about full-test anabolic steroids, which had already been outlawed in California. Schwarzenegger had admitted to using steroids during his career as a bodybuilder, but professed to be against them even before he became governor. Arnold saw supplements, however, as mostly safe and worth taking.

The bill Arnold vetoed had defined Performance Enhancing Dietary Supplements as a substance:

> designed or marketed to improve athletic performance or physical development by promoting body or muscle growth, stimulating or altering the cardiovascular system or the central nervous system, altering the perception of pain, or otherwise enhancing athletic performance or physical development above levels that would be anticipated under normal conditions with appropriate nourishment.

In other words, the stuff was designed to make you bigger and stronger than a person could normally be without doing something unusual to their body.

Unlike both prescription and over-the-counter drugs, Performance Enhancing Dietary Supplements are not tested or approved by the Food and Drug Administration. Congress had passed a law in 1994 that exempted these supplements from stricter regulations that applied to even basic food ingredients.

A Blue Cross Blue Shield study had found that more than a million kids ages 12–17 had taken these supplements in 2003. Public health officials were increasingly worried that using these supplements could lead to more dangerous steroid use down the road. The Center for Disease Control estimates that 3.7 percent of high-school kids have used illegal steroids, including about one of every twenty boys. A March 25, 2005, hearing in the California Senate identified poor education among coaches as a major factor contributing to the widespread use of supplements among teenagers. Coaches, in fact, would often tell kids that they needed to "get bigger" if they wanted to make the team, encouraging them to look to supplements as the solution.[4]

The bill had passed the California Senate by a vote of 24–11 and the Assembly by a vote of 54–24. Despite that strong support, Schwarzenegger vetoed the legislation on September 29, 2004.

In a statement, the governor said that steroids were already illegal, that this bill was problematic because the definition of dietary supplement was too vague, and that because of this the state Department of Health Services would be unable to draw up a list of supplements to regulate.

Arnold's rationale was puzzling because the bill had specifically told the Department of Health Services to base its list upon lists that had already been established by collegiate, professional, and Olympic sports organizations. If they could do it, couldn't the state of California? Governor Schwarzenegger said that the federal Food and Drug Administration should regulate these supplements, but the 1994 act of Congress had specifically tied the FDA's hands to do so by prohibiting the regulation of supplements as drugs or food additives.

Beyond the veto of the dietary supplement bill, Schwarzenegger has walked a fine line in denouncing the use of anabolic steroids. Dr. Charlie Yesalis, author of *The Steroids Game* and a recognized expert on the topic, says that Arnold "doesn't endorse anabolic steroids, but he stays, in my judgment, uncomfortably close to an activity that is inundated with drugs. . . . I wish he would use his celebrity and his fame and political clout in a way that would help the problem—rather than one that might exacerbate it."[5]

Steroids have been linked to liver cancer, jaundice, high blood pressure, kidney tumors, and body trembling. They may also lead to other problems. Rob Garibaldi, a high-school baseball star, began taking dietary supplements at age 15. After high school, he turned to steroids. His mother, Denise Garibaldi, believes the steroids caused psychological problems that contributed to Rob's failure to make the major leagues. Rob had turned down an offer by the Yankees to go to college, but ultimately killed himself at age 24 out of despondency. Rob's parents believe that his steroid use was "precipitated by his supplement use."[6] Rob's mother, Denise, testified before Congress about steroids, and in support of the legislation that Schwarzenegger eventually vetoed in California.

Upon learning of his contract with American Media, the Garibaldis filed a complaint at the Fair Political Practices Commission arguing that Schwarzenegger should have disclosed that the bill he vetoed would have hurt his own financial interests. The Garibaldis weren't just Democratic pawns. They had voted for Schwarzenegger in the recall election, as had another family from Vacaville that denounced Arnold's ties to the supplement industry.

Juiced-up Ads

While saying he is absolutely opposed to steroid use, Schwarzenegger has made statements that minimize their dangers. In admitting he had used them in the past, Schwarzenegger said in 1996 that:

> It was a risky thing to do, but I have no regrets. It was what I had to do to compete. The danger with steroids is over-usage. I only did it before a difficult competition—for two months, but not for a period of time that could harm me. And then afterward, it was over. I would stop. I have no health problems, no kidney damage or anything like that from using them.[7]

The advertisements in these magazines intentionally blur the line between dietary supplements and anabolic steroids. One advertiser, Fizogen, ran an ad with the headline "Not All Extremely

Powerful Muscle-Building Drugs are Smuggled Across the Border." The ad claimed its products were "extreme anabolic/androgenic agents" that promoted "intense muscle growth."[8] Others described their products as "grey market," boasted that they would "boost testosterone levels" and said "anything stronger would be illegal." One typical edition of *Muscle & Fitness* carried 110 pages of ads for these supplements.[9]

With Schwarzenegger receiving a direct percentage of revenues from ads sold in the magazines, which were almost all ads for dietary supplements, he had a clear stake in making sure that these supplement makers weren't too heavily regulated. The better they did, the better he did. If too many states banned supplements in high schools, then supplement makers might stop running ads in Arnold's magazines, which were read mostly by young people.

There are also indications that Schwarzenegger consulted with the industry about how to avoid further government regulation. One edition of *Flex* magazine described how Arnold had encouraged more than 20 supplement makers to fight efforts for further regulation. The article said that Schwarzenegger promised them that he was only a phone call away should they need his assistance.[10] In the May 2005 edition of *Flex*, Arnold wrote a column titled "In Defense of Supplements."

Once the details of Schwarzenegger's contract with American Media became public on July 14, 2005, there was an immediate outcry of disbelief and disgust. I joined Senator Jackie Speier and others to call on Schwarzenegger to immediately sever his ties with the publisher. My colleague Ned appeared on TV news stations that night in Los Angeles, Sacramento, Stockton, and San Francisco saying that the deal was a classic conflict of interest and that "it stinks."

Arnold's 180

Schwarzenegger spokesman Rob Stutzman first tried to dismiss the criticism. "There is no technical conflict," he said, because

Schwarzenegger hadn't personally solicited ads for the magazines and because he was getting his money from the publisher, not the supplement makers.[11] He pooh-poohed the entire outcry as simply, "The lemming attitude of the press. I don't think anyone else cares about this but you." The following morning, Stutzman stated resolutely that the governor planned on keeping his contract with American Media, and sneered that it was a "silly suggestion" for him to even consider dropping his agreement.[12]

But by that afternoon, the suggestion didn't appear so silly. Schwarzenegger abruptly changed course and personally announced in a phone call with the *Associated Press* that he would cancel the contract with American Media and give up the title of executive editor. He would not give back the money (more than $1.5 million) he had received to date and would continue to write columns for the magazines on an unpaid basis.

By dumping the story late in the day on a Friday, Schwarzenegger was using an age-old technique of politicians to bury bad news deep in the Saturday papers in the hopes that nobody would read about it.

Unfortunately for Arnold, it didn't work this time.

The *San Francisco Chronicle* ran a huge headline saying, "Governor to Quit Second Job," and the buzz continued for several days. One highlight was a spot on *The Daily Show*, where comic commentator Lewis Black ran a clip of Ned saying, "Anytime you have a public official who is taking money from companies with business before the state, it's a conflict of interest." Black then concluded the bit by quipping, "That's what happens when public figures enter the real world. They go from vanquishing the predator to having their ass handed to them by a guy named Wigglesworth." Ned had grown accustomed to his name inspiring chuckles, but suddenly it had landed him on America's funniest TV show.

Arnold was not amused.

Many Moonlighters, Not Enough Sunshine

Schwarzenegger's inherent conflict between his role as public official and his own private interests was far from unique, even if the amounts were well beyond what we normally see. Many California legislators earn income from a variety of outside sources including investments, businesses they own, and consulting work that they do.

Whenever public policy intrudes upon the interests of these private sources of income, there is a conflict of interest.

Indeed, just a few months earlier, newspapers expressed concern about Assembly Speaker Fabian Núñez's contract for $35,000 with a Los Angeles labor-affiliated group, called the Voter Improvement Program. We complained about the arrangement on our weblog, *Democracy's Daily Posts*, writing:

> It's bad enough when elected officials have a second job that may conflict with their duty to the public, but when that second job is getting paid $35,000 a year to provide political advice to a group whose backers have issues before you as an officeholder all the year 'round—it stinks. I imagine a lot of the folks that labor says it represents wouldn't mind a 10–15 hour a week job that pays $35k a year.[13]

Schwarzenegger himself had squarely criticized the speaker for this arrangement, saying, "It's all over the press now that he's receiving $35,000 from a nonprofit organization, that is from the unions. And excuse me, he's owned by them. He cannot make a decision without asking them for permission."[14]

When Núñez's labor contract was exposed in the media, he said he might be willing to give it up. A recent editorial that criticized him for the arrangement had caused him to think, "Do I want this distraction?"[15]

The same *AP* story that highlighted Núñez 's $35,000 contract also referenced Arnold's contract with American Media, saying that as compensation American Media donated $250,000 a year to the

California Governor's Council on Physical Fitness. Nobody from the Schwarzenegger administration stepped forward to correct this report as only the tip of the iceberg of Arnold's compensation.

Núñez eventually did drop the Voter Improvement Program contract prior to Arnold dropping his deal with American Media. But neither man pushed for policy changes that would prevent this type of thing from happening again.

Current California law requires legislators and state officials to file disclosure forms that list their sources of personal income. Then, when they are faced with making a public policy decision that could have an impact on those personal interests, they are supposed to recuse themselves. This policy failed to head off the supplement scandal because Arnold significantly dodged the disclosure requirements and he didn't recuse himself from considering the supplement bill.

The current disclosure system only requires public officials to list broad ranges of income they receive from various sources. Most of Schwarzenegger's business deals are done through a holding company, Oak Productions. So, it is Oak Productions that contracts with other business entities rather than Schwarzenegger himself. This is why Stuart Zakim of American Media could get away with saying that he wasn't paying Arnold a salary. Rather, American Media was paying Oaks Productions a consulting fee of one percent of its ad revenues with a guarantee of at least $1 million a year. To you and me, getting oodles of money to write a column sounds a lot like getting a salary, but technically this was a contract between two corporations.

The paperwork that Arnold did file for his conflict of interest disclosure lists Oak Productions as receiving undisclosed amounts from American Media. All in all, Schwarzenegger lists more than 20 different business deals that pay Oak Productions more than $10,000, but he is not required to provide any greater detail than that or list the actual amounts. All told, Arnold disclosed that Oak Productions was worth more than a million bucks and had generated more than $100,000 in income in 2003, but that was all the detail that was required. The corporate income falls within the

Arnold Schwarzenegger's Statement of Economic Interest

CHEDULE A-2 - Form 700, 01/01/05-12/31/05
vestments, Income and Assets of Business Entities/Trusts

1. Business Entity or Trust								2.	3.
ness Entity or Trust Name	Address	Bus / Trust	General Description	Fair Mkt. Value	Date Disposed	Nature of Inv.	Position	Gross Inc. Received	Source(s) of of Inc.
Productions, Inc.	3110 Main Street Santa Monica, CA 90405	Bus	Holds intellectual property and contract rights of Mr. Schwarzenegger's films.	>$1,000,000	n/a	S-Corp	None	>$100,000	See Attached
ping Iron America, Inc.	3110 Main Street Santa Monica, CA 90405	Bus	Film and trademarks holdings	>$1,000,000	n/a	S-Corp	None	>$100,000	HBO, Inc.
ess Publications, Inc.	3110 Main Street Santa Monica, CA 90405	Bus	Fitness books and trademarks	$100,001 - $1,000,000	n/a	S-Corp	None	>$100,000	Simon & Schuster
n Street Plaza, Inc.	3110 Main Street Santa Monica, CA 90405	Bus	Commercial real estate ownership	>$1,000,000	n/a	S-Corp	None	>$100,000	See Attached
Main Street., Inc.	3110 Main Street Santa Monica, CA 90405	Bus	Commercial real estate ownership	>$1,000,000	n/a	S-Corp	None	$10,000 - $100,000	1) Broadway Gymnastics School, Inc. 2) Hodgson Law
een Partners	3110 Main Street Santa Monica, CA 90405	Bus	Owned LLC interest in AP Entertainment, which was dissolved in 2005.	<$2,000	n/a	LLC	None	$10,000 - $100,000	AP Entertainment, LLC
point Investors	3110 Main Street Santa Monica, CA 90405	Bus	Owns preferred stock in CellGuide Ltd.	$100,001 - $1,000,000	n/a	Partnership	None	$0 - $499	None

Name	Mkt. Value	Gross Inc. Received
Oak Productions, Inc.	>$1,000,000	>$100,000

Schwarzengger only had to disclose that Oak Productions was worth more than $1 million and paid him more than $100,000 per year.

Arnold Listed American Media as one Source of Oak Production's Income, But Not the Fact His Contract Was Worth $8 Million.

Oak Productions, Inc.

20th Century Fox
American Media Operations
Anschutz Film Group
Beacon Communications
Classic Productions, Inc.
Columbia Pictures
Daniel Marshall Inc.
Lightstorm Entertainment
MGM/UA Services
Simon & Schuster
Sony Pictures
The Kid and I Productions, LLC
The Licensing Group Ltd.
UB Fintage Collection
VH1 Productions, Inc.
Vivendi Universal Entertainment, LLP
Warner Brothers Pictures, Inc.

Schwarzenegger attached this page to the report printed on the preceding page.

umbrella of Oak Productions, hiding the actual amounts from each source.

Part of the poor disclosure in Arnold's filing is due to the out-of-date nature of the law, going back to a period where anything above $10,000 was a ton of money. But, it's also the case that nobody ever envisioned that California's chief executive could have outside income that ranged in the millions, not tens of thousands. The California Supreme Court has ruled that requiring elected officials to divulge the exact amounts of their outside income is a violation of their privacy. But California can create categories such as $10,000–$50,000, $50,000–$100,000, $100,000–$250,000, and so on, that would give voters a better idea of just how extensive a public officials ties are to any given industry. Thresholds like this do exist for officeholders' personal income, but Arnold avoided this level of disclosure by having the deals housed within the holding company Oak Productions. There are fewer thresholds for reporting a public official's assets in a holding company.

Even after the supplement flap, Arnold refused to provide any more details about his extensive business arrangements. To this date, nobody knows if there are other deals out there like the American Media contract that could similarly present a conflict of interest.

A Structural Conflict

Arnold also got around the need to recuse himself from considering the supplement bill because of a bit of the law that says that if an elected official must take action on something, then he or she can't recuse himself. As governor, Schwarzenegger is the only person authorized to sign or veto legislation, so arguably he can't recuse himself from that responsibility even if he *does* have a conflict of interest.

A 1986 court ruling allowed then San Francisco Mayor Diane Feinstein to veto a rent control bill even though as a landlord she had a clear personal financial stake in the law. Likewise, Oakland Mayor Jerry Brown was allowed to promote redevelopment in the neighborhood where he lived, even though he would benefit personally from an improvement in the area's property values. As chief executives of those local jurisdictions, there was no surrogate who could sign or veto bills in their place.

One solution to this dilemma would be for the governor to delegate all bill-signing responsibilities to the lieutenant governor whenever a conflict of interest does arise. Current California law allows the lieutenant governor to sign bills when the governor is out of the state, although few lieutenant governors have exercised this power. However, had Arnold wanted to clear the air about any potential conflict in this situation, he could have asked the lieutenant governor to consider the bill on its merits, and sign or veto it accordingly, during one of his many out-of-state fundraising trips or vacations. If California doesn't want to count on the goodwill of our chief executive to recuse himself in situations like this, the state could tighten the laws to require it.

Alternatively, California could prohibit elected officials from receiving any outside income at all. Congress prohibits its members from earning outside income, and senators and representatives put substantial investments into blind trusts.

Members of Congress are also prohibited from receiving speaking fees or honoraria, which aren't that different from a payment to write a column. Similar rules apply to the Los Angeles City Council. California legislators earn a salary of $110,880 per year, more than any other state legislators in America.[16] On top of that, taxpayers pay them $138 for travel and food expenses every day the legislature is in session. If we're going to pay politicians salaries that are already much higher than what most of us earn, we have the right to demand that they work exclusively for us. If some politicians want to make money on the side, there are plenty of capable citizens who would be willing to act as public servants in their stead.

Did the *Enquirer* Sell Out?

Why would a man already worth hundreds of millions of dollars risk his reputation as governor over a contract worth only $8 million? To most of us, that's more than our families will make in ten generations, but Arnold made more than that without lifting his little pinky. Maybe it was sheer greed, but maybe Arnold had political reasons for doing business with American Media that were more important than the risk he took in signing the contract to write columns for the bodybuilding magazines.

As the summer of 2005 wore on, other facts came to light that suggested Arnold's contract with American Media went beyond his desire to make money and reached instead to an effort to quash gossip and media reports about Arnold's alleged womanizing that could have been fatal to his political career.

The *National Enquirer*, owned by American Media, had published unflattering accounts of Schwarzenegger's love life dating back to 2001. Yet, during the 2003 recall they published glowing accounts of the man, including a 120-page booklet that extolled his virtues as the symbol of the American Dream. In the final days before the recall election, the *Los Angeles Times* had published stories that many women claimed Arnold had groped them on movie sets. Yet the tabloids were strangely quiet about the juiciest piece of gossip around.

Is it possible that once it purchased *Muscle & Fitness* and *Flex* in 2002, American Media decided it had more to gain financially from partnering with Arnold than by trashing him?

On August 8, 2003, just two days after Schwarzenegger announced that he was running for governor, the *National Enquirer* signed a confidentiality agreement with Gigi Goyette. Ms. Goyette had previously claimed to have had an intimate relationship with Schwarzenegger that involved massages and other caresses that she described as "outercourse." Goyette had toyed with the idea of putting out a book detailing her life in Hollywood and saw the $20,000 confidentiality agreement as the first step in negotiating a book deal with the *Enquirer*. The *Enquirer* also signed a separate deal with one of Goyette's friends.

A confidentiality deal like this normally allows a newspaper to investigate a story and prepare it for publication without fear that some competing publication will scoop them by running the story before they can. But in this case, the *Enquirer* never published the story it had paid good money to secure.

Why not?

An unidentified employee of American Media told the *Los Angeles Times* that the *Enquirer* had "effectively bought the silence" of these two women in order to protect Schwarzenegger, who was a "de facto employee," and "important to their bottom line."[17] The only thing odd about that is that Schwarzenegger didn't enter into his deal with American Media until more than three months after they signed these confidentiality agreements to buy the women's stories. Schwarzenegger's spokespeople have said that he was unaware of these agreements.

Author Laurence Leamer has speculated in his book *Fantastic: the Life of Arnold Schwarzenegger*, that Arnold knew that if he entered into a business deal with American Media that they would be reluctant to trash him. When he met with David Pecker, the CEO of American Media, six months after AMI acquired the magazines from Weider, Arnold reportedly did not bring the subject up directly. "There was no discussion about the *National Enquirer*," Arnold insisted. "There were all sorts of people sitting there. It would have been inappropriate."[18] But Arnold admitted that he did not need to bring it up explicitly. "I think it's common sense. Do you want to work with someone who you are attacking? You don't have to say anything. You don't have to be sleazy and make deals. It's human nature."[19]

It is possible that Schwarzenegger, a consummate businessman, helped orchestrate his friend Joe Weider's sale of the two body-building magazines to American Media in November of 2002 as a way to win the cooperation of the *National Enquirer* and other tabloids during his political career. Or, maybe it was his friend Joe Weider's idea. When buying the magazines, Pecker had told Weider that he would not run anything negative about his protégé Schwarzenegger unless Arnold had new ethical lapses. This promise to not dig up old dirt was special treatment that the *Enquirer* gave to no other celebrity. Weider had relayed his conversations with

AMI to Arnold, letting him know that he'd told Pecker that if he wanted Arnold's help with the bodybuilding magazines, he would need to leave him alone in the tabloids.[20] November 2002, the time when AMI purchased Weider's magazines, is the same moment that Arnold launched his foray into politics with his sponsorship of Prop 49 for after-school programs. We may never know whether Schwarzenegger's ties to American Media began at the same time and with the same goal of preparing for the career change from actor to politician.

Who would have guessed that the *Enquirer* was capable of having its journalistic integrity compromised? Wasn't it already at rock bottom when it came to even its own readers' expectations? And, you may be wondering, what has this got to do with a book about money in politics?

The story of the *Enquirer* dropping stories of interest to its readers because of its parent company's conflicting business arrangements is unfortunately not a problem limited to the tabloids. General Electric owns 80 percent of NBC. Do you think you'll see stories that damage GE's bottom line on the NBC news? Fox News is owned by Rupert Murdock, who has his own political agenda. Disney owns ABC, and CBS was owned by Viacom until 2006.

Big business influences American politics not only by helping elect friendly politicians with campaign contributions and then spending millions to lobby those elected officials and lavish them with gifts. Major corporations get what they want by controlling the very information that citizens receive about what our politicians are doing. Think about that the next time you tune in to the news. The best defense for active citizens is to rely upon a variety of news sources, especially small, independent sources that make all of their money from providing news.

CHAPTER 11

THE NOT-SO-SPECIAL ELECTION

Voters Are Not Amused as Big Money Flows

By midsummer, 2005, Arnold was getting more and more desperate to cut a deal as his poll ratings fell through the floor. In the coming months, Arnold would learn that his opponents too had access to big money and dirty tricks. His powerplay was backfiring.

Off the Ballot

Beyond the magazine scandal, another glitch drained most of the gas from Arnold's REFORM1 Humvee. On July 7, 2005, redistricting reformer Ted Costa announced that he had discovered minor discrepancies between the language he had filed with the attorney general and the text that had been printed on the petitions he used to circulate the initiative.

The 16 differences in the drafts were minor but not meaningless. For example, the draft filed with the attorney general mentioned a three-day period for filing challenges to lines drawn by the redistricting panel, whereas the language on the petitions said four days. One version said judges would be "nominated" for the panel, while the other said they would be "selected." It was a simple clerical error that resulted from minor refinements being made to the initiative text and an aide accidentally filing an older version with the AG. Costa fessed up and took full responsibility. "The buck has to stop right here," Costa said. He then predicted "I've given the other side a little issue, and they'll put it together with other issues and try to keep us off the ballot."[1]

He was right.

Attorney General Bill Lockyer, a Democrat, went to court to remove Costa's redistricting initiative from the ballot. If the court disqualified the initiative, it would knock out Arnold's sole reason for holding a special election. The other initiatives could all wait for a 2006 ballot. The need to enact redistricting reform prior to the 2006 races was the only justification for conducting an extra election in 2005.

Then, in mid-July, the scandal of Arnold's multi-million dollar deal with the bodybuilding magazines erupted and he endured a week of terrible publicity. Arnold dropped the contract, but the damage was done. By this point, the Democrats saw no reason to negotiate on anything with a governor who had come out to destroy them and in the course of events had self-destructed.

On July 21, Art Torres, the head of the California Democratic Party, filed an ethics complaint with the Fair Political Practices Commission about Arnold's conflict of interest in vetoing the dietary supplement bill while at the same time taking money from magazines that derived most of their income from supplement manufacturers.

Republicans took it as a sign that negotiations were over. Kevin Spillane, a Republican consultant read the tea leaves: "Now we go to war, in all likelihood. Filing that complaint conveyed the level of seriousness the Democrats have for a negotiated settlement."[2]

The same day, the Sacramento County Superior Court announced that it would disqualify the redistricting reform measure from the ballot, based on the minor discrepancies between the language on file with the attorney general and the language circulated on petitions.

The Governator was down for the count.

Time to Throw in the Towel?

Within 24 hours, Kevin Spillane was ready to call off the war, even if it meant losing. He publicly told Schwarzenegger to cancel the special election, writing in a *Los Angeles Times* column:

> Ironically, the initial reason for the governor to call a special election this fall rather than wait for the June primary was so that the reapportionment initiative could be approved in time to trigger new districts for 2006. Now that there's no chance (barring a surprising appeals court reversal) for this to occur, it's time for the governor to consider a temporary tactical retreat in order to ensure the long-term success of his agenda. [3]

Democrat Garry South, who had advised Governor Gray Davis, smelled blood in the water and was ready for revenge. Negotiating a deal to cancel the election was the last thing on his mind. "A deal lets this guy off the hook," he said. "It would be one thing if the guy was still hugely popular or if a majority of voters wanted a special election or backed his reform package. But now, I'm not in favor of bailing him out."[4]

Arnold held firm and won an interim victory. On August 12, the California Supreme Court put the redistricting reform measure back on the ballot. The court ruled that the differences between the draft that People's Advocate submitted to the secretary of state and the one circulated for signatures were not large enough so that they would have misled or confused the people who signed the petitions. The court said that the measure should be put before voters, and if it passed it would then reconsider the legal issues posed by the discrepancies in the ballot. Redistricting reformers would at least get to take their case to the voters.

But days later, Arnold was rocked with more bad news. The *Associated Press* reported that Schwarzenegger had accepted a $50,000 contribution from Yuba County Entertainment LLC, a partner with the Estom Yumeka Maidu Indian tribe, which was trying to build a resort casino. Arnold had staked his political career on trashing Indian contributions, attacking both Cruz Bustamante during the recall and fellow Republican legislators who took Indian contributions while supporting the Indians' position on Prop 68 in 2004. Arnold quickly returned the cash, but the story was out.

Big Money for Arnold's Opponents

On August 17, Arnold got more bad news. The Federal Election Commission was going to allow members of Congress to raise unlimited contributions to oppose Arnold's redistricting measure. The FEC had ruled just a year earlier that the 2002 Bipartisan Campaign Reform Act had barred federal officeholders from raising unlimited soft money contributions, including big contributions for state candidates and ballot measures. They had prohibited Congressman Jeff Flake from raising contributions of more than $5,000 for a ballot committee in Arizona that was aimed, interestingly enough, at repealing that state's campaign finance laws. The FEC eventually applied this logic to Darrell Issa's fundraising for the recall, but it found no proof that he had asked for contributions more than $5,000.

Democratic Congressman Howard Berman and Republican John Doolittle jointly petitioned the FEC to reconsider its position. Congressman Berman's brother, Michael Berman, was the political consultant who California Democrats had hired to draw the 2001 districts. No less than 30 of the 32 Democratic members of Congress each paid Michael Berman's firm $20,000 to assure their interests would be protected and the state Democrats kicked in nearly $2 million more. Michael Berman made sure to protect his brother's career, carving up a district that would otherwise likely have elected a Latino Democrat into one likely to elect a white Democrat—like his brother. Groups like the Mexican American Legal Defense Fund were incensed and sued unsuccessfully to change the district. A deposition in that suit claimed that Berman told another representative, Brad Sherman, that he would make his district even tougher if he complained about the process.

John Doolittle was an ardent deputy of Republican Majority Leader Tom DeLay. These men knew that the 2001 districts had been a deal with the devil from the Republican point of view. In exchange for giving Democrats uncontested control of the California legislature, the Republicans got to keep congressional districts that would ensure 20 Republicans were elected from California.

This not only protected important senior Republican leaders like Doolittle; by DeLay's math it meant that the Republicans would maintain a lock on Congress for the entire decade, once he'd pulled off his own mid-decade redistricting in Texas.

Doolittle and Berman argued that because they were not up for re-election in the 2005 special election, indeed no candidate was, it didn't technically count as "an election." Therefore, they reasoned they should be able to raise unlimited sums of money. Berman's chief of staff, Gene Smith, argued that the fact that Arnold had created a loophole in California campaign finance law that allowed him to raise unlimited funds is what justified a new loophole in federal election law that would allow members of Congress to do the same thing. "You've got one side that can raise unlimited funds to say why they approve it, and the other side cannot put forward to the electorate the reasons why they oppose it, so the voters don't have the opportunity to hear both sides," he said.[5] The FEC staff recommended rejecting Doolittle and Berman's request, but a majority of the FEC commissioners overruled their own staff and granted the exemption. Scott Thomas, the one true reformer on the Commission, issued a stinging dissent:

> In essence, [Doolittle and Berman's] request boiled down to whether the November 8, 2005 California special election falls within the "any election other than election for Federal office" provision of §441i(e)(1)(B). If it did, the requestors could raise funds only to the extent the funds complied with the Act's contribution limitations and prohibitions.
>
> In my view, the clear phrase "any election" means just that—*any* election. This broad statutory language includes elections to decide ballot initiatives as well as elections to select public officials. I do not believe the statutory phrase "*any* election" is limited only to "candidate" elections. Indeed, if that was Congress's intent, it would have so stated.[6]

Nonetheless, Thomas lost while Berman and Doolittle won. Campaigns around Arnold's special election had managed to weaken both state and federal election law. In the spring, Arnold won his victory in court allowing him to raise unlimited sums of money for his ballot agenda and in the fall the FEC opened up a similar opening for his opponents. Now big money would flow unrestrained to both sides. Hollywood liberal Steven Bing loaned congressional opponents of redistricting reform $4 million to unleash against it.

Not to be outdone, Arnold launched another round of fundraisers in September. A dinner with Arnold at Sacramento's Sutter Club brought in $100,000 for a table of six. A Lake Tahoe fundraiser the next day brought in more money. On September 21, Arnold headed for Boston's Fenway Park for a Rolling Stones concert. The concert tour's corporate sponsor, Roland Arnall's Ameriquest mortgage firm, donated a block of 40 seats to the California Recovery Team, which scalped the tickets for $100,000 a pop. Steve Weiss of the Center for Responsive Politics commented that "politicians are always looking for more ways to raise money—but Schwarzenegger is one of those pushing the envelope and raising money in ways with a vigor that . . . we don't often see. Schwarzenegger is using his celebrity to his advantage," said Weiss, but that didn't seem to jibe with candidate Arnold who "ran a campaign in which he said he would not be beholden to special interests."[7]

The Stones maintained they had nothing to do with it and were not endorsing Arnold, just selling concert tickets. I told viewers on ABC's Bay Area Channel 7, "I don't have a problem if they spend that money to see the Stones, but when they're paying that kind of money to influence our election outcomes, there's distortion of democracy."[8]

One does have to wonder what Arnold's Republican donors thought when Mick Jagger proceeded to sing the Stones' new hit, Sweet Neo-Con, that included lyrics like "You call yourself a Christian—I call you hypocrite. You call yourself a patriot—Well, I think you're full of shit."

On October 7, Schwarzenegger received a $250,000

contribution from Wal-Mart heiress Christy Walton. That very day, he vetoed a bill that Wal-Mart opposed relating to insurance benefits. Schwarzenegger also vetoed a bill that would have ended a government subsidy for insurance companies and simultaneously a check of $105,000 found its way to one of Schwarzenegger's ballot committees from the American Insurance Association.

Perhaps the timing was just a coincidence. Another interesting coincidence is that both Wal-Mart and the American Insurance Association were among the 35 private interests that had hired Mike Murphy's firm to work for them, at the same time Murphy's firms had made $700,000 off work for Arnold and his committees.

Arnold's hunger for cash was so insatiable that he even got into a quarrel with President Bush. He asked the president to delay a planned October fundraising trip to California because it would compete with Arnold's own efforts to raise money. "In the next two months, it would be better if *we* just do the fundraising," he said, "Then let us go [past] our special election—and then *they* can pick it up again, the [Republican] national committee."[9] President Bush stayed the course and Arnold got over it. But still, the fact that he'd even ask indicated how desperate Schwarzenegger had become.

$ $ $

DONOR PROFILE: Texas oilman and corporate raider T. Boone Pickens gave Arnold's California Recovery Team $550,000 for his special election agenda in 2005. His clan has given more than 1,500 separate donations worth $1.4 million to federal candidates and parties. On top of that, Boone provided $2 million to the Swift Boat Veterans for Truth, who ran ads attacking John Kerry's war record in the 2004 presidential race, and $2.5 million to the Progress for American electioneering group. He ranks at 207 on the Forbes 400 list, with a net worth estimated at $1.5 billion.

$ $ $

Arnold was now on the defensive in regard to campaign fundraising, as opposed to the recall where he was the one throwing stones at Gray Davis. With the stones now in slingshots aimed at him, Schwarzenegger tried to back away from his previous positions. He claimed it was "absolutely wrong" that he ever criticized Gray Davis for raising money. "What I always said is politicians, in general, are raising money and have to do favors back," Arnold explained. "I never said raising money is not necessary . . . everybody does fundraising."[10]

Some voters saw it differently. Tim Kostner, a registered Republican who had voted for Schwarzenegger in the recall told the *Orange County Register*, "I thought anything would be better than Gray Davis." But now, he looks at Arnold and thinks, "If he got enough money, he'd build a casino in his mother's back yard."[11]

In the final month before Election Day, both sides faced campaign finance violations. Assembly Speaker Núñez returned $140,000 that he had received for his initiative committee after Republicans threatened to file a complaint. Steve Poizner, a candidate for insurance commissioner, returned $1.75 million to Arnold Schwarzenegger and the California Recovery Team from Poizner's ballot committee Redistricting California. Because Poizner's and Núñez's names were a part of ballot committees that they controlled, the contributions counted as a candidate-to-candidate transfer, which is subject to a limit of $3,300.

Overall, more money was spent to influence the outcome of the special election than for any other set of ballot questions in the history of America. Total spending by those interests promoting Arnold and his agenda reached $74 million. His opponents spent a total of $153 million. PhRMA spent another $84 million looking out for its interests. Just 30 donors gave a total of $189 million.[12]

The drug money not only went into TV ads, but to citizen groups who were willing to rent their good name to the drug companies. These included the NAACP, who opposed Prop 78 after its president, Alice Huffman, received $720,000 from PhRMA's ballot committee, of which only $400,000 went to the actual costs of a mailer. Some NAACP local affiliates received $2,500 or $5,000 from PhRMA's committee.

Assemblymember Mark Ridley-Thomas, an African American, criticized the group, saying that the position was "contrary to the interests of its constituency" and that "it is practically inconceivable to me that the NAACP would be twisted on an issue as fundamental as this. What's at stake is the credibility of the organization."[13]

The conservative Traditional Values Coalition, headed by Reverend Lou Sheldon, received $30,000 from PhRMA's ballot committee. It endorsed the drug-makers' position. The campaign also paid the slate mailer COPS (the California Organization of Police and Sheriffs) $200,000 to promote its position. COPS is known for selling its endorsements on many issues and on candidate races as well.

Marilyn Tenny, a 78-year-old resident of Escondido said she thought their money would buy the election. "The man who has the most money is going to win, isn't that the old saying?" she asked.[14]

Dirty Tricks

As the final days of the campaign drew near, the redistricting opponents pulled out their bag of dirty tricks. The No on 77 Committee, financed almost entirely by Democratic members of Congress such as Nancy Pelosi and their supporters, paid for a so-called slate mailer to Republican households. The mailing urged voters to "Support Arnold's Reform Agenda, but Vote No on 77." The intent was to fool Republican voters into thinking that people who thought similarly to them were planning to vote against redistricting reform. To accomplish this, some of the most liberal Democrats in the country had no problem urging people to vote for an anti-union measure, limits in teacher tenure, and even Arnold's spending cap. The mailings carried a notice about jury duty by the postmark—an old junk mailer's trick that fools people into reading the piece because they think it may be a summons to jury duty and that they would be shirking their civic responsibility if they just threw it out.

The redistricting reform opponents followed this mailing by one to Republicans that was signed by Congressman John Doolittle and former House Republican Majority Leader Dick Armey. It urged Republicans to defeat Prop 77 by explaining that Republicans had supported the 2001 redistricting scheme because it would ensure a Republican hold on all of Congress for the coming decade:

> By voting for Proposition 77, you may actually be voting to put Congress back in the hands of liberal Democrats. In 2001, all 45 Republican state lawmakers unanimously voted for the district lines that now exist—because they were the best set of lines possible to ensure Republican control of the House of Representatives.

This mailing was paid for, mind you, with funds raised by congressional Democrats through the "Citizens for Good Government" committee, which had received $610,000 from the No on 77 Committee. House Democratic leader Nancy Pelosi had contributed $25,000 to the No on 77 Committee.

To careful observers, the union printing bug gave away its true origins. Tom Kaptain, who put together the slate mailer, said its opposition to Prop 77 was purely a business decision, meaning the committee paid him for his slate endorsement.

The Democratic members of Congress, in going along back in 2001 and in continuing to fight Arnold on redistricting reform, were acting in their own self-interest to protect their individual seats even at the expense of their party's interest in picking up additional seats in Congress from more competitive districts that pitted them in closer races against Republican opponents.

On November 7, the day before the election, most people knew that Arnold was headed for a big defeat. Some true believers held out hope, however. Conservative Democrat Jill Stewart, who wrote a regular column about California politics, penned an opinion piece for the *New York Times* that reminded voters of Arnold's come-from-behind victory the year before on the effort to modify California's three strikes and you're out law. The reality, however, is that it is far easier for money and celebrity to defeat ballot measures than it is to pass them in the face of big-money opposition. It is difficult to persuade voters to adopt a new change, especially if it relates to issues that they do not know much about. It is much easier to sow confusion and skepticism, which is all it takes to win a no vote.

Election Day

As if to symbolize the problems encountered at every step along the path to the special election, Arnold showed up at his polling place on the morning of Election Day only to be told that he had already voted. A poll worker had entered in Schwarzenegger's name in testing Los Angeles County's new touch screen voting machines the day before. The error was fixed and Schwarzenegger was allowed to cast a ballot, but the event did little to instill confidence in either our voting systems or Schwarzenegger's campaign.

When the dust had settled, every one of Arnold's measures had lost. So had every other question on the special election ballot.

Final Results

When all the ballots were counted, the numbers looked like this:[15]

Prop	Issue	Yes votes	%	No votes	%
73	Minor's Pregnancy	3,676,592	47.2	4,109,430	52.8
74	Teacher Tenure	3,516,071	44.8	4,329,025	55.2
75	Public Union Dues	3,644,006	46.5	4,190,412	53.5
76	Spending/Funding	2,948,243	37.6	4,877,735	62.4
77	Redistricting	3,130,541	40.2	4,641,633	59.8
78	Rx Drug Discounts	3,199,193	41.5	4,508,873	58.5
79	Rx Drug Rebates	3,003,912	39.3	4,625,132	60.7
80	Electric Regulation	2,580,536	34.4	4,920,679	65.6

Source: California Secretary of State.

Arnold suffered a crushing defeat. Support for the redistricting measure had never been strong. It simply wasn't an issue that voters were losing any sleep over at night. A March Field Poll had shown that voters who knew nothing at all about the proposal opposed it 39 to 45 percent, while those who knew "only a little" supported it 46–42 percent. Voters who knew "some" or "a great deal" supported it 56–33 percent.[16] Arnold and his team were counting on the governor's personal popularity to bring this issue to the attention of voters who otherwise would have ignored it. They succeeded at that, but by Election Day Arnold's popularity had sunk and he proved a drag on the issue, not a boost.

Some observers think that the campaign finance rules put forth by the FPPC were responsible for Arnold's defeat. According to Dan Weintraub, a columnist for the *Sacramento Bee,* "The governor's staff has blamed some of those problems on an obscure state political regulation, later overturned, that would have strictly limited his fundraising if he controlled the committee that managed the initiative drive. Because of this rule, they said, his staff could not exercise quality control over the ballot measure drafting."[17]

Final Fundraising Numbers

All the measures had lost and there was only one case where the yes side has outspent the no side, the drug companies' Prop 78. This was consistent with past elections in California where big money can kill ballot measures, but has a hard time buying a yes vote. According to reports filed with the secretary of state, the following chart shows how much various groups spent on the special election.

The election was over. Arnold had lost, and so had democracy. California's campaign finance laws were weaker than they were a year earlier, voters were sick and tired of political bickering, and Arnold Schwarzenegger, the man who once looked like the champion of the little guy, now looked like a pawn of powerful special interests.

Final Fundraising Numbers for the Special Election

Prop 73 – Teenage Abortion	*Raised*	*Spent*
Yes	**$1,790,642**	**$1,863,234**
California Pro-Life Council	$263,296	$270,359
Life on the Ballot	$1,527,347	$1,592,874
No	**$5,373,121**	**$5,565,309**
No on 73 – Planned Parenthood	$5,303,276	$5,525,304
No on 73 – ACLU	$69,845	$40,006
Prop 74–77 Arnold's Initiatives		
Yes	**$73,288,300**	**$74,496,400**
Yes on 75 – Paycheck Protection	$4,690,840	$4,582,342
Californians for Fair Elections	$1,453,298	$1,730,754
Californians for Fair Redistricting – Bill Mundel	$1,229,747	$1,293,581
Citizens to Save California	$11,983,717	$12,008,531
California Recovery Team – Schwarzenegger	$44,140,959	$44,358,812
Small Business Action Committee	$1,127,798	$1,136,701
Redistrict California – Steve Poizner	$8,519,476	$9,243,153
Reform California (74, 75, 76) – Sheldon Adleson	$123,500	$123,562
Common Cause Committee for Prop 77	$18,964	$18,964
No	**$154,612,222**	**$152,895,373**
Alliance for Better California – labor groups	$39,703,191	$39,769,022
No on 74 – teachers and school board members	$14,472,469	$14,501,799
No on 74 and 75 – Alex Padilla	$0	$77,476
No on 75 – Darrel Steinberg	$27,304	$29,804
No on 75 – labor groups	$54,122,095	$53,315,139
No on 76 – labor groups	$27,770,067	$27,770,067
Mary Haishi – No on 74–76	$13,500	$13,677
Protect California's Future – No on 74–77	$2,492,000	$2,257,724
No on 77 – Steve Bing, members of Congress	$9,186,445	$8,354,745
Californias for Fair Representation – No on 77	$6,633,326	$6,614,097
For Judicial Restraint – No on 77	$191,825	$191,825
Prop 78/79 Drug Company vs. Consumer Groups		
Yes on 78 and No on 79	**$81,317,485**	**$84,360,130**
PhRMA	$80,394,902	$83,584,641
Biotech Industry	$922,583	$775,489
No on 78 and Yes on 79 – consumer/health groups	**$811,356**	**$808,227**
Prop 80 – energy re-regulation		
Yes on 80 – consumer and labor groups	**$542,466**	**$551,134**
No on 80 – energy companies	**$2,693,807**	**$2,642,892**
Total	**$320,429,399**	**$323,182,749**

CHAPTER 12

THE SECOND MONEYMOON

Bipartisan Business As Usual

Chastened by his embarrassing defeat in the special election, Arnold charted a major course correction for his administration in 2006—the year in which he would personally ask voters to re-elect him. He would work with Democrats to get things done rather than waging war against them. And, while continuing to raise money, lots and lots of money, he would no longer push the envelope and explore new legal loopholes as he had in 2005. Meanwhile, legislators were happy to work with Arnold, raise their own money, and pretend to make progress on reform while actually engaging in business as usual.

Arnold's new direction paid off. Rather than trading insults with legislative leaders as he had in 2005, by mid-2006 he was swapping compliments. One notable politician proudly told voters:

> In the last couple of months, we've proven that California can come together and set our ideological differences aside to move forward, and I'm proud to say that our governor has California back on track. California is once again, my friends, on the move thanks largely to this man, the governor of our great state and a good friend of mine, Governor Arnold Schwarzenegger.[1]

This gushing praise came from Fabian Núñez, the Democratic Assembly leader and the man who was purportedly chairing the campaign for Democratic candidate Phil Angelides to replace

Schwarzenegger as governor. How did Arnold engineer such a remarkable turnaround? For one, he proved that he does not hold grudges and extended an olive branch early to Democrats in the legislature. But, just as importantly, he picked agenda items that he knew would meet approval not only from Democrats but from other entrenched interests in Sacramento.

The Other Kennedy

Voters have always known that Schwarzenegger, though a registered Republican, has strong ties to Democrats through his marriage to Maria Shriver, daughter of Eunice Kennedy Shriver and Sargent Shriver. Conservatives have always been wary of Schwarzenegger's true Republican credentials, but his appointment of Susan Kennedy (no relation to Maria's family) as his chief of staff in 2006 raised new hackles.

Kennedy had served as a top advisor in the Gray Davis administration and Davis then appointed her to the Public Utilities Commission. Prior to that, she led the Northern California chapter of the National Abortion Rights Action League. By appointing a lifelong Democrat to head his administration, Schwarzenegger sent a clear signal to both the left and the right that 2006 would be a dramatically different year from 2005.

One immediately troubling aspect to Kennedy's appointment was that Schwarzenegger agreed to pay her two salaries. One from the taxpayers, of $131,000, to cover her official job as his chief of staff where she would be responsible for the interests of all Californians. Schwarzenegger also announced that Kennedy would receive a second salary of $100,000 from his re-election campaign to pay for her work to win Arnold a second term.

Kennedy explained the need for the extra cash by saying, "I'm 45 years old; I got a mortgage to pay. And staying in government was not in my plan."[2] Most Californians clearly manage to pay their mortgages for less than the $230,000 that Susan Kennedy required. The median individual income in California was $43,107 in 2005. Californians who bought homes in October, 2006 faced average monthly payments of $2,287. Making these payments would require an annual household income of $91,480 if a family wanted to pay 30 percent of their salary for housing.

Kennedy said that the taxpayers would still be getting full value for their dollar in paying her chief of staff salary because all her work for Arnold's re-election would be done after hours and on vacation time.

But this explanation troubled both conservatives and liberals. Steve Frank, publisher of the conservative *California Political News & Views*, noted that Kennedy's appointment:

> Gives ammo to the Democrats. They threw Gray Davis to the dogs. Susan Kennedy was his chief partner in his pay-to-play schemes and now she's back at it. Has she done anything wrong? Probably not. Does it look bad? Absolutely. [3]

Liberal critic Doug Heller was quick to use this ammunition, charging:

> What's amazing is that you've got a situation where Schwarzenegger has become worse than Gray Davis. It's almost like a Schwarzenegger movie where the hero kills the villain—and takes over his personality.[4]

Gray Davis, George Deukmejian and Jerry Brown had all barred the practice of paying double salaries to staff from campaign funds when they were governor. Phil Angelides promised he would also avoid the practice if elected governor. Meredith McGehee, a policy director of the Campaign Legal Center, observed that federal law prevents officials from using campaign funds to pay bonuses or salaries for government staff. The Center was launched by Senator John McCain at a time when government reform was a priority for him. McGehee explained that:

> At the federal level, it's clear that the statutory prohibition of supplementing an executive branch employee's income is a safeguard to ensure that their primary and sole responsibility is to those who pay them. When you allow special interests, through their campaign contributions, to supplement the executive branch employee's salary, you are opening the door to divided loyalties. And that's not good public policy.[5]

Karen Getman, the former head of the California Fair Political Practices Commission, went so far to say that the example proved how loose ethical standards had again slipped in politics after a brief period of better behavior following scandals in the 1970s. "Between what's happening in Washington and the Schwarzenegger administration, it's as though Watergate never happened," she lamented.[6]

Other facts eventually surfaced that reinforced the concerns of government watchdogs. There appeared to be strong connections between actions that Kennedy took while still on the PUC, donations to Schwarzenegger's political committees, and Kennedy's salary. On November 14, 2005, just days after the disastrous special election and during the time Schwarzenegger was considering appointing Kennedy as his new chief of staff, AT&T donated $25,000 to Schwarzenegger's re-election campaign. Four days later, Kennedy voted on the PUC to approve a merger of AT&T and SBC. On December 5, Schwarzenegger's campaign paid $25,000 to Susan Kennedy. Also in December, PG&E donated $44,600 to Schwarzenegger's campaign, right around the time that Kennedy considered matters on the PUC that could impact PG&E.

The Utility Reform Network estimates that the AT&T/SBC merger will cost consumers some $330 million. Bob Finkelstein, executive director of the group, criticized the Kennedy payment, saying, "the timing is pretty damning."[7]

Adam Mendelson, a spokesman for the Schwarzenegger campaign dismissed the attacks as politically motivated. "Susan

Kennedy was paid by the campaign for her work advising the governor on campaign activities," he explained. "There is no conflict for work done on a political campaign."[8] Interestingly, Mendelson himself received a second salary from Schwarzenegger's campaign for $13,000 during the fall of 2006 and then a campaign bonus of $75,000 on top of the $123,000 he earned as the governor's communication director.

Phone Lines Carry Movies and Money

It turned out that AT&T had a lot more at stake than simply getting its merger with SBC approved. One of the biggest issues to dominate the legislature in 2006 was approving a request by AT&T to offer TV shows over its Internet and phone lines. The move was designed to let phone companies compete with cable companies in providing TV entertainment. Cable firms had contracts negotiated with localities across California to provide service in each area. The phone giants didn't want to have to negotiate similar deals, claiming it was unwieldy. Phone companies were also facing new competition from cable providers that were offering high-speed Internet and phone services bundled with video programming.

AT&T and other phone companies tapped Assembly leader Fabian Núñez to champion their bill. Then, they poured in the cash. AT&T spent nearly $23 million to pave the way for their legislation including:

- Holding a swank dinner event for legislators at the Monterey Bay Aquarium.
- Providing $1,238 worth of Lakers' tickets and refreshments to Senator Martha Escutia, the head of a key Senate committee, and her family.
- Hosting a golf tournament at Pebble Beach to raise $1.7 million for the California Democratic Party.

Cable companies were naturally concerned about the potential competition. When negotiating local contracts, cable firms often had to meet requirements to provide service to all residents, not just selecting those easy to serve while leaving rural viewers out of luck. Sometimes they had to provide local access channels to community groups, or to carry city council meetings so citizens could keep tabs on local government. If phone companies could negotiate directly with the state for a contract, they could potentially avoid these requirements and be at a competitive advantage to the cable firms.

Comcast spent $3 million during the same period to make sure that AT&T's move didn't come at their expense. They too used basketball tickets as bait, taking Assemblymember Lloyd Levine out to see the Sacramento Kings. Their efforts succeeded in winning an amendment that would allow cable companies to also bypass local officials and negotiate for statewide contracts. The only opponents left to the bill were consumer groups, who claimed it would not lead to any real savings, and local governments who had seen their power taken away from them by the state. Regina Costa of The Utility Reform Network argued that the bill will "just allow people to come in and gouge you."[9]

Even professional lobbyists were stunned by the sheer amounts of money poured into the issue, an indication of just how much profit companies stood to make once it went through. "I don't recall this kind of money being spent, this much drama," said Dennis Mangers, president of the California Cable and Telecommunications Association, which spent $196,000 to influence the legislation.[10]

AT&T's bill passed the Assembly by a vote of 77 to 0. Across the building in the Senate, only four members voted against it: Chesbro, Dunn, Migden, and Speier. It was then signed into law, at Susan Kennedy's recommendation, by Governor Schwarzenegger. The last time an industry-backed bill met such widespread approval and consensus from legislators on both sides of the aisle was the brilliant idea of Enron and others to deregulate California's energy markets. Remember how well that turned out?

But AT&T wanted more. In addition to getting their merger approved and opening up access to sell TV shows to millions of viewers, the phone companies wanted to install the high speed lines needed to provide these programs on state property. And, they wanted to do it for free. In 2000, Level 3 Communications had agreed to pay California $6.40 per foot for installing its high-speed lines. When the state wanted to charge similar fees to other companies, Pacific Bell challenged the idea in court. California won the court case, but after AT&T acquired the company in the Susan Kennedy–approved merger, it appealed the case.

Sunne Wright McPeak was Schwarzenegger's Secretary of Business, Transportation, and Housing at the time. She had initially backed the decision to charge phone companies a fee. But, in the spring of 2006, the Schwarzenegger administration decided it wouldn't charge any fees to the phone companies, thus ending the court case appeal by AT&T. McPeak was approached several months later to take a position as president of the Emerging Technology Fund, financed by Verizon and AT&T. Due to this offer, McPeak then recused herself from deliberations about the fee policy. Schwarzenegger finalized the decision on October 27, 2007, with an executive order. McPeak, wearing her new hat as president of the Emerging Technology Fund, praised the decision, saying "It's going to be a very important thing for this state to bring us up to the world standard."[11]

Consumer advocates criticized the move as giving away something of substantial value while receiving nothing in return. It certainly didn't look like a move from a governor who was worried about closing the gap in a chronic state budget shortfall as much as it looked like a freebie to corporate America.

Beyond McPeak's convenient job offer, other revolving doors that emerged in 2006 included Northern Star Energy's hiring of Joe Desmond. Northern Star Energy was attempting to build a liquefied natural gas facility on California's coast and Desmond had previously served as Schwarzenegger's chairman of the California Energy Commission. In this role, he was a key advisor to Schwarzenegger on the natural gas proposal. He had served temporarily in another key position, but had failed to win legislative confirmation to that post because lawmakers felt he was too closely tied to industry. David Maul, who had also worked for the Energy Commission, went to work for another natural gas company with plans to operate on the coast as well, the Texas-based Tidelands Oil and Gas. Mike Murphy's consulting firm also received a multi-million dollar contract related to the project, which Schwarzenegger will ultimately have to approve or reject.

As a way of saying thanks for the excellent service it had received from California's governor, AT&T put a nice cherry on top of their already generous scoops of political spending—a half-million contribution to Arnold's favorite charity. The six-figure check to the After-School All-Stars took the total amount AT&T has given the group since Arnold's inauguration in 2004 to $1.2 million. Schwarzenegger founded the group in the 1990s and Bonnie Reiss, a longtime confidant and aide to his administration, sits on the board of directors. Schwarzenegger and Maria Shriver donate money to the charity themselves.

Shelia Krumolz, executive director of the Center for Responsive Politics noted that, "there is a benefit to [Schwarzenegger] regardless of his technical affiliation with the charity. It's one of the charities he supports, and so [the contribution] is certainly noted by the governor. Bob Stern added that companies often make contributions such as this to "be on the good side" of public officials.[12]

Perhaps approving huge telecom mergers, allowing telecom firms to provide TV programming through different rules than cable companies have historically followed, and then allowing those firms to use state property for free really is in the best interests of all Californians. If so, then AT&T shareholders got ripped off. A company should not have to spend upwards of $25 million to get good ideas that will serve the general public approved, even if it does mean that the company will turn a profit in the process. What would this mean for all the other good ideas that don't have $25 million behind them? But, if these government actions turn out to benefit AT&T at the expense of taxpayers and consumers, then it will be the public that got ripped off. AT&T should not be able to spend $25 million to purchase policy that will make it billions at the expense of everyone else. Either way, something is seriously wrong.

Arnold Moves to the Middle

While helping AT&T might have helped with the campaign fundraising, both Arnold and the legislature must have known it wouldn't really help them with the voters. With both the governor and legislators receiving low marks in polls, they began a process of working out compromises to deliver results that they could take to the voters in November.

Arnold had vetoed an increase in California's minimum wage in both 2004 and 2005. But in 2006, he signed a boost in the wage from $6.75 to $8 after negotiating out a clause that would have guaranteed the wage would keep rising with future inflation.

Arnold signed legislation to cut the price of prescription drugs after he'd vetoed legislation previously to allow importation of drugs from Canada at cheaper prices.

Schwarzenegger worked with legislators to negotiate a massive package of bonds to place before voters in the November election. The model was reminiscent of bond measures 57 and 58 that Arnold had championed with Steve Westly in 2004 and a far cry from the partisan battlelines drawn in the special election initiatives.

For the first time in seven years, the governor and the legislature managed to agree on a budget before the July 1 deadline.

Arnold and legislative leaders each had their own political reasons for choosing to work together in 2006. Arnold was up for re-election and badly needed to repair his standing with voters. His highly partisan attacks and massive fundraising in 2005 had sullied his reputation and dragged down his poll numbers. Legislators, for their part, wanted to repair their own standing with the voters, which in many polls was actually worse than the governor's. A 2005 Field Poll found that only 27 percent of respondents approved of the job the legislature was doing, down from 51 percent four years earlier.

The cooperation between Arnold and the legislature certainly did not help Phil Angelides, who needed to show voters that Arnold should be replaced. It's possible that legislators simply didn't expect Angelides to win and therefore knew that they'd be dealing with Schwarzenegger for another four years. If so, why antagonize him? But, another factor is that legislators likely wanted to improve their own standings with the public. Gerrymandered districts and campaign war chests meant that any individual legislator was almost guaranteed re-election. But, the unresponsive behavior and unaccountable attitude that this entrenchment encouraged in individual politicians was contributing to an overall decline in public approval of the legislature in general.

But whatever the reasons, the cooperation was real. The Republican governor and Democratic legislature did come together and get many things done. While election years can sometimes lead to partisan grandstanding, just the opposite proved true in this instance.

The Big Green Accomplishment

The trophy accomplishment of Arnold's 2006 legislative agenda was the passage of a bill to set caps on greenhouse gas emissions by 2020. The legislation, sponsored by Assembly Leader Fabian Núñez, was the first of its kind to pass in the United States and drew international praise.

Schwarzenegger staged a grand signing ceremony for the bill and used it as the centerpiece of his re-election campaign to establish his environmental record. But while the bill was moving in the legislature, Schwarzenegger's administration negotiated behind the scenes to weaken it.

As the bill gained momentum in April 2006, Schwarzenegger cautioned that the state should move slowly or else "we could really scare the business community." Karen Douglass, of the group Environmental Defense, said that Arnold's comment on global warming "isn't what we were hoping to hear," and that it represented a bit of a "Jekyll and Hyde approach"[13] compared to his previous pro-environmental statements.

As it became clear the bill could pass, Schwarzenegger tried to amend the bill by taking enforcement authority away from the California Air Resources Board and giving it to a special new board that would include nine of his top appointees, including members of the business community. The new board would have the authority to gut the regulations called for in the bill if it found that they would have a negative impact on the economy.

In the end, Núñez and the legislature held firm against a number of concessions that Schwarzenegger had sought in backroom negotiations and placed a strong bill on his desk, betting that he would sign it. An advocate at the Natural Resources Defense Council who was heavily involved in the negotiations described the tension: "It was touch-and-go until the very end as to whether or not the governor would sign the bill."[14] To his credit, he did. Arnold then made sure he got the recognition he was due and then some.

But there were other important environmental bills with lower profiles that Schwarzenegger vetoed. These included a bill by Assemblymember Joe Nation to require that half of all cars sold in California by 2020 be powered by alternative fuels and a bill to reduce emissions in California's ports. Three of Schwarzenegger's four appointees to the Coastal Commission have been pro-development and his other appointments included many industry proponents. His environmental record has been mixed to be sure.

When critics suggested that Schwarzenegger's contributions from Chevron and other oil and big business interests called into his true environmental intentions, Terry Tamminen, who served as Schwarzenegger's environmental secretary at the time sounded a bit defensive. He explained that Arnold needed to raise this money in order to stay in office and be a champion for the environment. Taminen claimed that Arnold "would be the first to tell you he didn't want to take contributions from anyone. But unfortunately that's the way the system works."[15]

Tamminen is exactly correct. Whether or not Chevron's contributions influenced Scharzenegger's actions in office, they definitely played a role in keeping him in office. The question for Chevron, and for the rest of us, is whether or not Schwarzenegger was more likely to protect public health and the environment than the candidates he defeated. We know Chevron's answer. The other question is, if Schwarzenegger dislikes the system as much as Tamminen asserts, why hasn't he lifted a finger to change it?

Commerce vs. Conservation, Shades of Gray

The Chamber of Commerce had strongly opposed the greenhouse gas emissions cap that Schwarzenegger signed into law. His support marked the first major break that Arnold had with his closest allies in the business community. Yet on 14 other bills that the Chamber cared about, Schwarzenegger took their side. That's a 93 percent rate of compliance with Chamber requests. During 2005, Schwarzenegger racked up a 90 percent score on the Chamber's top priorities and in his first year he had batted a thousand by taking the Chamber's side every time.

For comparison, Schwarzenegger received a score of 50 percent from the California League of Conservation Voters in 2006, down slightly from 58 percent in the two previous years. Gray Davis had received environmental scores from the same group of 85 percent in 2001, 72 percent in 2002, and 100 percent during the recall year of 2003.

Davis had also done reasonably well for the Chamber of Commerce. He agreed with the Chamber on 66 percent of the bills that reached his desk in 2000, 57 percent in 2001 and 71 percent in 2002. But during the recall year of 2003, Davis only sided with the Chamber 31 percent of the time. It is worth noting that during his most intense period of public accountability, Davis sided with environmentalists and not with big business. Maybe environmentalists should have been happier about the recall process than they appeared to be in 2003.

Faking Campaign Finance Reform—Again

While Schwarzenegger and the legislature did work together in 2006 to get things done on many issues, when it came to reforming California's broken political system they failed yet again. One reform that might help level the playing field between business and environmental interests would be to provide candidates who swear off accepting large private contributions with public funds to run their campaign. This allows the good guy candidates of both parties to compete with those who are backed to the hilt by deep-pocketed special interests.

Activists began calling for full public financing in California as early as 2000. At first, the idea generated little attention. But by April 2004, the idea had passed the Assembly Elections Committee and momentum began to build. In the 2005 legislative session, the bill went nowhere despite an impressive turnout of supporters at an informational hearing. But in early 2006, clean money again passed through the Assembly Elections Committee by a vote of 4 to 3 and passed on the Assembly floor by a vote of 47 to 31. This marked the first time that either house of the California legislature had passed a significant campaign finance reform since the 2002 effort to gut Prop 208 and replace it with the far weaker limits of Prop 34. Governor Schwarzenegger, the man who had run for office on a pledge to clean up Sacramento, took no position on the bill.

Don Perata's Senate was no more eager than Schwarzenegger to embrace clean money. During the Senate Elections Committee hearings, senators came up with a million excuses for why the bill wasn't perfect. The bill was eventually pulled from the committee without even an up or down vote. Don Perata's office received more than 600 faxes from supporters, but it wasn't enough to convince him to move the bill. It died a quiet death, without senators being forced to take a public position and allow their constituents to hold them accountable.

The Dog Ate My Redistricting Reform—Again

Perhaps nothing better justified the cynicism that voters have for their elected officials than the charade put on by Assembly Leader Fabian Núñez and Senate Leader Don Perata to avoid changes in the how political districts are drawn.

After the defeat of Schwarzenegger's redistricting reform in 2005, both legislative leaders promised that they would come forth with their own redistricting proposal in 2006. Don Perata acknowledged that the voter defeat of the initiative did not mean that voters were offering a vote of confidence that said, "Hey, we really like you guys." Rather, Perata agreed that reform was needed and promised: "We have a bill . . . that we are going to push down and get it to the governor. Set up a real independent commission that will take effect when the next census is taken. And get the legislature forever out of a conflict of interest. We're committed to doing that."[16]

Indeed, on August 16, the California Senate passed a redistricting reform bill by a vote of 27 to 11. Outgoing Senator Jackie Speier explained her support by noting that she had observed three cycles of drawing political districts and

> all it was about was cutting deals for individual members that wanted to make sure they would have a comfortable seat to run in the future. The reason why the people don't like it is pretty obvious. We're taking care of ourselves. And they would like to see us run in districts where we, in fact, are not the architects.[17]

Fabian Núñez promised his support for the bill in the Assembly and supposedly asked that the Senate send the bill over to the Assembly immediately to meet an end-of-the-session deadline. Then, a funny thing happened. Somehow, the bill never got there in time. Maybe a dog chewed it up.

"I asked for the bill more than once," said Núñez, "and directly with Senator Perata I asked for the bill and did not get it." Perata said that he was merely following standard procedure in waiting a day to have the bill walked across the capitol building to the Assembly. Then, when it was delivered, the Assembly rejected it. A Núñez spokesman said that this was because the Assembly had adjourned.[18] Somehow, seven other bills passed by the Senate that day were delivered on time, and received by the Assembly in time for a final vote. Maybe the dog didn't like those bills.

Núñez cried crocodile tears over the mishap. "I'm deeply disappointed. Deeply disappointed that we didn't get this done."[19] Even though the deadline had passed to place something on the 2006 ballot, Núñez could have still taken the Senate's reform bill to the Assembly, which could have put it on the 2008 ballot. His disappointment was evidently not so great as to warrant that action.

Just as legislators had come close to negotiating a deal on redistricting in the summer before the special election, they had somehow managed to fail once again on the same topic. It could hardly be because they weren't familiar with the subject matter.

Dan Schnur, who co-chaired a coalition of good government groups that had supported the redistricting reform effort, summed up his frustration:

> For the last several days, the legislature has been pretending to act, but they never had any intention of passing any legitimate redistricting reform. The key here for the legislature was presenting the appearance of action while actually not doing anything. They succeeded very effectively.[20]

The Plot to Kill Term Limits—Again

One reason that redistricting reform may have tanked in 2006 was that legislative leaders hatched an idea to tie it to changes in California's term limit laws. If legislators were going to have to swallow a reform they didn't like, maybe they could tie it to something that they did.

California voters enacted term limits by passing Proposition

140 in 1990 with 52 percent of the vote. The measure limited politicians to serving no more than three two-year terms in the Assembly and two four-year terms in the Senate, for a total of 14 years if they moved from one house to the other.

Most legislators don't like term limits, even those who might never have been elected had a vacancy not been created by a termed out predecessor. In 2002, Senate leader John Burton spearheaded an initiative to allow legislators to bypass the term limit requirements if they could gather (or pay others to gather) sufficient signatures from voters within their district. Politicians raised $10 million to support that measure, Prop 45, but it was defeated with 58 percent of the vote. A 2004 Field Poll found that 75 percent of registered California voters thought that terms limits were a good thing, so an outright repeal of term limits does not seem politically feasible.

By 2006, legislators were again anxious to change the term limits law. Assembly Speaker Fabian Núñez favored an approach that would allow politicians to spend 12 years in any one chamber. He began discussing the idea as part of a package of reforms to be included with redistricting reform.

Combining the term limits and redistricting proposals had at least two advantages for Núñez. First, he could potentially negotiate Schwarzenegger's support (or at least neutrality) for a relaxation of term limits by going along with Arnold's proposal for redistricting reform. Secondly, Núñez knew that he needed to improve the legislature's standing with the public before voters would be ready to consider extending term limits.

A major goal of the second moneymoon was to repair both Arnold's and the legislature's image with voters. This would position them to take another stab at changing term limits laws and redistricting laws in 2007. One wrinkle lay in the way. In order for changes in term limits to take effect quickly enough to allow Fabian Núñez and Don Perata to remain in their respective legislative leadership positions, the change would need to occur before the June 2008 primary. Yet these changes must also be approved by California voters, and there was no election scheduled prior to that primary. Calling a special election was clearly off the table given the disastrous results of the last one. What to do?

Arnold and the legislature crafted a clever solution. They would hold a special primary election in early February 2008 for presidential candidates only. This provided a plausible excuse for holding an extra election—it would boost California's clout in the presidential primary which has always been locked up long before Californians have cast their ballots. A term limits extension initiative was hastily filed by allies of Fabian Núñez and then rewritten and refilled after the first version failed to include the necessary special exception to allow Don Perata to maintain his seat in the Senate. Insiders held little doubt that the real reason for the February 2008 presidential primary was to offer Núñez and Perata one last shot at holding on to their seats.

Last-Minute Shenanigans

The final days of the legislature are notorious for last minute deals with bait and switches that would make a mattress salesman blush. The close of the 2006 moneymoon proved no exception. During the final four days of the legislative session, some 600 bills were pending. Many of them, however, did not look anything like they had when they were introduced. Through a process called "gut and amend," legislators can completely change a bill at the last minute so as to provide little public scrutiny of the subject matter. It's a process ripe for special interest handouts.

Assemblymember Betty Karnette took a bill she had introduced about Medi-Cal and gutted it at the last minute to instead give the Boeing corporation a $100 million tax break. Boeing had contributed almost $600,000 to California politicians since 2000, including $5,500 to Karnette and $35,000 to Schwarzenegger. The gambit failed when it was reported in the media.

Computer companies wanted to get rid of a requirement that they take out bonds to reimburse taxpayers if they failed to deliver on their contracts (remember the Oracle company during the Gray Davis administration and CGIAMS during the Schwarzenegger administration?) Assemblyman Jerome Horton expressed surprise to learn that one of his bills had been amended with this giveaway. His staff then corrected him and admitted that they had been involved along with the office of Assemblyman Alberto Torrico. Senator Debra Bowen asked "Why do we need to do this in jam job at the end of session?" Once the bill was clearly dead, Horton told the press that if his own bill had made it to a floor vote, "I wouldn't vote for it." He said that somehow the provision had been added to his legislation as the "nature of the rush" of the end of the legislature.[21] Indeed.

Assemblymember Mark Leno took a bill aimed at reshaping a tourism board and added a provision to allow car rental companies to avoid telling consumers at the time they make their reservations about certain airport fees they would pay at the time they pick up their car. The bill passed at a late-night committee hearing and was passed the next day in the Assembly with under three minutes of debate. "This is so typical of what happens at the last minute," said Bob Fellmeth of the Center for Public Interest Law, who opposed the bill as anti-consumer. "All sorts of horrible things go sweeping through."[22]

Car dealers also got a special bill squeezed through that allowed them to increase "document processing" fees a consumer pays when buying a new car by $10. Senator Tom Torlakson took a bill of his that dealt with air-quality issues and replaced them with the fee increase in the final week of the legislature.

These last-minute examples demonstrated the lasting power that campaign spending can have. Legislators perhaps remembered what had happened to Assemblymember Cindy Montañez when she stood up to the car dealers only to be defeated in a future Democratic primary by their money. (see Chapter 3 on the first moneymoon.)

Murray's Legacy

Perhaps no legislator attempted as many below-the-radar maneuvers in 2006 as outgoing Senator Kevin Murray from Culver

City. In addition to playing a leading skeptic in helping drag down both clean money and redistricting reforms, Murray seemed to have a penchant for legislation that would help narrow interests, including politicians themselves.

Near the end of the 2006 session, legislative leaders allowed Murray's senate bill 145 to skip the normal committee votes and head straight to a floor vote with little public notice. This bill allowed politicians to create personal slush funds called office-holder accounts—a practice that Prop 34 had banned but that many legislators had been circumventing by simply creating new campaign committees to run for re-election or another office. Murray's bill allowed legislators who were in their final terms, such as he was in at the time, to keep raising money even though they faced no more campaigns. (See Chapter 7 for how Willie Brown had launched a phony campaign for insurance commissioner for this purpose.) Bob Stern suggested that the move to skip committees was aimed at preventing public interest groups from having "time to get all riled up and get people to oppose it."[23] Arnold signed this bill and promptly set up his own committee to raise up to $200,000 annually. He quickly took in $20,000 each from Paul Folino, Robin Arkley, William Robinson, and Avis car rental.

Murray was unsuccessful in passing a last-minute bill aimed at extending the tenure of William Burke on the South Coast Air Quality Management District. Burke is married to Los Angeles County Supervisor Yvonne Brathwaite. When *Capitol Weekly* blew the whistle on the scheme, the amendment was eliminated.

Earlier in the year Murray had attempted to slip through a bill that appeared to be designed to benefit just one person—Ron Burkle. Burkle is a grocery store billionaire who was going through a messy divorce and preferred to keep the matter quiet. To keep things under wraps, Burkle had invoked parts of a privacy law that had been passed (for his apparent benefit) in 2004 under the leadership of John Burton and signed by Schwarzenegger. But the courts had then thrown out those provisions.

So Murray introduced legislation to allow one party in a divorce case to seal the proceedings from public view if they contained financial information. There's no direct evidence that Burkle directly asked Murray for the bill, but Burkle is well known as one of the most prolific donors and fundraisers in California and someone capable of helping those who help him. Murray acknowledged that he knew Burkle was following his actions. "Is (Burkle) interested in it? Sure. Clearly, his name is on the court case. Clearly, it's not lost on anybody that he's involved somewhere."[24] The bill stalled in May after Fabian Núñez objected at the request of female legislators and advocacy groups. Media outlets also opposed the idea as a restriction on basic freedom of information. Burkle tried to buy 12 newspapers from the Knight-Ridder chain, including the *San Jose Mercury News* and *Contra Costa Times*. He later made a bid for the *Los Angeles Times*.

To keep big donors in the beer and wine industry happy, Murray sponsored a bill to ease rules on samples that liquor salesmen could give restaurant and bar owners. Schwarzenegger signed the bill after he'd received more than $100,000 from the Southern Wine and Spirits of Nevada association, which lobbied for the change.

A final Murray endeavor was an attempt to allow donors who give between $10,000 and $30,000 to politicians to avoid current disclosure rules that require them to register as major donors with the secretary of state. This rule makes it easier for reporters and watchdogs to track the donations of large donors to various candidates, PACs, and ballot committees. To his credit, Arnold Schwarzenegger vetoed the bill when it reached his desk. That veto has been his sole campaign finance accomplishment to date.

Pledging Allegiance to Campaign Cash

During the final days of the legislative session, *Orange County Register* reporter Brian Joseph was trying to write a story on last minute fundraising when he stumbled on an interesting observation. Legislators were holding lots of fundraisers, but they weren't reporting many donations in the required 24-hour disclosure window. For instance, Assemblyman Chuck DeVore had held a fundraiser on August 15, but the next day he reported no new contributions to his campaign. After finding 14 other similar examples, Joseph called me to ask how that could be.

We soon learned that lobbyists and other donors were showing up at fundraisers and making pledges to contribute to a politician, but not actually writing the check. This allowed the lobbyists to get access to legislators during a crucial time, but avoid having to report their contributions until later. I had known this process had been used for many years, but I had not grasped how widespread it had become. It has become commonplace for campaign consultants to maintain two lists for politicians: those who have pledged contributions and those that actually have given them. Only the second list is reported to the public, but one consultant said that "99 percent of the time, pledges are good. I don't know a lobbyist who would make a commitment he couldn't keep."[25] The pledge system, at a minimum, seriously undermines the goals of the California Political Reform Act's requirement to disclose large contributions within 24 hours. It also opens up the possibility that a donor can make a pledge to a politician on one day, request action on a bill the next, but wait to send in the check until after they have seen how the politician voted.

The pledging scheme reveals the flaw in the arguments of those who say we should have full-disclosure of campaign finances, but no limits on the amounts given. Limits, they claim, only drive big money further underground, making it harder to track. But the fairly simply ploy of offering pledges instead of actual checks proves that donors and politicians will find ways to avoid disclosure whenever it furthers their own aims, whether there are contribution limits or not. If we want to avoid the corrupting power of contributions, we need to limit them to a size that ordinary people can afford to give, or provide a way for candidates to run for office without accepting any contributions at all.

One thing is certain—the number of fundraising events certainly skyrockets at the end of a session. There were at least 90 fundraisers scheduled by legislators in August compared to just four during July. At least $3.5 million came in during the month of August in checks of $1,000 or more. On one day, August 15, no fewer than 25 fundraisers were scheduled. Outgoing Senator Joe Nation expressed dismay at the process. "It's how the system works but there is something wrong with the system," he said.[26] Even some lobbyists griped. Barry Broad, a lobbyist for the Teamsters complained "the whole thing has turned into an almost 24–7 crazy, obsessive system. All this money is corrosive. It is eating away at the credibility of democratic government."[27]

Things have become so bad that Willie Brown, a notorious fundraiser in his days as Assembly leader, was shocked, saying that lobbyists have become in effect a third chamber in the legislature:

> There wasn't the same aggressive fundraising there is now when I served. We kind of had an understanding you minimized what you did in Sacramento. Events in Sacramento are strictly for the third house. They aren't civilian events. They are events for people who understand why they have to give.[28]

Donors Sign Checks, Arnold Signs Bills

Legislators weren't the only ones raising money during crucial decision-making times. Despite his calls to ban fundraising for legislators when they were considering the budget, Schwarzenegger had no problem accepting contributions as he was considering legislation during the bill-signing window of September. He scheduled at least 22 fundraisers that month.

Former Republican Governor Deukmejian, who had criticized Gray Davis for similarly timed fundraisers, was also critical of Schwarzenegger. "Personally, I think that should be avoided because it is a very sensitive time," he said.[29]

During the last week of the legislature, Schwarzenegger held a fundraising trip to Florida where he raised a half-million bucks. One donor was the Geo Group, private prison company. (Prison reform would become a major issue for the governor to tackle in

2007 after talks broke down in 2006, and outsourcing California's prisoners was one option on the table.) The car dealer AutoNation also contributed $22,300 to Schwarzenegger at this event, knowing that they would have several bills that they lobbied on awaiting Schwarzenegger's veto or approval. On August 30, Schwarzenegger accepted $22,300 from Home Depot, the maximum amount allowed by law. The same day the Senate sent a bill to his desk that the company had lobbied on. EZ Lube contributed the maximum $22,300 to Schwarzenegger in the fall, days after being accused by the California Department of Consumer Affairs of ripping off consumers by doing unnecessary oil changes on their cars.

Months later, after he was re-elected, Schwarzenegger would criticize lawmakers for taking contributions from interests who had business before them. "I know what goes on in our building," he charged. "Everyone is in there, everyone is trying to get influence. And then they do fundraisers at night. At five o'clock, they are in the Capitol, and two hours later, they're doing fundraisers. If you don't link those two together, it's a little bit obvious."[30] Nine days later, he held a $250,000-per-person fundraiser in his Brentwood home for his California Recovery Team.

The rush of last-minute fundraising, even when some of it is hidden by collecting pledges rather than checks, helps illustrate the connection between the decisions politicians make and the contributions they receive. But focusing too much on the timing can lead to phony solutions. Even if there were blackout periods enacted on fundraising during the budget session, the end of the legislature, or during the governor's bill signing period, it would be easy enough for lobbyists and special interests to tell legislators what they want and reward those who meet their demands with contributions while punishing those who dare defy them by funding their opponents.

In rejecting Arnold's initiatives in 2005, voters had reminded politicians that they wanted them to do the people's business, not play political games. It was part of the same message they had sent during the recall of 2003. In 2006, Arnold and the legislature did get down to business. But the primary message of the recall, to sweep special interests and big money from Sacramento, had all but been lost.

CHAPTER 13

THE 2006 ELECTIONS

California's Song Remains the Same

While the second moneymoon continued the relationship between special interests and politicians of both parties, the reasons behind the phenomenon go much deeper than the cozy relationship between lobbyists and legislators. Legislation and other favors to benefit donors is only the tail end of the process, which, at its heart begins with these narrow interests using huge sums of money to elect the politicians of their choosing in the first place. Once that's done, the project of schmoozing them to do their bidding is almost perfunctory because politicians know that they are more accountable to the donors and party bosses who gave them their jobs than to the voters who merely ratified the decision.

The 2006 California Democratic primary set new records for spending to influence election outcomes. Perhaps not coincidentally, it also set the record for the lowest voter turnout. The November general election broke records for spending on initiative campaigns and candidate campaigns alike with the funds coming from a small group of astronomically large donors. In short, the promise of the recall to put an end to business as usual had not been realized.

Westly Replicates Checchi

Steve Westly dumped $35 million of his own dough into an unsuccessful bid to win the Democratic primary in the 2006 governor's race. The only person who had ever come close to spending this much of his own money for a California election was Al Checchi, who spent $39 million in his 1998 loss to Gray Davis. Both men seemed out to prove that the new way to become California's governor is to first make enough money to buy the election. Both men were almost right.

Westly had always wanted to be a politician. Back in his days as an undergraduate at Stanford, he was elected student body co-president and walked precincts for congressional candidates (that sort of thing was still done in those quaint days before elections were completely sewn up by big money and gerrymandered districts). In 1981, he became the California Democrats' youngest officer ever when he was elected as the northern California party treasurer. In describing those days to a reporter, Westly reminisced, "I knew I'd continue to be politically active and maybe someday, if I did well, I'd run for office."[1] In 1989, he lost out to Jerry Brown in a bid to become the chair of the California Democratic Party.

At age 37, Westly woke up one morning with an epiphany: "I've got my MBA from Stanford, that's pretty good. I've been out of school for 12 years. I'm not making much money. I've got to fix this."[2] He was making about $95,000 a year at the time.

That epiphany may have had something to do with advice Westly had received from John Gardner, a reformer who had founded the reform group Common Cause back in the 1970's. "He looked me right in the eye," recounted Westly, "and said 'Steve, go out and make some money first. Don't become dependent on the system like all the rest of them.'"[3]

Once there was a time when mentors would have told a young man interested in public service to get some experience by running for city council or maybe working for a state legislator. Not any more. If you want to succeed in politics today, the advice is to get rich first. "You're at one level when you're a hard working person interested in politics," explains Tom McEnery, a former mayor of San Jose who co-taught a course at Stanford with Westly. "But you're at another level when you're a hard working person interested in politics who has $200 million of your own."[4]

Westly did indeed set out to make some money. After casting

about at a number of ventures, he wound up at eBay, right before the Internet auction house really took off. He walked away with a fortune worth more than $200 million. He could have earned much more, but his desire to get back to politics pulled him away.

Perhaps learning from the failed efforts of Checchi, who had no political experience, Westly first set out to win a lower office before using his money to take a run for the top job in California. In 2002, Westly spent more than $5 million of his own money to win office as controller. This would provide a resume that would be credible enough to mount a bid for governor in 2006.

Angelides Replicates Davis

Westly's opponent in the 2006 primary was Phil Angelides, a proud liberal who had also followed the trail of first becoming personally wealthy before entering politics. But in the 2006 primary, Angelides would rely primarily upon money from others, as had Gray Davis in the 1998 showdown against Checchi. Like Davis, Angelides would win.

Angelides grew up in Sacramento and, like Westly, had a lifelong interest in politics. While still in college, he ran unsuccessfully for the Sacramento City Council. After graduating from Harvard, Angelides went to work for Angelo Tsakopoulos, a housing developer in the Sacramento region. Three years later, Angelides formed his own development company, but he continued to partner with Tsakopoulos in many different deals. While Angelides has never disclosed his net worth, he did earn more than $11 million from development ventures between 1998 and 2004 according to tax returns that his campaign made available to the media.[5]

Like Westly, Angelides used his money to buy a stepping-stone office. He chaired the California Democratic Party from 1991 to 1993. Then Angelides ran for state treasurer in 1994, spending more than a million dollars that he had earned as a developer. He lost. He tried again in 1998 and won after spending nearly $5 million.

Angelides' pockets were deep, but not as deep as Steve Westly's. To compete, Angelides went out and raised money from traditional Democratic constituencies, especially labor unions.

An Ugly Primary, with Corruption Sub-theme

Westly and Angelides fought a bitter campaign with both sides slinging handfuls of mud at each other. The candidates were similar on many issues, but they sparred over who would raise taxes, who had most opposed Schwarzenegger, and who would better protect the environment. Both sides raised concerns over the other's fundraising and ethics.

Westly took out ads charging that Angelides had accepted more than a half-million dollars in campaign contributions from oil companies. Angelides fired back that Westly had invested in many of those same companies.

Angelides hit Westly with ads claiming that he had accepted campaign funds from "corrupt Chicago businessman" Joe Carri.[6] The charge was accurate. Carri was convicted in 2006 of criminal charges in a pension fund scandal in Illinois. Of course, Angelides had also sought funds from Carri, but he didn't get any.

Carri and his associates raised $50,000 for Westly. "What's relevant here is Steve Westly's activities after that point on behalf of Joe Carri," charged Angelides.[7] Carri's company did receive a $5 million investment from the California fund Westly controlled.

Westly had also used his position as controller to help the bookseller Barnes & Noble avoid a multimillion-dollar tax bill. In an e-mail to his campaign staff, Westly said that the company was pleased with his actions and that it would be a good time to ask them for a campaign donation.[8] Westly defended his actions, saying "I think it's appropriate to ask people for support after you've made decisions based on what you think's right."[9] What would Westly's mentor John Gardner, who had since passed away, have said to that?

After the Barnes & Noble story broke, Westly announced that he would support a policy that would create a minimum time period before officials, including the controller (who sits on the tax board), could approach a donor for a contribution after making a tax board decision that impacted the donor. This is a phony solution, much like Schwarzenegger's proposal to ban fundraising during budget negotiations. Donors will quickly figure out which politicians are doing things that benefit them. They'll give those politicians money in order to keep them in office so they can help them again in the future, even if it means delaying a donation to play by the rules.

Tsakopoulos Replicates Soros

While California law forbid anyone from giving more than $22,300 to a candidate for governor in 2006, federal law forbid a donor from giving more than $2,100 to a candidate in the 2004 presidential campaign. In that campaign, millionaire George Soros proved how easy it was to bypass that limit. He gave a reported $27 million to Democratic-leaning electioneering groups to try to defeat President George W. Bush. Peter Lewis, another liberal billionaire, gave $24 million in the same way. Republicans got into the act as well, funneling huge checks to Republican-leaning electioneering groups.

Angelo Tsakopoulos decided to try a similar ploy in California. After being approached by the California firefighters' union, Tsakopoulos and his daughter Eleni Tsakopoulos-Kounalakis gave $8.7 million to an independent electioneering effort to support Phil Angelides for governor. This was by far the largest state-level independent expenditure in U.S. history and, other than the 2004 presidential race, it topped federal records as well.

The Tsakopoulos money paid for TV ads to blanket the state with a positive message about Angelides at a time when he was lagging 13 points behind in the polls. Many political observers in California agree that without these ads, Angelides would not have won the nomination.

$ $ $

DONOR PROFILE: Angelo Tsakopoulos is the Sacramento region's biggest developer. Along with his family, he had given more than $5.8 million to California candidates and issue committees before giving $8.7 million to the Californians for a Better Government Committee to help Phil Angelides win the 2006 Democratic primary race for governor. The family directly gave Angelides $228,000 for his bid for governor and a total of $3.2 million over his political career. The family generally gives to Democrats, but they recently gave $100,000 to a conservative Republican running for the Placer County board of supervisors. Tsakopoulos also gave $779,000 to the Tracy Hills Citizen Planning Association to promote one of his development projects in the Sacramento Delta.

At the federal level, Tsakopoulos and his associates at AKT Development have given more than $680,000 to candidates and parties. Bill Clinton rewarded Angelo for his largesse with a stay in the Lincoln bedroom.

Tsakopoulos spent $221,000 lobbying California government from 2002 to 2005. Tsakopoulos personally complained to legislators about a bill that required developers to prove they had adequate water supplies before building new homes.[10] He was once fined by the federal Environmental Protection Agency for violating the Clean Water Act.

$ $ $

This was not a case of a big donor buying access. As a long-time friend and business partner with Angelides, Tsakopoulos had virtually unlimited access even before making such a contribution.

Rather, this was a case of buying an election or, perhaps more accurately, buying it back. Steve Westly thought he had placed the winning bid for the auction already, but the Tsakopoulos money caught him off guard. "Were it not for outside help" from Tsakopoulos, grumbled Westly's campaign manager Garry South (a former Davis consultant), "this race would be essentially over."[11]

Even counting the money from his developer allies, Angelides still had less money on his side than Westly did. So the money from his developer allies did not really give Angelides an unfair edge, it merely helped erase an unfair advantage that Westly had held. But the question remains, do we want our elections to be determined by what millionaires decide to spend, either on their own campaigns or others?

Angelides Uses the Cruz Loophole

Desperate to keep up with Steve Westly's spending, Phil Angelides turned to the same tactic that Cruz Bustamante had used to boost his popularity during the recall campaign—a ballot committee. Angelides formed a committee called Standing Up for Our Kids to support Proposition 82, an initiative that called for providing free preschool for all four-year-olds. He transferred more than $750,000 to this committee from Standing Up for California, an old ballot committee that he had established just before the Fair Political Practices Commission rules kicked in that set limits on candidate-controlled ballot committees.

Angelides used the money to send out a mailer that featured himself endorsing Prop 82 along with U.S. Senators Barbara Boxer and Diane Feinstein. These two popular politicians had endorsed Angelides and the mailer was a way to reinforce that connection. It used the same themes as Angelides' candidate campaign mailers.

Steve Westly cried foul. "The issue is not support for Prop 82, the issue is that Phil Angelides is violating campaign finance law," cried Westly spokesman Jude Barry.[12] Had Arnold Schwarzenegger not gone to court to void that campaign finance law, Barry's charge would have been correct. But, thanks to Arnold, it was now once again legal for candidates to use unlimited funds for ballot committees that they controlled.

TheRestofUs.org looked for evidence that Angelides' Standing Up for Our Kids committee was spending money on slush fund activities that boosted his candidacy without having anything to do with Prop 82. This is what Schwarzenegger's California Recovery Team had done, spending money on a website and PR stunts to promote his candidacy that had nothing to do with ballot measures. But we found no evidence that Angelides was doing the same thing. It was against the spirit of campaign finance reform, but it was legal.

Meathead Copies Terminator, with Less Success

Beyond the candidate races, the 2006 primary provided another venue for ballot initiatives and yet another example of the mixing worlds of candidate and initiative politics. Just as Schwarzenegger made his foray into politics with the Prop 49 initiative for after-school programs, Rob Reiner (who had played Archie Bunker's son-in-law Meathead on the TV sitcom *All in the Family*) was widely seen as having ambitions to run for governor. Reiner was hoping to use Prop 82, which would have provided funding for universal preschool in California, to reinforce his standing as a credible political player.

Reiner had a long history of working on issues to help young children. In 1998, he had championed Prop 10, a ballot measure that increased tobacco taxes and used the money to promote early childhood development programs. Reiner went on to head the commission charged with spending those funds, known as the First Five Commission because of its focus on the first five years of a child's life.

As chairman of the First Five Commission, Reiner urged California to adopt a universal preschool program. When the legislature balked, he organized an initiative effort. Reiner and his family dumped $4.6 million of their own money into the campaign.

But there were allegations that the First Five Commission was inappropriately using government money to promote this initiative effort. When proponents were circulating petitions to qualify Prop 82 for the ballot, the First Five Commission spent $23 million on TV ads promoting preschool. The commission claimed the ads were simply to encourage parents to send their children to preschool, but troubling evidence surfaced that they were actually designed to boost public support for taxpayer-financed universal preschool.

A June 28, 2004, contract between Reiner's First Five Commission and the Greer Margolis Mitchell Burns (GMMB) ad agency notes that the target audience for the ads would be "groups with relatively low levels of support for Preschool for All, such as middle and upper income populations, and people with no children in the house."[13] Why would people with no children in the house need to know about the benefits of preschool unless it was convince them it was worth taxpayer money to fund it?

The contract referred to polling work done by Peter Hart Research, known for advising Democratic candidates. Frank Greer, a former Bill Clinton media consultant, headed the GMMB ad agency. The deal looked a lot more like a political campaign than an effort to conduct public education about preschool.

After initial advertising aimed at people with no kids, the contract called for a second step:

> During this phase, our primary targets are those with high support and low demand for Preschool for All, such as Latinos—especially Spanish speaking Latinos, and low-income populations with young children. . . . As a reminder, these are populations who clearly understand the benefits of Preschool for All, but for whatever reason, have not yet come to the conclusion that the state should do more.[14]

If these citizens already understood the benefits of sending their kids to preschool, why spend state money to tell them the benefits? Clearly, the reason was to boost their support for a state program like Prop 82.

The First Five Commission had been spending a lesser amount of money on an ad campaign designed to reduce the effects of second-hand smoke on young children. But in 2005, the time when the Prop 82 Committee was trying to qualify its initiative, the commission abruptly dropped the smoking ads and dumped a year's worth of ad dollars into a single calendar quarter. Those ads were all about preschool and that calendar quarter was the exact time that Reiner's ballot committee was gathering signatures.

TheRestofUs.org and others called for Reiner to step down from the First Five Commission. He eventually did, right about the same time he hired a political spinman to get him out of what was turning into a public-relations disaster. Who did Reiner turn to? Mark Fabiani, one of the political consultants that Gray Davis had hired to get him out of the energy crisis.

Fabiani had about as much luck rehabilitating Reiner as he did Davis. Prop 82 went down to defeat. After the loss, Reiner refused to be interviewed, but Fabiani did tell reporters that the door remained open to a future Reiner bid for office. "There will always be room for people who have a vision of what they want to achieve and the means to achieve it," he predicted.[15]

But what about those people who have a vision, but not the means? Is there room in today's politics for another Abe Lincoln, who was born in a log cabin, or for another Thomas Jefferson, who spent most of his life on the verge of bankruptcy? What does it mean for government of the people when the prerequisite to run for office is to first make or raise enough money to buy the election?

Slate Mailers—Guilt (or Approval) by Association

The 2006 California primary saw the continued use of so-called slate mailers—the postcards that voters receive in the mail making a host of endorsements for candidates and ballot measures. Often a voter will see a slate taking the same position that they hold on issues or candidates the voter is familiar with, and then take it on faith that they probably have it "right" on other lower profile issues. What voters often don't know, unless they read the very fine print on these cards, is that some or all of the "endorsement" positions on the slate mailer were sold to the highest bidder.

For example, the Democratic Voters Choice slate urged voters to vote against Rob Reiner's Proposition 82 on the primary 2006 ballot after receiving more than $30,000 from a business group opposing the initiative. The California Democratic Party and most of its elected officials, however, actually supported Proposition 82 and have no affiliation at all with the Democratic Voters Choice, which simply told its readers to "Vote Democratic!" as proof of its credentials. The Democratic Voters Choice was little more than a money making creation of Burbank political consultant Tom Kaptain, who paid himself $70,000 in 2006 to operate the slate.

In another example, Lynn Diane Olson, a candidate for superior court in Los Angeles County, spent $75,000 to be endorsed on at least 18 slate card mailers. She defeated Dzintra Janavs, a respected sitting judge, even though her experience amounted to owning a bagel shop and four other businesses. She had not focused on legal issues in 14 years and was rated as "not qualified" by the Los Angeles County Bar Association. Although she was a Democrat, the Republican-leaning slate Citizens for Representative Government listed Olson as the "Republican choice" and "well qualified" after receiving a payment from her. Allan Hoffenblum, the political director for the slate, was embarrassed when confronted about it and admitted he hadn't screened her application carefully. He explained that the process he used to make her endorsement decision was that, "She requested it, she sent in her money and she got on the slate."[16] How representative.

At least one voter, Frank Daly, told reporters that he regretted his vote for Olson after learning more about her. "I voted for this lady solely on these pieces sent to me," he lamented. "I don't really trust a lot of those things anyway, but I didn't have any other avenue to base my decision on."[17]

Slate mailers can be as much about making money as conveying a message. The COPS Voter Guide received a million dollars from candidates in 2004, but only spent $751,079 on the mailers. That leaves a tidy sum left over as profit.

Garry South, a political consultant who ran Steve Westly's campaign for governor described the slate-card operators as shakedown artists. "What they try to tell you," he claims, is that 'the other guy is trying to buy my slate but I'd rather have you, so I'll give you a price break. If you don't do that, I'm going to have no choice but sell to the other guy."[18]

A Big Spending General Election

With no opponent to speak of in the Republican primary, Arnold sat back and watched Democrats Steve Westly and Phil Angelides tear each other to shreds while Rob Reiner self-destructed. Arnold kept his head down, went back to his style of working with both parties in the legislature and, of course, kept raising money.

On June 30, 2006, Arnold Schwarzenegger agreed to pay a $202,200 fine for the California Recovery Team's failure to report expenditures it made during the 2005 special election in a timely fashion. The Fair Political Practices Commission found 143 delinquent reports that involved some $25 million in spending. Compared to the overall abuse by Schwarzenegger and others of using ballot committees as a way to get around limits on contributions to their candidate campaigns, the violation was pretty minor. Arnold had disclosed the information, just not in the correct fashion and on the right timeline. Nevertheless, the fine was appropriate as a signal to prevent future evasion of disclosure laws by other politicians. This was the second largest fine ever paid by a candidate for campaign finance violations, second only to Cruz Bustamante's fine of $260,000. But, the delayed penalty again showed the weaknesses of California's system to enforce campaign finance laws only after elections are long over.

Once the primary was over, Schwarzenegger stepped up his campaigning and his fundraising. In all, Schwarzenegger raised $46 million for his re-election campaign. He spent $30 million of that during the general election. By comparison, Angelides raised $47 million over the entire campaign, but spent most of that during the primary. For the general election, he had only $11 million to spend. He did however, benefit from roughly $20 million spending by the Democratic Party and outside groups, roughly half of which came in the general election. Further, some of the spending by both Angelides and Westly during the primary was in opposition to Schwarzenegger. So while Arnold had considerably more money during the final four months, over the course of the year he was significantly outspent.

But looking over the entire election cycle, Schwarzenegger vastly outspent Angelides when you consider the spending he did to promote himself through his ballot committees as well as his candidate committee. Schwarzenegger's donors for his re-election were not substantially different from his donors to his ballot committees. He drew most of his support in large checks, often from business interests.

Arnold's New Majority is not the Moral Majority

In the 1980s, a conservative Christian group called the Moral Majority gained national prominence in part by pooling contributions from small-donors to political candidates. But ideological small donor groups are somewhat passé in 21st century California politics. One of Arnold's biggest sources of funds came from an organization called the New Majority, a confederation of about 250 businessmen in Southern California. They reportedly dole out about $7.5 million a year collectively.

Members of the New Majority gave or raised more than $10 million to Schwarzenegger's causes in his first three years as governor. Republican consultant Allan Hoffenblum described them as "checkbook Republicans—individuals who are wealthy and raise big bucks to support moderate candidates. They are not dominated by religious right issues."[19] The rise of checkbook Republicans has significantly altered the debate within the California Republican Party, which was previously dominated by activists who were more motivated by social issues than concerns of the Chamber of Commerce.

Paul Folino, who began investing in Schwarzenegger back with the Prop 49 campaign, is a leading New Majority donor, giving more than a million dollars to Schwarzenegger's campaigns. Folino described how New Majority saw Schwarzenegger: "Our view of the world links up very closely with the governor's—you have to consider the governor is a *moderate* Republican," he explained (emphasis added).[20]

Other New Majority donors included investment banker Frank Baxter and Lawrence Higby, who helped found the group. Higby is a former Nixon aide who runs Apria Healthcare, which had a small contract with the State of California. More importantly, with health care reform on tap as a major concern for 2007, Higby had a clear interest in decisions made in Sacramento. Donald Bren of the Irvine Company (profiled in Chapter 3) is another prominent New Majority figure. A.G. Kawamura, an orange grower and past chair of the Western Growers Association whom Schwarzenegger appointed to be his food and agriculture secretary, gave $15,000 to the New Majority Fund and $21,200 to Schwarzenegger.

Kawamura wasn't the only big donor to receive an appointment. Schwarzenegger appointed GAP founder Donald G. Fisher, who wound up giving him a total of $223,500 to his campaigns, to the board of education. Arnold appointed Douglass Barnhart and Kelly Burt to the prestigious Del Mar Fair board. He had received about $140,000 from each of them. Schwarzenegger also placed Gary Hunt, New Majority's finance chairman, on the board of his California Recovery Team, steering millions of dollars into Schwarzenegger's ballot fights.

Other major donors to Schwarzenegger's campaign included auto dealers, who reportedly gave Arnold nearly a million dollars compared to $11,000 to Angelides' campaign. Angelides had said that he would have signed the bill Schwarzenegger vetoed that would have required 50 percent of new cars to run on alternative fuels by 2020. The president of the California Motor Car Dealers Association, Peter Welch, expressed concern that the bill would limit the selection of cars dealers could offer and raise costs. Welch stressed that the difference between Schwarzenegger and

Angelides on his groups interests "is night and day. The choice is very stark."[21]

Agricultural interests likewise sided with the governor, giving him more than a million bucks while just a pittance for Angelides. Ag interests were concerned about bills dealing with groundwater monitoring and workers compensation for farm workers, among other items that reached Schwarzenegger's desk.

Prison Guards Talk Tough, Carry a Small Stick

During the summer of 2006, Schwarzenegger negotiated with one of California's most powerful unions, the prison guards, over a host of issues ranging from their contract to the construction of new prison facilities. Schwarzenegger prides himself in not taking contributions from labor unions, but in this instance the unions tried to find a way to have an impact anyhow. The prison guard union made it known that it had a war chest of $10 million that it was willing to spend on the governor's race. Rather than giving the money to Angelides, the guards intimated they would spend it on their own campaign trashing Arnold. If they did get what they wanted, they would stay neutral, or possibly even endorse Schwarzenegger. Try as he might to deny that reality, Schwarzenegger was not immune from the prison guards' money, even if he refused to accept it as a direct donation (had they wanted to give it in the first place). In standing up to them, Arnold would need to placate other donors in order to have the funds necessary to defend himself against the guards.

When Arnold did not cave into the prison guards demands, they moved into attack mode. On September 20, a story ran in the *San Francisco Chronicle* citing unnamed sources saying that "a coalition of the state's most powerful public employee unions has agreed to start an independent campaign opposing the re-election of Gov. Arnold Schwarzenegger that could cost as much as $25 million."[22] To conduct that campaign, the prison guards formed a political fund with the teachers and firefighters union. The guards initially provided $2 million, the teachers $820,000 and the firefighters $80,000.

In the end, though, it was a lot of talk but little action when it came to spending against Schwarzenegger. The groups spent roughly $450,000 on mailings attacking him. Perhaps the unions concluded that Schwarzenegger was going to win anyhow, so spending money against him was a lost cause. Perhaps they never intended to spend so much, but leaked phony announcements to either pressure Schwarzenegger in negotiations or to encourage other donors to give to Angelides by making him look more financially viable than he was.

Schwarzenegger had used the union bogeyman as his major reason for why he had to raise so much money from his own set of special interests. He needed to compete with what his opponents would spend against him. In the end, though, he found himself with $30 million to spend in the general election, roughly three times what his opponent had and well more than any union would unleash against him.

All in all, the prison guards spent $11.7 million over the 2005–2006 election cycle. Of this, nearly half was in independent expenditures in candidate elections. Another $4 million went to ballot questions, primarily during the 2005 special election.

Arnold Breaks Fundraising Records

Over the course of a relatively brief political career, Schwarzenegger has raised a staggering amount of money from other people whether he needed to or not. The money includes:

Californians for Schwarzenegger '03:	$17.3 million
Total Recall Committee '03	$ 3.9 million
California Recover Team in '04	$18.7 million
California Recovery Team in '05	$34.8 million
Citizens to Save California '05	$10.7 million
Workers Comp Initiative '04 (to qualify)	$ 4.5 million
Schwarzenegger '06 (re-election)	$46.3 million
Total	**$136.2 million**

An analysis by the *Associated Press* found that more than 75 percent of Schwarzenegger's funds came in amounts exceeding $10,000.[23] That's hard to square with Arnold's statement during the recall campaign that 90 percent of his funds came from regular people, like those who owned local grocery markets and shoe stores.

These figures don't include money he raised for Prop 49 in 2002 ($8.8 million) before running for governor, money he raised with Steve Westly for Prop 57 and 58 ($2.7 million) while he was governor, or his own personal contributions to his campaigns ($19.8 million) When you include those figures, the total that Arnold has spent to advance his political career comes to $167.5 million.

By comparison:

- Diane Feinstein raised $9.4 million to be re-elected in 2006. To face the exact same electorate, Schwarzenegger raised $46.3 million.

- Michael Huffington spent $27.5 million in an unsuccessful attempt to defeat Diane Feinstein in 1994. At the time, this was viewed as an astronomical amount.

- John Corzine of New Jersey spent $65 million to run for the U.S. Senate in 2002 and then $44 million to run for governor of New Jersey in 2005.

- Gray Davis spent $120 million over seven years compared to the $167 Schwarzenegger spent in five years.

- Al Gore raised $132 million in 4 years to run for president in 2000. Arnold raised more than that in four years to campaign in just one state.

- Michael Bloomberg spent $157 million over 4 years to run two races for NYC mayor. Arnold spent $167 million over five years to run in a larger electorate, so pound for pound Bloomberg arguably still holds the record. Bloomberg, however, really didn't need to raise it from others.

Of Schwarzenegger's spending, at least $70 million went into radio and TV ads, but significant amounts went for other expenses including nearly $15 million to his consultants, $5 million for travel and hotels, $5 million for putting on public events, and $2 million for polling.

In November 2006, Californians chose between two men for governor. Both were personally wealthy and would never have made it in politics otherwise. Both had made millions as real-estate developers (Arnold built a 30,000 square foot apartment and office complex in Santa Monica and owns a shopping mall in Ohio.) And both had received millions of dollars in backing from developers (Angelides from Angelo Tsakopoulos, Schwarzenegger from Donald Bren, Alex Spanos and others). This striking similarity is no accident. When we allow big money to dominate campaigns, both parties wind up with candidates sympathetic to major economic sectors like real estate.

The similarity also reveals the faulty reasoning behind those who suggest that full disclosure of campaign contributions is enough. Voters knew full well both men were backed by developers. But what are they to do if they want a governor who is not hand-in-hand with real-estate interests? How can voters trust that more houses won't be built in flood plains, that taxpayers won't get unfairly dunned with bills for levy improvements, or that suburban sprawl won't continue to eat up California's farmland and open spaces? Under our current system of campaign finance, we can't.

Arnold Re-explains Himself

During the course of the campaign, news outlets frequently asked Schwarzenegger about his pledge during the recall not to take money from special interests. He argued that people had not understood him correctly, "What I said is: I'm financially independent," and that anyone who contributes "buys into my philosophy," not the other way around.[24]

In another interview, he asserted:

> What's wrong with fundraising is not the fundraising, but when you are vulnerable and you want to do favors back. That's what I said will never happen in my administration, because I'm financially independent. I don't need to take money from anybody.[25]

There are some who would claim that Schwarzenegger's administration certainly did offer favors to its donors, like appointing Brent Wilkes to the Del Mar Fair board or letting Hilmar Cheese exceed its water polluting permit. But even if we take Arnold at his word, do we want decisions about government to be determined by small numbers of large donors "buying into" candidates, or instead by voters agreeing with candidates in a system where every vote counts equally? Whether Arnold needs the money personally is not the question. Nobody has ever contended that Arnold was personally getting rich off his government service. But nobody claimed that about Gray Davis either.

During a TV interview shortly before the 2006 election, Schwarzenegger kept talking the talk of a campaign finance reformer:

> Money in and favors out. That is what is wrong. And I see it sometimes, and you know it bothers me. This is why I want to reform the system and this is why we have to stay on it and keep working on it until we find a way of reforming it.[26]

When reporter Marci Brightwell pointed out that he had promised to reform money in politics during the recall and yet had not yet done so, Schwarzenegger admitted, "You are absolutely correct. More work needs to be done."[27] So it does.

Millionaire vs. Moneygrubber for Ins. Comiss.

Big money placed a role in other general election races beyond the governor's contest. Cruz Bustamante, termed out of his position as lieutenant governor, made a bid to stay in elected office by running for insurance commissioner. In doing so, Bustamante provided perhaps an even better example than Gray Davis of how non-wealthy candidates must prostitute themselves to special interests in an attempt to keep pace with self-financed millionaire candidates. As with Davis, the public soured on Bustamante because of his apparent connections to private interests.

Bustamante's opponent, Silicon Valley businessman Steve Poizner, had spent about $5.75 million from his own bank account in 2004 in an unsuccessful bid to win a seat in the Assembly. It added up to nearly $62 for every vote he received. Undeterred, he maintained a strong interest in California politics. He led efforts to pass Schwarzenegger's redistricting initiative during the 2005 special election.

As someone in a position to entirely fund his own campaign, Poizner was easily able to draw distinctions between himself and Bustamante. Poizner's ads hit Bustamante hard for taking more than $150,000 from insurance companies. This was true, although Bustamante had returned $133,000 of these contributions he had taken just prior to the primary election. This led Poizner to charge, somewhat credibly, that Bustamante simply hadn't received enough money from the firms to make it "worth it" compared to the negative publicity he would receive. Further, it appeared that Bustamante held on to significant amounts of money with ties to insurance companies and funds from other entities that the commissioner regulates. He also used some insurance company money to pay off debts from his 2003 campaign during the recall.

Poizner spent a total of $14.8 million on his campaign (not counting $1.25 million that his campaign gave to the special election Prop 77 redistricting initiative). He had donated $14 million to his campaign from his own pocket. Bustamante spent $2 million. Poizner won with 51 percent of the vote compared to 39 percent for Bustamante. Californians will never know who would have won had both sides spent an equal amount of money.

Non-wealthy elected officials in California should take note of the fate of Gray Davis and Cruz Bustamante. As incumbents, they can raise huge amounts of money from special interests as a means of holding their current office. But unless they reform the very system that got them elected, they run the risk of being the next victim of public backlash when they run for another office and face a millionaire opponent who can outspend them without having to sully their reputation by taking special interest money.

Trying to Control the Controller Election

Big money even found its way into the usually dull race for state controller. Intuit, the company that makes Quickbooks and TurboTax accounting software, spent generously to support Tony Strickland's campaign against John Chiang. They did it in a way that only an accountant could love.

On October 20, 2006, Intuit made a contribution of $1 million to an independent political committee called Alliance for California's Tomorrow, a California Business and Labor Coalition. That group recorded the contribution on October 24. Two days later, the committee spent $934,000 on an ad campaign supporting Strickland. Despite its title, from 2005–2006 the Alliance recorded contributions from zero labor unions, 40 corporations or trade associations, and two individuals—both business executives.

While he served on the board of equalization, Chiang had championed efforts to make it easy for low-income families to file tax returns, thus decreasing the need for these people to by Intuit's software. This provides yet another example of where no favors needed to be asked or granted in order for money to have its corrupting influence. Intuit knew which candidate was bad for its bottom line. The company it spent its money accordingly.

A group of Indian tribes formed a political committee known as Team 2006 that spent $958,000 on behalf of Strickland.

Chiang, in turn, benefited from $1.4 million in independent

expenditures by labor unions and other Indian tribes, which lead to an almost level playing field in terms of overall spending although Chiang had more than twice as many donors. Chiang's own candidate campaign raised $2.9 million from 3,980 donors, for an average contribution of around $728. Counting the outside groups, he thus had $4.3 million on his side. Strickland's campaign raised $2.3 million from 1,891 donors, for an average contribution of $1,216. Adding in the Intuit and Indian spending, his side had $4.1 million. In the end, Chiang won with 51 percent of the vote compared to 40 percent for Strickland.

Team 2006—Indian Givers

Indian tribes looked well beyond the controller's race for places to spend money and buy influence in the 2006 elections. A few key legislative races drew big bucks in response to the legislature's failure to approve compacts that Schwarzenegger had negotiated to expand Indian gambling operations. The tribes had locked horns with labor unions over a provision to allow workers at tribal casinos to form labor unions and many Democratic lawmakers balked at approving the compacts as a result. While the tribes had previously given 70 percent of their funds to Democrats, they shifted their support in 2006 to include more Republican candidates. Five tribes formed a PAC called Team 2006 and dumped in more than $9 million.

Daniel Tucker, chairman of the Sycuan tribe, described their actions as selfless, even noble: "We're just helping to move California forward by supporting strong leaders—Democrats and Republicans—who will move the state in the right direction."[28] Golly, who could object to that?— so long as we all agree what the "right" direction is.

Beyond the money spent to support Strickland in the controller race, Team 2006 spent $493,000 to support Senator Jeff Denham, $520,000 for Nicole Parra, $281,000 on behalf of Shirley Horton, $404,000 for Bonnie Garcia, $196,000 for Guy Houston, $51,000 backing Jenny Oropeza, and $122,000 backing Audra Strickland (married to Tony Strickland).

The spending was intended to send a message to future legislators to think twice before crossing the tribes. But, as with the prison guards, some of the tribe money was more talk than action. On November 28, Team 2006 returned $6 million of the $9 million it had raised to its member tribes. By appearing to be major players during the campaign, the tribes tried to build their power and influence while still getting to hold on to most of their cash.

The Party Loophole

By 2006, both the Democratic and Republican parties had perfected a scheme that allowed big donors to bypass the limit of $3,300 that they could contribute to a state legislative candidate. Donors could give up to $27,900 to a state or county party political committee, which could then give an unlimited amount of such contributions

California Legislative Campaign Loopholes

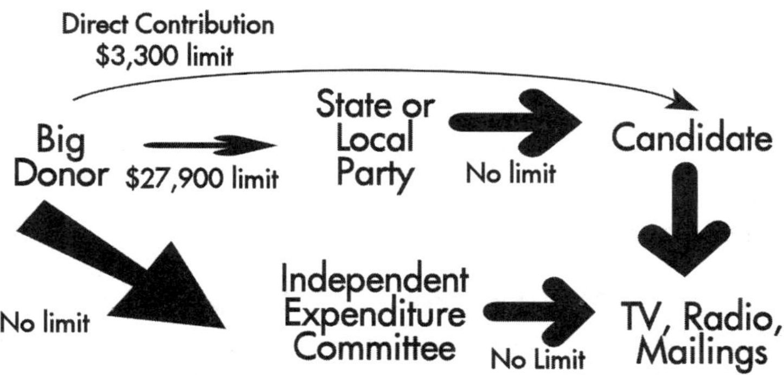

to a candidate. Or, a donor could give an unlimited amount to a party if the party spent that independently of the candidate.

At least $10 million flowed through county party committees as a way of evading the contribution limits that apply to candidate committees. Republican Gerry Machado received $1 million of his $1.6 million budget from contributions that flowed through the California Republican Party and the Sacramento County Republican Party.

The Democrats did it as well. Democrat Maxine Sherard raised $700,000 of her total of $842,000 from party committees.

In addition to county committees, many funds also flow through campaign committees run by legislators, especially those who chair important committees. San Francisco Assemblymember Mark Leno, for instance, gave $114,000 to other candidates. Leno conceded that participating in raising money for other members is considered a key part of being on the party's leadership team:

> Clearly, if you look at who is chairing committees and who is participating, there would be some correlation. Those that do not participate at all really become nonplayers.[29]

To his credit, Leno has worked hard to change the current system, supporting campaign finance reform proposals in the legislature and on the ballot. He is in the unenviable position of needing to play by the current rules, even though he thinks they do a disservice to democracy. "Just because I don't like the system we are using doesn't mean that I'm not going to take part in it" he explained.[30]

Democratic committees in Stanislaus and San Luis Obispo counties channeled a combined $1 million into legislative races in 2006 after being virtually inactive in previous years. San Diego County Democrat committee funneled $625,000 to a candidate running in the Stockton area, Cathleen Galgiani, who also received $625,000 from the Sacramento Democratic Committee. Each committee recorded numerous contributions of $27,900 from corporations, labor groups, and incumbent lawmaker committees—the amount from any one donation that a party is allowed to directly contribute to a candidate.

Nicole Parra received at least $780,000 from Democratic county committees that were not even in the region she represents. In the end, less than 5 percent of the funds raised by Parra and her opponent came from people who could actually vote in the race, the rest was from outsiders. Team 2006, the group of Indian tribes, spent $355,000 on its own TV ads in the race.

Democratic spokesman Steve Maviglio, who had worked for Gray Davis, defended the money shuffle. "We're following the law," he explained. "These are the new rules of engagement under Proposition 34."[31] Indeed they were. Maviglio neglected to point out that those rules of engagement had been drafted by politicians for the clear purpose of gutting the previous rules of engagement and replacing them with rules that placed party machines as central gatekeepers for most campaign funds that would flow to key races.

When asked if the Democrats had stolen the county loophole idea from Republicans, who had first used it in 2002 to move money from the 21st Century Insurance Company into several legislative races, committee chairman Jess Durfee replied: "Certainly. We've got to stay competitive."[32] Republican consultant Dan Schnur agreed that the avoidance of campaign limits had become thoroughly bipartisan by 2006: "Neither party has the corner on this."[33]

But, even this loophole had its limits.

In April 2006, the Viejas tribe gave senate candidate Jeff Denham $3,300, the maximum amount they were allowed to directly contribute to his campaign under the fairly weak campaign finance rules of Prop 34. But later that fall, the Native Americans and Peace Officers gave $300,000 to the Monterey County Republican Party on September 11, 2006. On September 14, the committee received $50,000 from the California Tribal Business Alliance and the next day another fifty grand from the Viejas Tribal Government committee. That makes a grand total of $400,000 in tribe money in the course of four days. On September 26, the Monterey Republicans gave Denham $250,000. Four days later, they gave him another $150,000 for a grand total of; you guessed it, $400,000 over four days. It was an accounting scheme that Enron would have been proud of.

Denham's campaign manager, Shant Apekian, conceded that

Denham had actively helped raise some of the funds that county committees funneled to his campaign. The money "certainly plays a big role," he said, stating an unfortunate but obvious reality of current California campaigns.[34]

The only problem? It might not have been legal. If indeed the contributions were given to the Monterey Republican Party for the purposes of passing on to candidates, and if indeed that's what the party did, it would have been a violation of the $27,900 limit. Perhaps realizing this, Denham returned $390,000 in contributions to the Monterey Republican Party during the final two weeks before the election. He also returned $200,000 of the $290,000 he had received from the California Republican Party.

Denham should have known a thing or two about the need to walk this line carefully. He was named as a recipient of illegally laundered funds from the Kern County Republican Party in a memo by the California Fair Political Practices Commission. The memo concluded that the 21st Century Insurance Company had violated the law in 2002 when it first engineered this loophole in the first elections held under Prop 34. It is also possible that Denham simply concluded he didn't need the funds, so returned them to be spent elsewhere, or that the funds were originally sent as part of a ruse to make Denham look financially strong to scare off donors from backing his opponent.

It is worth noting that even the porous limits of Prop 34, which was intentionally designed to funnel big money through political parties on its way to candidates, had enough bite to impact what the tribes wanted to give to Denham. This serves as a reminder once again that limits on money in politics do have an effect and that limits more stringent than those in current California law would have an even greater impact.

The Independent Expenditure Loophole

Beyond the $27,900 that a big donor could funnel directly to a candidate by giving it first to a party committee, a fat cat, corporation, union, or tribe could spend an unlimited amount of money on their own TV ads and mailers attacking or supporting candidates. This technique is often used in primary elections, where the party is reluctant to get involved on behalf of any candidate. It is also used in general elections as a way of masking the true source of the money.

Outgoing Assemblymember Tom Umberg chaired a hearing in the fall of 2006 and invited me to testify. "I think the process has been completely turned on its head," he lamented. "I think accountability is at an all-time low."[35]

In one legislative primary held in the spring of 2006, the candidates themselves spent $1.47 million compared to $1.63 million spent by outside groups. Another primary race saw candidates spend $1.24 million compared to $1.41 million in independent expenditures.

The disclosure rules in California are such that in the final weeks before an election, candidates must disclose contributions of $1,000 or more within 24 hours of getting them. Independent PACs must disclose that they've spent money to attack or praise a candidate within 24 hours after doing so, but they can amass the funds ahead of time without tipping off their opponents.

Rob Stutzman, the political consultant who steered Arnold's special election agenda, was frank about his reasons for using independent expenditure groups to delay disclosure of his actions. "It's the same reason the U.S. military develops stealth bombers. You don't want your opponents to see you coming."[36]

Yet despite all these advantages, in the general election where party committees could play a role, donors generally preferred to channel their money through the parties rather than spending it independently. This is a reminder that while independent expenditures remain a loophole, it is one donors and certainly candidates generally prefer not to use unless they have to due to laws put in place to limit candidate contributions. This is likely because money spent independently is less helpful to a candidate in winning a race, and therefore also less likely to buy influence with that candidate once elected than money that the candidate gets to spend as they please. Independent ads can raise issues that a candidate would rather avoid and can sometimes even backfire and hurt the candidate they are intended to help by generating sympathy for any opponent or depressing turnout among both sides' supporters.

Big Money Floods Ballot Questions

Campaign spending on ballot measures by corporations and individual wealthy donors broke new records in 2006. While it is worth following the money in ballot questions in its own right, it is important to recognize that ballot-question spending is increasingly intertwined with the fate of candidates. When a candidate takes a stands on ballot initiatives, it is purportedly because their endorsement will help the initiative pass. But as political consultant Darryl Sragow explained, it can also be helpful to the candidate. Endorsing or opposing initiatives can be an "easy way, in shorthand, to convey a lot of information to voters very quickly."[37] Unlike candidate campaigns, there are no limits on contributions to initiative campaigns and several ballot questions drew donations that were larger than any seen on the candidate side.

The Infrastructure Bonds

The legislative leaders who backed passage of the infrastructure bonds they had negotiated with Schwarzenegger raised big money to help ensure their passage on the November ballot. Bond questions 1A–1E provided funding for road building, housing, school construction, and flood prevention. In all, politicians and their allies spent more than $17 million in support of the bonds which faced relatively little opposition. Overall the bond campaigns helped both Schwarzenegger and Democratic legislators by reminding voters that they had worked together to put them on the ballot.

Bond proponents found they had to raise and spend more

Spending on November 2006 Ballot Measures

	Topic	Yes*	No	Result
1A-1E	Infrastructure Bonds	$17,355,261	-	Passed
Prop 83	Penalties for Sex Offenders	$2,002,239	-	Passed
Prop 84	Water Quality	$10,759,187	-	Passed
Prop 85	Teenage Abortion Notification	$5,157,860	$10,467,219	Failed
Prop 86	Tobacco Tax	$14,638,611	$59,904,076	Failed
Prop 87	Alternative Energy, Oil Tax	$58,641,071	$92,875,096	Failed
Prop 88	Education Property Tax Increase	$5,992,836	$506,677	Failed
Prop 89	Public Financing of Campaigns	$4,794,224	$5,460,494	Failed
Prop 90	Eminent Domain and Land Use Laws	$1,450,660	$215,850	Failed
Total		$120,791,948	$169,429,412	

*Yes spending includes cost of gathering signatures to qualify the initiative

money than they expected due to the fact that ad rates had been inflated by the big spending of other initiative campaigns. "We were buying TV time in a market that was stratospheric, one that we had not seen before," complained Senate leader Don Perata.[38] Campaign director Paul Heffner elaborated, saying the spending on other initiatives is, "Driving the rates up fairly significantly. With the rates higher, our money doesn't go as far as we want it to go."[39]

The bond example is a reminder that paid political speech is to some extent a zero-sum game. The more one person or group speaks, the less others are able to speak. This is partially because there is a limited amount of TV advertising time to purchase, so the more time one interest buys the more it prices others out of the market. But more fundamentally, voters have limited amounts of time to consider political arguments. Between holding down jobs, raising families, and taking care of their lives, voters quite reasonably start tuning out political ads, throwing out mailers, and switching stations when they've heard what feels like more than enough. Undeterred, political advertisers, just like commercial advertisers, spend more and more money trying to break into the voters' consciousness. The reality of current campaign financing means that only the few interests that are heavily backed by deep pockets can succeed, and when they do, it becomes that much harder for others to find space in the political bandwidth.

Prop 86—Tobacco Snuffs Out Other Voices

Public health organizations like the American Cancer Society and American Lung Association supported Prop 86 to assess an additional 13 cents a pack tax on cigarettes and use the proceeds for public health programs. They raised $14 million to support their effort, an impressive amount for public interest groups.

Some concerned citizens formed a political committee called Californians Against Unaccountable Taxes, A Coalition of Taxpayers, Businesses and Law Enforcement. Of the $27 million raised by this committee, $25 million came from the R.J. Reynolds Tobacco Company.

Phillip Morris funded a separate opposition campaign that it called Stop the $2 Billion Tax Hike, a coalition of business, law enforcement and taxpayer groups, and Phillip Morris USA. Of the $39 million raised by this committee, $35 million came from Phillip Morris, $2.6 from U.S. Smokeless Tobacco, and $1 million from tobacco producer Commonwealth Brands.

R.J. Reynolds had warned its shareholders that its earnings would be depressed if Prop 86 passed. Company spokesperson Frank McConnell explained:

> It is in our best interest to fight the proposition. The impact to our business of Prop 86 passing is far greater than the amount of money we will spend opposing it.[40]

Have we reached a point where public policy questions will be determined by simple calculations by private interests on whether or not it will be cheaper for them to change or defeat a law than it would be to abide by the law?

Schwarzenegger opposed Prop 86 while Angelides supported it. Prop 86 was defeated after receiving 48 percent of the vote and being outspent $14 million to $60 million.

Prop 87—Big Oil Buries the Competition

Concerned about dependence on foreign oil in the wake of the September 11 attacks, Hollywood Executive Anthony Rubenstein came up with the idea of taxing oil production in California and using the proceeds to finance research and development of alternative energy. Rubenstein called Berkeley energy expert Dan Kammen on Christmas day of 2004 to brainstorm the idea. Every other state in the U.S. charges a tax on oil pumped out of its ground, so parts of the idea were hardly new.

In some ways, Prop 87 is the classic example of a regular person taking a policy idea to the voters through the initiative process. Rubenstein had no previous environmental or political experience, just a passion for his idea. He wasn't doing it as a platform to run for future office or to advance his career.

But in its eventual financing, Prop 87 was far from ordinary. Hollywood mogul Stephen Bing, a high school friend of Rubenstein's, financed the bulk of Prop 87's budget, contributing $50 million out of the total $60 million budget. This was the largest amount that any individual has ever spent to influence the outcome of any single ballot question in the history of the world. While a small percentage of Prop 87's funding came from people that had financial interests in alternative energy, it is doubtful that Bing would have personally gained from its passage. Oil companies released a gusher of money to defeat Prop 87, spending $93 million in all. Chevron gave $38 million, AERA energy $33 million, Occidental Petroleum $10 million, and BP and ConocoPhillips $3 million a piece. Compared to the $4 billion that the tax would have cost them, this was still pennies on the dollar.

The oil companies argued in their ads that the tax would lead to higher prices because it would cause California oil production to shrink. Energy experts countered that this was faulty logic because the price of California's gas is determined by worldwide oil-markets.

Despite his efforts to appear pro-environment, Schwarzenegger opposed Prop 87. Angelides supported it.

Prop 87 broke all previous records for money spent on a single ballot question. Even opposition spokesman Scott Macdonald had a hard time justifying the money the oil companies spent on his campaign or the money spent by its proponents:

> The money spent is obnoxious. It is bad. No one says $150 million spent on a proposition is money well spent. But our people spent the money because they were under attack.[41]

Media consultant Steve Swatt observed that with the Prop 86 and 87 campaigns corporations were using cash to compensate for their lack of credibility:

> These are two of the most P.R.–challenged industries. To make up that credibility problem, they have to spend huge amounts of money. When you have a wealthy, deep-pocket special interest that is at risk because of one initiative, they will write checks like there is no tomorrow because so much is at stake.[42]

Of course, the general reputation of various corporations depends largely upon the public learning of their behavior through communications that they don't pay for, usually news stories. When voters hear about Exxon's behavior after the Valdez oil spill, or Mobil funding research to prove global warming doesn't exist, or tobacco company executives testifying before Congress that their product is safe despite their own studies to the contrary, it is justifiable for voters to become skeptical. Does it make sense to allow these companies to compensate for that well-earned reputation by purchasing campaign ads to overwhelm their opponents?

Unlike the oil companies that opposed Prop 87 or the cigarette firms that opposed Prop 86, Stephen Bing's donation appeared to be based upon which opinion of what would benefit California as a whole. But as with the huge donation by Angelo Tsakopoulos to benefit Phil Angelides, the money allowed one donor's opinion to rise above others.

Prop. 89—A Failed Effort at Reform

After running up against big money from hospitals and HMOs whenever they pushed for health-care reforms, the California Nurses Association made a bold attempt in 2006 to pass one of the most sweeping campaign finance reform proposals ever considered in U.S. history. With little previous experience in campaign reform issues, they perhaps did not know what they were in for. The measure failed badly on Election Day.

Prop 89 would have provided candidates who rejected big private funds with public money to run their campaigns. To prove they were viable, candidates would need to raise large numbers of $5 contributions from people within their district but after they had qualified they would be prohibited from raising a dime from anyone.

To provide a steady source of funds for the clean money program, Prop 89 called for an increase in the corporate tax rate by 0.2 percent, taking it to a level where it was during most of the 1980s and 1990s under governors Deukmejian and Pete Wilson.

Beyond the public financing proposals, Prop 89 included a number of other campaign finance reforms comparable to those found in other states including lowering the limits on contributions to legislative candidates from $3,300 to $500 and from $22,300 to $1,000 for gubernatorial candidates. It also called for an aggregate limit of $15,000 per year on all contributions to all candidates and political parties that applied to individuals, labor unions, and corporations. Prop 89 further tightened some disclosure requirements.

But Prop 89 also tried to break new ground. It would have closed the ballot measure loophole used by Bustamante in the recall and Schwarzenegger in the special election by placing a $10,000 limit on contributions to all candidate-controlled ballot committees. This would have essentially restored and improved the reform that the FPPC had tried to enact, only to be foiled by Arnold's lawsuit (see Chapter 6). Further, Prop 89 called for a $10,000 limit on what any corporation could contribute to a ballot measure campaign from its corporate treasury. To spend more on that, corporations would have to raise funds from their shareholders and executives much as non-profit groups raise money from individual donors and labor unions raise it from their members.

Prop 89 managed to unite most interests that currently hold power in Sacramento against it. Richard Claussen, the political consultant who worked for Schwarzenegger and other Republican interests, and Gale Kaufman, who battled Claussen in the special election on behalf of Democrats, joined forces to oppose the reform. Arnold Schwarzenegger, the self-proclaimed reformer, opposed Prop 89 while Phil Angelides, to his credit, supported it. The California Teachers Association and the Chamber of Commerce both opposed Prop 89. The measure would have dramatically reduced the power of both labor and corporate interests in candidate campaigns by limiting what they could give candidates and allowing other candidates to run viable campaigns completely free of labor and corporate money. The nurses union had given money to candidates in the past, but they were evidently willing to give up what leverage they had gained through their donations for the opportunity to work with legislators who were not beholden to any financial interests at all. The nurses qualified Prop 89 in near record time by mobilizing many nurses to volunteer to gather signatures in addition to using paid signature gatherers.

Opponents tried to claim Prop 89 was part of a "secret" plan by the nurses to pave the way for policy ideas that they support, such as providing universal health care coverage. But it was hardly a surprise that the nurses' frustration with the current campaign finance system stemmed from their experience in trying to put forward health care ideas. Rose Ann DeMoro of the nurses explained:

> There's nothing secret about the fact that we believe that health care reforms and others like it should be instituted. Right now, we can't have an honest policy debate because of the money the corporations and special interests can spend.[43]

It would be convenient for reformers to say that Prop 89 was killed by huge special interest spending. Opponents spent $5 million against the measure, with contributions from many of the deep pockets that currently dominate California politics: Chevron ($250,000), PhRMA ($200,000), California Hospitals Committee ($200,000), ConocoPhillips ($100,000), Occidental Petroleum ($100,000), Exxon/Mobil ($100,000), the California Business PAC ($395,000), the Farm Bureau ($75,000), and AT&T ($50,000). Several insurance companies put in $100,000 or more each, including Blue Cross, Mercury, State Farm, and Zenith.

But in truth, the money spent against Prop 89 did not dramatically outweigh the funds spent in favor of it. Big money did not buy this election result.

Others claimed that Prop 89 went down because it tried to do too much. Many proponents of clean money feared that the public financing provisions would be dragged down in the polls by the restrictions on corporate money, but polling showed that just the opposite was true. Others fretted that some of the provisions dealing with ballot measures could be thrown out by the courts. As *Los Angeles Times* columnist George Skelton put it, "Prop 89 would be the most dramatic step ever, anywhere, in campaign finance reform. It may be too big a leap—for voters and the courts."[44]

But, the fact is, most of Prop 89 would have been upheld in court even if some provisions were struck. Further, Prop 89 could just as easily have failed even if it were much less ambitious. The reason? The language that summarized the lengthy text of Prop 89 on the ballot was confusing and uninspiring. When a late summer poll asked respondents how they planned to vote on Prop 89 after reading them the ballot summary, only 25 percent responded yes while 61 percent responded no. This was before a single ad aired against it or a single mailer went out trashing it.

The ballot summary had been prepared by attorney general Bill Lockyer. He had the job of distilling the 17 pages of Prop 89 into a 14-word summary. He chose these words: "Political Campaigns. Public Financing. Corporate Tax Increase. Campaign Contribution and Expenditure Limits. Initiative Statute." Had these words been put into a sentence, they might have at least made sense: "Taxes corporations to provide public financing for political campaigns. Applies contribution and expenditure limits to candidate and initiative campaigns." By emphasizing a tax increase and failing to explain that candidates who receive public funds must reject all private contributions, this clarified summary would probably still have not met with strong voter approval, but at least voters would have known what it was.

An analysis by the Campaign Finance Institute found that over the past 30 years, public-opinion polling has found consistent support for providing public financing for candidates. However, the support varied dramatically based upon how the question was worded. When questions were presented in what the institute described as neutral terms and describes the accompanying limits that candidates must abide by to receive public finds, polling support is consistently in the 50–65 percent range. When the context for the question includes highlights of corruption and tells respondents that candidates who accept public funds must reject all private funds, support is in the 65–70 percent range. But when the question emphasizes the cost of the program, mentions tax increases, and does not detail how it works, support can drop to 20 percent.[45] That finding is certainly consistent with the 25 percent Prop 89 received in polls and on Election Day.

When ballot wording is favorable to reformers, voters have approved of public financing initiatives. In 2005, voters in Albuquerque, New Mexico adopted a public financing proposal by a vote of 69 percent to 31 percent. Massachusetts voters approved a public financing measure in 1998 with 67 percent of the vote. Maine enacted a full public financing law in 1996 with 56 percent of the vote, and Arizona saw 51 percent support for its clean money initiative in 1998. A 2005 poll found support in Arizona had grown to 66 percent as voters had become more familiar with how it worked. Connecticut legislators passed a public financing bill in 2005 after polls there found 76 percent support for the idea. Even California voters had previously supported a partial public financing system in 1988, giving 53 percent support to Prop 68. (This measure never became law because a competing measure received even more votes.)

Had the Prop 89 ballot summary read: "Reduces political contributions, provides public funds to candidates rejecting private funds, limits corporate ballot contributions," it likely would have passed. This summary is certainly as accurate as the one drafted by the attorney general, yet another reminder of the power of that office to describe ballot measures to the electorate.

Bottom Line: More Money than Ever

The 2006 election simply continued the trend of ever-increasing amounts of money in politics. While some of the recent increase at the federal level has been due to a resurgence of small donors, the same has not been true in California. Rather, the role of big donors, who are not necessarily reflective of the views of most citizens, has grown significantly.

Analysis by the California Nurses Association found that campaign funds coming from those who give $5,000 or more have gone up in California as follows:

2001	$100 million
2002	$266 million
2003	$174 million
2004	$441 million
2005	$625 million[46]

Commentator Scott Collins aptly pointed out that spending at this level is no longer about getting your own speech out so much as restricting the ability of your opponent to communicate:

> Political advertising on this scale is not even about the message anymore. It's about mass. Media strategists have spent the last five decades weaponizing TV; now it's all about employing an overwhelming force of propaganda. Trying to stomp the other side's PR during a campaign is an unstoppable spiral, an arms race with no option of détente. The high-paid strategists don't want to just run their own ads; they feel compelled to drown out the other guy's voice.[47]

Independent voter Matthew Krohn summed up his feelings about the record levels of political spending:

> It's an orgy. We're being bombarded by all sides with information that is not usually very accurate. It's not just the state elections—it starts in Washington. So much more could be done with that money.[48]

Inaugurating a New Era of Checkbook Politics

After winning re-election handily, Schwarzenegger set the tone for his new administration by throwing a series of extravagant inauguration parties financed by; you guessed it, special interests. The donor list, heavy with health care and oil interests, provided a clue that the big items on the state's agenda for 2007 would include health care reform and implementation of the greenhouse gas bill passed in 2006. Just one out of six inaugural parties was open to members of the public.

To honor Schwarzenegger, the following companies kicked in $50,000 for the bash:

Adams Steel
AT&T
E&J Gallo
California Grocers Association
California Association of Realtors
California Chamber of Commerce
Chevron
Oracle
New Majority California
PG&E

Those giving at the $15,000 level included:

21st Century Insurance
Allstate Insurance
State Farm
Pacific Life Insurance
Farmers Insurance
Mercury General (insurance)
The California Hospital Association
The California Medical Association
The Assn. of CA Life and Health Insurance Companies
The California Business Roundtable
Anheuser-Busch
ConocoPhillips
Occidental Petroleum
Sempra Energy
California Independent Petroleum Association
California State Building & Construction Trades
Cemex (cement producer)
The Irvine Company
Union Pacific Railroad
Boeing
William Robinson
California Motor Car Dealers Association

Microsoft
Comcast Cable
Time/Warner Cable
PhRMA

Cemex, a Mexican cement company, was battling with the City of Santa Clarita over a quarry it wanted to operate there. The donation to the inaugural committee came just weeks after city officials had lobbied the Schwarzenegger administration to defeat the proposal

Bob Stern characterized the Cemex donation as a simple calculation:

> They want to have good will or influence a decision. If they don't have something pending in the jurisdiction they are unlikely to contribute. It's a business decision; they have to justify it as a business decision.[49]

In total, Schwarzenegger disclosed that he had raised at least $1.4 million for the event in private donations. In comparison, Gray Davis had raised little for his second inaugural event in 2003, a folksy barbecue held just ten months before he would be recalled. People wore blue jeans. Schwarzenegger managed to swear himself in for around $200,000 right after the recall. Three years later, it was back to black ties and lobbyists. The man who had promised to sweep the special interests from Sacramento instead threw them a party.

CHAPTER 14

What Arnold's Done Right

And Others Have Done Wrong

It would be easy to read this book and conclude that Arnold Schwarzenegger has failed to live up to the promise of the recall election. He said he would sweep special interests from Sacramento. He has not. However, it would be wrong to conclude that Arnold has done nothing to try to improve California's democracy. His failed attempt to reform legislative redistricting was a noble and fair-minded effort. Likewise, it would be wrong to assume that Arnold alone is responsible for fundraising scandals. The state's biggest scandal during Arnold's first term had nothing to do with Schwarzenegger but rather dealt with a Democrat, former Secretary of State Kevin Shelley who was forced to resign in disgrace. Finally, while most legislators did not run for office on a pledge to clean up Sacramento as Schwarzenegger did, legislators of both parties failed to enact meaningful campaign finance reforms even when given opportunities to do so. Arnold surely does not deserve all of the blame for California's continued culture of corruption.

Rigged Elections

California's current political districts are the result of a dirty deal between the Democratic and Republican Parties. Political districts are redrawn every ten years, after the census, to make sure that each district has roughly the same number of voters. Democrats controlled both houses of the legislature after the

2000 census and therefore controlled the process for drawing new political lines. They had an inherent interest both as a party and as individual legislators to draw new districts that would help ensure a Democratic majority remained in the California legislature and in its congressional delegation.

Republicans, while in the minority, had two tricks up their sleeve to keep some influence over the process. First, they threatened to refer the new district lines to a voter referendum if the Democrats were too greedy and drew districts that blatantly disadvantaged Republicans. This threat, turned out to be "a bluff that we orchestrated well," according to Jim Brulte, the Assembly Republican leader at the time.[1] Evidently, the Republicans weren't really planning to spend the money on a referendum, but managed to fake it.

Second, the Republicans threatened to sue in federal court. The Federal Voting Rights Act requires that district lines be drawn in a way that doesn't artificially diminish representation of ethnic minorities. The Voting Rights Act was passed for good reason after southern states had used gerrymandering to deprive African Americans of fair representation. But, the VRA has also led to many lawsuits.

In the 1970s, courts drew California's political districts after a political impasse between the legislature and Governor Reagan. The districts drawn by the judges produced elections that resulted in significant change in the makeup of the legislature. Likewise, in 1990, a deadlock between the Democratic legislature and Republican Governor Pete Wilson resulted in retired judges drawing districts. In the 1990s, districts drawn by these "special masters" saw ten different congressional districts change party hands, as did six state senate districts and 14 state assembly districts.[2]

Faced with the chance that their district lines could be rejected in a voter referendum or tossed by the courts, the Democrats decided to cut a deal with the Republicans. Republicans used their leverage to get congressional districts that protected all but one of their incumbents. They consulted with Karl Rove in the White

House, who assured them that, "If you can deliver 19 Republican seats, we'll hold the Congress of the United States."[3] California delivered 20. Even in the watershed election of 2006, California still elected 19 Republican members of Congress—Rove lost his congressional majority elsewhere.

In return for protecting the Republican congressional delegation, Democrats were able to draw state legislative lines that protected Democrat incumbents by adding Democratic voters to their districts. The result of this bipartisan gerrymander was to preserve the status quo. Democrats gave up the opportunity to win significant gains in Congress or to get a two-thirds majority in the California legislature, but each Democrat legislator got their own career protected. This also allowed California's congressional delegation to maintain high levels of seniority, which aided these members once Democrats regained control of Congress in 2006. Republicans, in turn, basically gave up any chance to win back the state legislature. Legislators' self-interest in keeping their own districts intact overrode their party's interest in trying to pick up seats. The deal was remarkably successful. In the 2004 elections, none of the legislative or congressional seats in California changed party hands. Just one changed hands in 2006 when Congressman Richard Pombo lost his seat in an election that swept many Republicans out of office nationally.

When Schwarzenegger began talking about changing not only the process for drawing political districts but also scrapping the current districts that entrenched current incumbents safely in power, he ran up against a bipartisan buzz-saw. Democrats in the legislature had absolutely no interest. Don Perata, the Democratic leader of the Senate said, "This is a nonstarter here. . . . No one in my district gets up in the morning and makes coffee and says, 'What are we going to do with redistricting?'"[4]

Most congressional Republicans were also opposed to the idea. John Doolittle, who had been Tom DeLay's loyal lieutenant, said, "California now has more clout in the House of Representatives than at any time in previous history. It would seem to me self-defeating if we set in motion forces that could result in the loss of

[Republican] seats in California, which in conjunction with a loss of a handful of seats elsewhere in the country could spell a return to the minority for Republicans in the House. I just don't think that's a risk worth taking."[5]

Duke Cunningham, who was later convicted of accepting bribes in exchange for defense contracts, said, "We're just going to have to sort it out. I don't want to have to give up the majority in the House because we screwed up reapportionment."[6]

As it turned out, Republicans lost the majority in the House due to Cunningham's corruption, while the redistricting reform failed to pass.

Not all Republican congressmen were so self-centered. Darrell Issa who had bankrolled the recall when most of the Republican establishment still feared or dismissed it, said, "To assume that I'm the best person to draw up my congressional seat is lunacy. And it isn't better when the majority party of the legislature does it."[7] Bill Thomas, who was preparing to retire, chided incumbents of both parties by asking if they really thought that, "The only way they can stay in office is to hang on by their fingernails in a district that was gimmicked to allow them to stay in? Who would be proud to stay in a district [like that]?"[8]

Not only did Arnold take on Democrats in the California legislature and Republicans in California's congressional delegation, he lent his support to redistricting reform in Ohio. Unlike Jeb Bush, who helped raise money for Schwarzenegger's redistricting reform in California while opposing the same reform in his own state of Florida, Arnold was consistent in his support for the idea. Republicans controlled Ohio's redistricting process, so Republican politicians in Ohio opposed taking the process out of their hands and giving it to a bipartisan commission. Rising above his own party's self-interest, Schwarzenegger tape recorded a message to be left on the answering machines of Ohio voters expressing his support for a redistricting initiative on the 2005 ballot.

Schwarzenegger won the support of nonpartisan organizations CALPIRG and Common Cause for his redistricting reform efforts in California. Even though some of their members were angry with Schwarzenegger over other actions he had taken, both of these groups staunchly backed Schwarzenegger's redistricting proposal and faced tough questions for doing so.

"How could the respected good government group sign on with a governor who's been criticized for his supercharged fund-raising? Why was Common Cause embracing a plan that's picked up little or no backing from other nonprofit groups?" asked an *Associated Press* story.[9]

Chellie Pingree explained that just because Common Cause backed the governor on redistricting didn't mean they would not criticize him on other issues: "We're well-known at times for criticizing and supporting the same person on the same day. That's who we are."[10]

The League of Women Voters remained opposed to the Schwarzenegger's redistricting initiative and most of his agenda even though the League does support the concept of redistricting reform.

TheRestofUs.org joined in support of the redistricting initiative, even though we had battled Schwarzenegger's fundraising for this and other ballot proposals. Dan Weintraub, a columnist at the *Sacramento Bee*, used the support from the good government groups to debunk a misleading mailing that attacked the redistricting reform initiative as a power grab:

> The real insult is that the warning about "power-hungry politicians" was paid for by—you guessed it—power-hungry politicians, and mailed by the California Democratic Party. While Proposition 77 has been endorsed by Gov. Arnold Schwarzenegger, against the advice of many of his Republican Party colleagues, it is also backed by Common Cause, TheRestofUs.org and CALPIRG, three very independent, grass-roots groups that have been fighting for years to put the job of redistricting in the hands of an independent commission. Some power grab.[11]

Ironically, had Arnold avoided the massive fundraising and confrontational approach, he might have been more successful. If Arnold had not bundled his redistricting reform with other issues and rhetoric that was intentionally designed to stick it to Democrats and labor unions, he might have been perceived as acting more fairly by the voters.

Further, had Arnold truly gone to the people and appealed for small contributions, he might well have won. Schwarzenegger could have maintained the moral high ground and spread his message through the news media which loves to cover him rather than taking the low road of big money, expensive consultants, and glitzy TV ads that in the end dragged his special election down with them in the cesspool of big money campaigning.

Kevin Shelley

Speaking of cesspools, a book covering money in California politics in the early part of the 21st century would not be complete without mentioning Democrat Kevin Shelley. Shelley resigned as secretary of state on February 4, 2005, after a troubling series of allegations. Arnold reacted to the crisis reasonably well, although he has done nothing to prevent such an incident from happening again.

After serving as majority leader of the California Assembly, Shelley was elected secretary of state in 2002. Shelley was a man of considerable talent, experience, and most of all, ambition. By most accounts, Shelley did a highly competent job of administering the recall election in a fair and nonpartisan way. Further, he made the bold but correct move to require California's electronic voting machines to produce a paper receipt that could be used in the case of computer malfunction or for a recount in contested elections. But in the end, Shelley's blind lust for power did him in.

Stealing State Money

In August of 2004, the *San Francisco Chronicle* reported that a San

Francisco nonprofit organization, the Neighbors Resource Center, had paid several consultants and contractors significant sums of money. Those people, in turn, had donated similar amounts to Shelley's campaign for secretary of state. Shelley had received $125,000 from the following sources:

- *Eric Zhu* gave Shelley $25,000 on December 28, 2001, just weeks after he received $27,000 in "project management" fees from the Center in two payments in late 2001. Zhu told the press that he had never done any work for the Center.[12]

- *Gemini Advisors, run by Jeffery Chen,* gave Shelley $25,000 on March 5, 2002, after receiving $26,000 from the Center on February 8, 2002. Jeffrey Chen had been a financial officer for the Center.

- *Cabrillo Construction, headed by Joseph Chen,* gave Shelley $25,000 on November 1, 2002, after receiving $30,000 in "development fees" from the Center on October 30, 2002—just days before the general election. In September 2004, Chen told a grand jury that he was acting as an intermediary to pass through a campaign contribution. His lawyer claimed that Chen refused to fake an invoice for the services when the Center asked him to do so.

- *Steve Chen* gave Shelley $25,000 on December 28, 2001, after receiving $25,000 from the Center on December 1. None of the Chens are related to each other. A grand jury subpoenaed Steve Chen in September 2004 to testify about the contribution and he told them that he didn't even know who Kevin Shelley was at the time of his "contribution" and that he never did any work for the Center in return for the $25,000 it paid him.[13]

- *James Li* gave Shelley $25,000 on June 30, 2002. Days later, the Center paid him $60,750 for engineering work. Li is Joseph Chen's brother-in-law. Law enforcement officials claim that the nonprofit had faked an invoice from Li to justify the payment from the government grant.[14]

Making matters considerably worse, Shelley had earmarked a $500,000 grant for the Center from the California taxpayers while he was majority leader in the Assembly. The money was to build a community center, but construction never began. It appeared that the Center had converted money that Shelley had allocated to it right back into Shelley's campaign.

Laundering Private Money

The one thing all the fishy donations had in common was Julie Lee. Lee both founded and directed the Neighbors Resource Center. She was a close friend of Shelley's and one of his principal fundraisers. She had arranged for the $125,000 in contributions that wound up in Shelley's campaign coffers from people who supposedly did work for the Center. Lee also contributed $20,000 to Shelley herself. Beyond that, Lee appears to have given Shelley an additional $80,000 through elaborate real estate transactions where she directed buyers of her properties to make payments to Shelley instead of to her.

Patrick Hsu—On September 30, 2001, Lee instructed Hsu to write a $50,000 check to Shelley's campaign as a down payment on a property she sold him five days earlier on 25th Avenue in San Francisco.

Eliana Maldonado—She signed a statement on October 20, 2004, that she had made checks out to a realtor in a property transaction with Julie Lee, only to find out later that the realtors had "donated part of that money" to Kevin Shelley on September 27, 2002.[15] That amounted to two contributions, worth $30,000. Maldonado had purchased the house from Yei Hei Chan for $600,000, who had bought it from Lee for $550,000 that same day. When investigators in the secretary of state's office contacted Maldonado for failing to report her contribution to Shelley, she told them that she didn't even know she had made a contribution.

That investigator alerted both Kevin Shelley and the FPPC about a potential money-laundering situation. Shelley did nothing to follow up, casting serious doubt on his claims to have no reason to suspect that Lee's contributions were tainted.

California law prohibits anyone from making a contribution that hides the true source of the funds. In this case, it seemed clear that the money was coming out of Lee's pocket, but being attributed to Hsu and Maldonado. Bob Stern explained the reason for the law is that:

> The public has a right to know who is financially backing candidates prior to the time of the election. If a candidate is receiving large sums from a special-interest group, from a person who was awarded a state contract, even from a relative or the candidate herself, the public may want to take that into account before voting—or before the candidate votes or participates in an issue of particular interest to the voter or the public.[16]

Don't Ask, Don't Tell

Shelley denied any knowledge of Lee's actions and said he hadn't asked her about the donors she had recruited for him. "I didn't ask, because I trusted Julie Lee," he said. "It is not uncommon for donors in the Asian American community to be successful with friends and associates to raise significant dollars."[17]

It is hard to believe Shelley's claim of ignorance. Consider:

- Lee had personally handed many of these checks to Kevin Shelley. He absolutely knew about them and had the opportunity to ask Lee where they came from.

- Many of these checks were the largest contributions Shelley had received from an individual at the time. The $50,000 from Hsu was the largest individual contribution Shelley had ever received, other than a $200,000 loan that came late in the campaign. Shelley claimed he had never spoken with Hsu, not even to thank him for the contribution.

- Shelley was known to be a hands-on fundraiser. Every politician takes care to personally thank major donors and establish a relationship with them so they'll give again. It's incredibly hard to imagine that a prolific fundraiser like Shelley wouldn't have tried to contact these donors to personally thank them unless Lee gave him some reason not to.

- Campaigns routinely check the background of large donors. Julie Sandimo, who did fundraising for Shelley said that this was standard practice on the campaign, "especially if we don't know them. Obviously, we're going to say, 'Where did this come from?' There's a vetting process: Who sent this check? What was the amount? Are they a U.S. citizen? You have to do a vetting process. That is normal. There definitely would have been more scrutiny under that time period for that vetting process."[18]

As the *San Francisco Chronicle* editorialized, "It almost takes a suspension of disbelief to think that a politician of Shelley's seasoning would not want to know why some people he did not know—and had no obvious stake in the outcome of the statewide race—would be making big donations."[19]

One final suspicious circumstance around the Lee contributions was the fact that Kevin Shelley hired Julie's son, Andrew Lee, to work in the secretary of state's office shortly after he was elected. The job paid nearly $58,000 a year. Andrew Lee didn't necessarily have the strongest resume. He'd made a go of a career as a rap music star, only to see that fizzle. His mother decided that politics would be a good career and groomed him for a campaign by giving an unpaid position at—surprise—the Neighbors Resource Center. Lee ran for the San Francisco Board of Supervisors in 2002 with the backing of his mother and her friends Mayor Willie Brown and Kevin Shelley. Even that race was tainted with allegations that Lee used a public giveaway of high-efficiency light bulbs that was sponsored by his mother's nonprofit and Mayor Willie Brown during the peak of the electricity crisis to improperly support his candidacy. Andrew Lee spent $184,000 of his own money on the race. He finished fourth.

The secretary of state's office accepted applications for the position that Kevin Shelley hired Andrew Lee for only from 8 a.m. to 2 p.m. on the Wednesday before Thanksgiving. The hiring looked a lot more like a favor to Julie Lee than a careful and exhaustive search to find the most qualified candidate for the job.

An Election Won With Illegal Funds

Even if Shelley did not know about Lee's illicit activities, it is undisputable that they helped him win his race. Shelley was running against the popular former Secretary of State March Fong Eu and personally wealthy Michaela Alioto in the 2002 Democratic primary for the secretary of state. A month prior to the election, a Field Poll showed Shelley in third place. But that was before he turned on the gushers of campaign cash.

Shelley raised a total of $3.5 million for both his primary and general campaigns. He raised some $1.5 million before the primary, including the Lee-laundered contributions from Patrick Hsu, Steven Chen, and Eric Zhu. March Fong Eu, on the other hand, raised only $368,566 for her campaign. In the Democratic primary, Shelley defeated Eu by only 140,379 votes after out-raising her by more than four to one. At least $100,000 of Shelley's illegal funds came before the primary.

In the general election, Shelley defeated Republican Keith Olberg by 286,294 votes after spending twice as much as Olberg. It is distinctly possible that had Shelley not received the $205,000 in illegal contributions through Julie Lee, that he would never have been elected as secretary of state.

Money isn't everything in winning elections, but it's close. In the 2002 election cycle, the candidate who spent the most money won 97 percent of state races.

HAVA Lotta Money?

Once in office, Shelley continued a pattern of behavior that suggested he was abusing government resources for his own personal political advantage. In September 2004, newspapers broke the story that Shelley had used federal taxpayer funds allocated to California through the Help America Vote Act to pay a multitude of Democratic operatives. Three quarters of the consultants that Shelley hired with HAVA funds were tied to the Democratic Party or other left-leaning organizations, including:

- Eric Jaye, who had worked on Shelley's 2002 campaign, received a no-bid contract worth $49,000. Jaye never billed the state for the work and wasn't paid. He did create a voter turnout website, which featured a big photo of Shelley, but volunteered his time for this.

- Renne Holtzman, wife of the treasurer to Shelley's campaign, received a no-bid contract for $70,000.

- Clark Lee received $45,750 for two contracts. Lee was a member of the California Democratic Party's executive committee and worked on the campaign to oppose the Gray Davis recall.

- Jay Hansen lobbies for the State Building and Construction Trades Council, which had directed $60,000 in contributions to Shelley. He got HAVA contracts for $13,250.

- Jason Vega attended a John Kerry presidential fundraiser hosted by Eleni Tsakopoulos-Kounalakis as a HAVA consultant for Kevin Shelley. Vega had previously served as the deputy director for the 2003 inaugural committee for Gray Davis. He had a HAVA contract for $8,000. Tony Miller, who served as special counsel to the secretary of state's office after the HAVA scandal broke, said that Vega's work activity report ". . . doesn't look good. It is hard to justify when you see something like this submitted."

- David Yaroslavsky received a HAVA contract for $25,000 and used the money in part to attend a California Democratic Party fundraiser, a use clearly not permitted by HAVA. He also did "vital" voter outreach work like presenting the French Foreign Consul with a plaque from Kevin Shelley on Bastille Day. In his work report to justify the state money he'd earned, he reported, "it was a very enjoyable soiree."[20]

Arnold Schwarzenegger handled Shelley's HAVA scandal reasonably well. While the California Republican Assembly called for Shelley's resignation early on, Schwarzenegger largely stayed out of the issue. He did take steps to freeze some of the HAVA funds that were under Shelley's control until he could be assured that they were being spent responsibly. This move irked some county clerks who were eager for the money, but in the end proved a responsible course of action.

The California state auditor conducted a thorough investigation of the funds spent by the secretary of state's office under the Help America Vote Act. That audit concluded that:

> Because the office disregarded controls and exercised poor oversight of staff and consultants, its use of HAVA discretionary funds to pay for activities unrelated to HAVA led to questions about the improper use of these funds. Also, the office failed to document the time spent by its staff members on HAVA activities, as required when salaries and wages are charged to a federal fund source. Staff activity reports submitted by two of the employees we reviewed, as well as 62 of the 169 staff activity reports submitted by regional outreach consultants, reported attendance at events—some of which were partisan in nature—that appear to be unrelated to HAVA purposes. Finally, a law firm retained to provide legal advice on issues related to HAVA performed unrelated work such as writing

> speeches for the secretary of state that had little if anything to do with HAVA and also invoiced and was paid for services that did not conform with the terms of its contract.[21]

In 2006, the federal Elections Administration Commission ruled that California must repay its own election administration fund $2.4 million and the federal government another half million in funds that were mismanaged by Shelley's administration.

Office Politics

We've all heard of the phrase "office politics," but Shelley gave the words a whole new meaning by abusing his taxpayer-financed state office and staff to support his re-election campaign.

Shelley's most blatant abuse was accepting a $2,000 check from Suresh Patel in his official secretary of state office. Patel is a hotel owner from Santa Cruz who had a run-in with the tax collector. After one of Patel's employees filed an expensive worker's compensation claim, the state had assessed Patel $97,296 for the claim.[22] When he refused to pay it, the Department of Revenue was looking to put a lien on his property. Patel stopped in to talk with Kevin Shelley about it, and to give him a campaign contribution that he had promised earlier but never sent in. He recounted the interaction like this: "I think I probably went in there and said, 'Here's the check that I promised you on your campaign donation,' and then we sat down and we talked about the tax issue."[23]

Shelley chatted with Patel for about ten minutes and then asked his staff to leave the room. Five minutes later, Patel left, and Shelley waved the check in his hand while bragging about his fundraising ability. According to a Shelley's deputy at the time, "He was gloating about the money that he got from the guy. The first thing he did was gloat. He held up the check and handed it to [his staff] for processing."

California law expressly prohibits accepting campaign contributions on state property. Bob Stern of the Center for

Governmental Studies noted, "You'd think the secretary of state, of all elected officials, would know these rules. . . . This is exactly what this is designed to stop—someone coming in, asking for a favor and giving a check at the same time. It's like being paid to do a governmental function."[24]

Shelley also reportedly had a habit of asking his state employees to do campaign work. Shelley allegedly fired Bryson Roberts after he refused to stuff envelopes and make fundraising calls for Shelley's campaign while on government payroll.[25]

Slow Rolling Wheels of Justice

By December 2004, Kevin Shelley was under investigation by no less than eight law enforcement agencies, including the FBI and the state attorney general. Yet criminal investigations can take a long time. The burden of proof for sending someone to prison is justifiably high, and prosecutors often need to build a case against high-ranking officials by first going after low-level scoundrels who will then provide evidence in return for more lenient sentences. Julie Lee was only indicted on April 7, 2005, for her role in stealing state money to funnel into Shelley's campaign.

All too often, politicians pretend that the standard for holding elected office should be the same standard for staying out of prison—innocent until found guilty by a jury of your peers. Even as allegations mounted against Kevin Shelley, one Democratic lawmaker said, "Some of us think we ought to keep our mouths shut until the half-dozen investigations come to a conclusion."[26]

But voters should hardly have to wait until a politician is in jail before replacing someone of questionable character with a more honest public servant. By fall of 2004, TheRestofUs.org was suggesting a campaign to recall Shelley. The *Sacramento Bee* editorialized on September 2, 2004, that Shelley should not resign, only to reverse itself weeks later, saying:

> As the state official in charge of elections, Shelley bears a particular responsibility to safeguard the

> public's trust in democracy. He clearly has shirked that responsibility and eroded that trust. . . . Shelley should resign immediately. If he does not resign, the legislature should call a special session and begin impeachment proceedings.[27]

Resignation is in many ways an unsatisfactory resolution to political scandal. The only good thing is that it removes a questionable politician from office quickly. But the downside is that the public never gets to hear the full charges and evidence against the alleged wrongdoer. That is exactly what happened in Shelley's case.

A Timid Watchdog

The Joint Legislative Audit Committee (JLAC) is the primary tool that the California legislature uses to investigate alleged wrongdoing by officeholders. The JLAC had aggressively pursued allegations of Insurance Commissioner Chuck Quackenbush's abuses in the insurance scandal that led to his resignation in 2000. The committee had also done a good job of investigating the dubious no-bid contract that the Davis administration had granted to Oracle. But Assembly Speaker Fabian Núñez had refused to re-appoint Dean Florez, the legislator who chaired the audit committee during the Oracle investigation. Florez called the move to keep him off the watchdog committee, "very disconcerting."[28]

Nicole Parra, the new chair of the Joint Legislative Audit Committee took her time in investigating Kevin Shelley. She scheduled a hearing on January 11, 2005, but after initially announcing she would require Shelley to testify, she allowed him to send a representative in his stead.

Shelley began a bizarre public negotiation with the Democrats who controlled the legislature by openly musing that he might resign. That would allow Arnold Schwarzenegger to appoint a Republican replacement, something the Democrats wanted to avoid. Democratic leaders probably wanted to have Shelley stay in office but announce he would not run for re-election, thus preserving the chance that the office would remain in Democratic control. By threatening to quit, Shelley was calling their bluff as to whether they would really investigate him.

In response to Shelley's Hamlet-like statements on resignation, Nicole Parra announced that she would require Shelley to testify, but would limit the scope of the testimony to Shelley's use of HAVA funds. While there were certainly improprieties there, they were less likely to involve impeachable offenses. The campaign finance laundering and use of state property and workers for his own campaign fundraising were far more serious charges.

Parra and the Democrats in the legislature may have wanted to avoid discussing campaign money laundering in their investigation of Shelley because they thought that other politicians had engaged in the same thing. After all, people who live in glass houses ought not to throw stones.

When questioned about a potential agreement to limit the scope of the JLAC investigation, Republican Assemblyman Greg Aghazarian said, "I would be troubled if that were the fact. We shouldn't be having these backroom deals and hiding the people's business from California."[29] But secretly, many Republicans may have felt it was helpful to have Shelley stay in office over a long drawn-out scandal that would keep Democrats in the news for doing bad things over many months.

On January 26, 2005, the day that Parra announced the diminished scope of the JLAC hearing, Shelley dropped his talk of resignation. His spokesman relayed that Shelley, ". . . said there's much work to be done in his office and he plans to carry out his duties. He seems to be in a very work-oriented mood."[30]

But in the end, the ongoing scrutiny must have taken its toll. Late in the day on Friday, February 4, 2005, Kevin Shelley announced he was resigning from office. Earlier that day, Assembly Leader Núñez had announced that JLAC would not require Shelley to testify if he resigned. When he did, they dropped their investigation.

To replace Shelley, many called on Schwarzenegger to

appoint a caretaker candidate. Someone who would serve out the remainder of Shelley's term but agree not to run for re-election. Former Republican Senator Ross Johnson was often mentioned. While this would have been a truly classy and nonpartisan move, Arnold could also have appointed a rabid Republican and forced the legislature to either reject him and look partisan or swallow the decision and face a Republican ideologue, who would then be poised to run for higher office.

Schwarzenegger took a middle route and appointed Bruce McPherson, a moderate Republican senator from Santa Cruz. Many observers on both sides of the aisle agreed that McPherson did his job admirably. McPherson avoided endorsing candidates or ballot measures while serving as secretary of state to ensure that the office remains nonpartisan. In the end though, voters decided they wanted someone other than Arnold's choice for the position, choosing Democrat Debra Bowen to replace him in the 2006 election.

Perhaps remembering the suggestions he received to fill the Shelley vacancy, Schwarzenegger appointed Ross Johnson to chair the California Fair Political Practices Commission in 2007.

In the first five years of the 21st century, California saw two statewide officials resign due to money in politics scandals: a Republican (Chuck Quackenbush) and a Democrat (Kevin Shelley). The state has recalled a governor, Gray Davis, for the first time in its history. Given those remarkable, and sad, events, you would think that politicians of both parties would realize that something is seriously wrong and take steps to correct it. You would be wrong.

Arnold should get at least partial credit for talking the talk on campaign finance reform. One of his early promises upon taking office was to push a reform measure that would ban politicians from raising funds while they were working on the state budget. This is a pretty measly reform that is easily circumvented by having big donors simply write checks before and after budget season. But even if his solution was half-baked, Arnold was at least admitting that there was a problem with money in politics. That's more than

Gray Davis ever did.

More significantly, after having his hat handed to him in the special election, Arnold made broader statements about the role of campaign cash beyond influencing the budget process. Schwarzenegger told columnist George Skelton that in private discussions with Common Cause President Chellie Pingree over the redistricting proposal on the ballot, he committed to taking a serious look at campaign finance reform. "The way [campaign financing] is going, it has become like a circus. The ones benefiting from it are the television stations. Look at the amount of money they are making right now," said Arnold.

When asked if he would consider Pingree's favorite reform, a system of full public financing of campaigns based on a successful system in her home state of Maine, Schwarzenegger replied, "Absolutely. Whenever you open up a can of worms, you've got to let everything come in. Every idea. We'll have those debates and then put an initiative on the ballot if the legislators don't want to vote for it."[31]

His staff followed up on the commitment with substantial conversations with reform proponents. Despite this, Schwarzenegger opposed Prop 89, the one true campaign finance proposal on the ballot during his first term. He also steered clear of more modest public financing proposals put forth in the legislature by Assemblywoman Loni Hancock. While he has yet to embrace any form of comprehensive campaign finance reform, Arnold has at least shown a willingness to consider it. Again, that's more than you can say about Davis.

While Arnold certainly didn't champion campaign finance reform, the same was true of the Democratic California Senate. After the courts said that the Fair Political Practices Commission did not have authority to limit the money that Arnold and other candidates could raise for ballot committees they controlled, Assemblymember Lois Wolk introduced a bill to enact a $5,600 contribution limit on all candidate-controlled ballot committees. The Assembly passed that bill by a vote of 43 to 29, with all but one Republican voting against it. But when it moved over to the

Senate, the elections committee killed the reform by a vote of one to three (two Republicans, one Democrat), with two abstentions (both Democrats). Democrat Debra Bowen (since elected to be Secretary of State) was the lone supporter. The Democrats in the legislature were happy to criticize Arnold for his special election fundraising, but when it came time to do something about it, they balked.

Likewise, after Arnold's conflict of interest with the body-building magazines and his veto of the dietary supplement bill, Senator Jackie Speier vowed to introduce legislation that would ban both legislators and statewide officials from earning outside income. After all, taxpayers shell out six figure salaries to state legislators; you'd think for that kind of money we could have them working exclusively for us. Unfortunately, the idea went nowhere.

Senate President Don Perata even introduced legislation to weaken oversight of campaign finance violations. His bill would have made it harder for investigators to use letters from donors that come with political contributions as evidence. For instance, if a donor included a letter that said "good luck in your re-election," but the politician deposited the check in an account to pay off a past campaign debt instead of for a re-election campaign, the Fair Political Practices Commission could not use the letter as evidence of the donor's intent. The commission's director said, "It gives us great unease that they would be shifting the rules for enforcement cases in legislation at all."[32]

In 2004, the FBI confirmed that it was investigating Perata's campaign financing, including his campaign's ties to his son. Campaign accounts controlled by Perata contracted with Exit Strategies, a consulting firm run by his son, for more than $743,000 from 1999 to 2004. During that time, his son's firm paid Perata more than $138,000 for "rent" and "consulting fees."[33] Perata also received payments in excess of $100,000 in consulting fees from his friend Timothy Staples while at the same time helping some of Staples's clients in the legislature. The FBI is also investigating lobbyist Lily Hu to see if she illegally funneled payments to Perata. Perata has raised nearly $1 million in unlimited donations to pay high priced lawyers to defend him.

Things began looking up in the legislature in early 2006. After seeing the public opinion beating that Arnold took over big money in the special election, suddenly legislators saw an opening to make themselves look good in comparison. In that backhanded way, Arnold has indeed spurred the reform movement in California, because suddenly Democrats favored reform after years of stonewalling it. In January 2006, the Assembly passed a bill to provide full public financing for state campaigns by a vote of 47–31. The bill did not make it out of Don Perata's Senate, but the California Nurses Association adopted and strengthened the idea and qualified it for the November 2006 ballot as a citizen initiative.

Further, Arnold's failed attempt to enact redistricting reform on the November 2005 ballot spurred earnest legislative negotiations in 2006 and 2007. Arnold remained in the background, rather than grandstanding or trying to bully the legislature. It remains to be seen if real redistricting reform will come to California, but Arnold has made a good faith effort to help this happen. That's a big deal.

CHAPTER 15

Ideas for Improvement

A Citizen's Guide for Taking Back Democracy

Let's face it; what's going on with our democracy can be downright depressing. If you've made it to the end of this book, you are probably wondering why you should even bother thinking about the role of big money in politics, when it seems like there's nothing that you can really do about it. Politicians, and the powerful interests that back them, always resist reforms that would take away some of their power and give it back to the people. When citizens are able to push for modest improvements, the courts reject them, or politicians find ways around them. When that fails, they repeal the reforms when nobody's watching.

But, the fact of the matter is that as a citizen of the United States of America, you have a vested stake in getting this stuff fixed. If we cop out and refuse to take on the challenge of making government more accountable, then we can expect the government to keep responding to wealthy private interests and screwing the rest of us every chance they get. We may never get all the big money out of politics, but we may never eliminate gang violence, terrorism, or global warming either. But that doesn't mean we can not, or should not, take steps to reduce these problems.

What's more, as a citizen of the United States of America, there are a lot of things you *can* do individually, and, more important, that we can all do together, to reduce the role of big money in politics. Here are a few ideas:

Vote

There's a bumper sticker floating around out there that says, "Don't vote, it only encourages them." In fact, just the opposite is true. Political consultants have made entire careers out of figuring out how to run campaigns where the primary purpose is to discourage people from voting. If reasonable people get fed up with all the mudslinging and attack ads, it means that only the ideological zealots turn out to vote. That's exactly what the consultants want to happen. Smaller voter turnout makes it easier for them to manipulate the outcome.

Many people don't vote because they want to send a message to all the politicians that they are disgusted with the whole thing and want nothing to do with it. As I quoted retired biology professor Emil Bernstein in chapter 1, sometimes citizens even call for a voter boycott. A better way to send a message to the politicians would be to show up at the polls and cast a blank ballot. Alternatively, you can vote for some races where there is a candidate you support, vote on the ballot measures, but leave blank the races where you think both candidates are standing up for special interests instead of you. Some people also cast protest votes by supporting minor party candidates, writing in the name of a candidate they would support, or even writing in "None of the Above." All of these choices are perfectly legal, although in most states election officials are not required to count these votes unless someone has registered as a write-in candidate. (Nevada requires a tallying of votes for None of the Above.) These protest votes could send a much stronger message than simply staying home, which is what they want you to do. The 2006 California primary election saw a record low turnout of 28 percent.[1] Governor Schwarzenegger had no serious competition in the primary and voters were not enthused about either Phil Angelides or Steve Westly on the Democratic side. Imagine the statement it would have sent if 56 percent of voters turned out, with 28 percent voting for a candidate and the other half casting a protest ballot rather than staying home.

Many voters feel like they don't know enough about the

candidates to be able to choose between them, but one piece of information we do have about most candidates is their party. Political parties don't stand for as much as they used to, but they can still give the voter a basic sense of what a candidate's values and positions are. When there are a lot of candidates on the ballot, relying upon a candidate's party is a reasonable step for a voter to take. Our elected representatives do this all the time when they are called to vote for measures in the legislature. When a given member of the legislature hasn't read a bill that's up for a vote, they look for advice from people they trust, including their political party. Voters can do the same thing.

Ignore the Ads

One big mistake is to rely upon candidates' own ads as the primary source of information about how to vote. You wouldn't buy a car just because you saw a TV ad that showed it looking really cool driving down a desert racetrack followed by the fine print, "Done by a professional driver only on a closed course. Do not try this at home." Instead, you might go read a review in *Car and Driver* magazine or *Consumer Reports*. Almost certainly, you'd go test-drive it for yourself, or ask someone who owns the same model, rather than taking the company's word for how great their car is. The last person you'd trust as a source of information would be the salesman at the dealership who you know perfectly well has a self-interest in giving you biased information.

Likewise, why would we vote based primarily on what politicians tell us, when we know full well that they'll tell us anything just to get elected?

When it comes to information, whether it's about candidates or cars, we should all remember one simple fact: you get what you pay for. If someone is paying to put on an ad that you watch for free, keep in mind that the information is more for their benefit than yours. But, if you're seeking out the information through buying a magazine or a newspaper, you're probably getting more reliable facts.

So, the first rule is to ignore all the ads. Use TiVo or a digital video recorder to screen out all the commercials when you watch TV. Or better yet, when you encounter a political ad, turn off the TV or radio. The broadcasters will eventually figure out that they are losing ratings when they sell all those crummy attack ads.

Especially ignore any postcards that come in the mail that include a list (or slate) of paid endorsements from a group you aren't familiar with. Like the mailers done by the Democrats who opposed redistricting (outlined in chapter 14) or the mailer that helped elect a bagel shop owner to be a judge (chapter 13), these are usually done with the clear intent of confusing you by including some endorsements of candidates that are of the same party you are. That way, you wind up thinking, "people like me oppose ballot measure XX." In California, paid endorsements on slate mailers must be marked with a little asterisk. Look for that, and the minute you see it toss the whole thing in the recycling bin. The more people toss this junk, the less likely we'll keep seeing it. Candidates will eventually have to go back to honest campaigning.

Of course, nobody can completely ignore all the ads. Advertising experts who sell everything from soda to politicians have figured out ways to subliminally break into our brains even when they know we're trying to keep them out. Especially with negative ads, these pitchmen know that if they can repeat an attack enough times, it begins to sound like the truth. The best defense against these shysters is the minute you hear an ad trashing a candidate, especially if it's accompanied by the grainy looking black and white photos and the eerie music in the background, go immediately to the website of the candidate being trashed. In this day and age, most rapid-response campaigns will have already posted a rebuttal to the sleazy attack and you'll at least be able to hear both sides before you make your decision.

Get Your Own Sources of Information

Rather than relying upon candidate ads, voters can go on the offensive and look for information ourselves. One source, of course, is candidate websites. Here, you're still getting biased information, of course, but by going to all the candidates' websites you can reduce the unfair advantage that candidates with the deep pockets have by giving them all a fair shot to tell you what they stand for. Increasingly, even candidates who refuse to take big checks can get their message out to voters through the Internet, but that only works if we give them a chance by visiting their websites.

Voter guides are another great source of information. California and a handful of other states allow candidates to purchase space in the official voter guide that is sent to each household. Ideally, candidates would be able to submit 500-word statements for free. Again, you are still getting your information straight from the horse's mouth, but at least all candidates are competing for your vote on a level playing ground. If you live in a state that does not provide candidate statements in the voter guide, this is an easy thing to push a secretary of state to start including. Many newspapers also compile voter guides that contain statements from all the candidates, so look for that in your local paper or on its website. Project Vote Smart, a nonprofit and nonpartisan organization, also compiles voter guides based on the responses that candidates submit on questionnaires. Check out www.vote-smart.org.

Newspapers and magazines generally are better sources of information than candidates themselves. Yes, all newspapers have a bias, but if you read them regularly you probably know what their bias is and whether or not you agree with it. You might decide to vote the opposite way from your local paper's endorsement, but even there you've learned something. The fact that you are paying 50 cents for the paper means it's probably higher quality information than an ad that someone else is paying for you to see.

Likewise, you can subscribe to alternative newspapers or websites or join ideological organizations with values similar to yours and look for their endorsements to guide you in voting. As a member, you're paying them to provide you with information, so they're more likely to be accountable to you and other members. This only goes for membership-supported organizations, of course.

Be on the lookout for front groups that claim to be "citizens for good government," or a "coalition of smart people, heros, and business leaders" but are really funded by corporations or a handful of fat cats.

Watch Debates—and Punish No-Shows

Perhaps the best source of information about a candidate comes from a debate. This is the one forum where they cannot control everything that is said and they have to deal with questions from a moderator or their opponent(s) that they've been ignoring for the whole campaign. Most incumbents and front-runners avoid debates like the plague, precisely because they're the best way for voters to learn what they're really about.

When the front-runner refuses to debate, TV stations then refuse to cover the event and the whole thing fizzles. But it's time that stations and voters started standing up to this nonsense. If a candidate doesn't have the guts to defend their actions in an honest debate with their opponents, what right do they have to represent us in office? Just like they did in the recall, TV and radio stations should decide to cover debates even if the front-runner refuses to show up. Viewers should reward the stations by tuning in. Then, voters can punish candidates who duck debates by refusing to support them on Election Day.

Ask a Friend

Most people don't have as much time as they would like to follow politics. Between getting the kids to bed, paying the bills, and keeping the lawn mowed, who has time to go out and research all the candidates? But most of us also know at least one person who follows politics the way most people follow sports. They check all the political blogs to get the low-down on everyone running for every office, from president to dogcatcher.

Since you know them, they're usually a trustworthier source

of information than any ad, newspaper, or voter guide you'll every run across. As you're looking at your sample ballot, give them a call. By relying upon each other for voting information rather than the politicians, we can start taking back our government.

Give Money!

It sounds crazy, but one of the best things you can do to get big money out of politics is to put some of your own money into politics through making small contributions to candidates you support. The best candidates out there are the ones who have the guts to stand up to powerful interests, but of course those folks aren't going to raise much money from the fat cats for their campaigns. That's where the rest of us skinny cats have to step up to the plate to give them a fighting chance. I know it doesn't seem like much, but scraping together a $10 or $25 contribution to give to a candidate you really believe in can make a big difference, especially if we all do it. Even with the decks stacked against them, small donors gave significant boosts to the presidential campaigns of John McCain in 2000 and Howard Dean in 2004. Small donors can play an even bigger role in local campaigns.

Write Letters

Politicians may listen more to the powerful interests that fund their campaigns, but that doesn't mean they won't listen at all to the rest of us. Most folks are so discouraged that they don't even bother contacting their elected officials any more. But for that reason, many officials, especially state legislators, don't get much mail. Even one or two personal letters written with conviction can make an impression. Better yet, send a letter to the editor of your local paper. Politicians have staff people who diligently clip letters to the editor for their bosses to read regularly. Let the politicians know when you are upset with their individual behavior. But also let them know about the need to push for comprehensive reform.

Promote Systemic Reform

Beyond these simple steps that we all can take as individuals, there are a lot of reforms that we can push for that would make it harder, but not impossible, for the big money boys to buy our election results. Just like we lock our doors when we go out to make it harder, but not impossible, for someone to break into our house, these are common sense reforms that we should be pushing for. If you live in a state like California, which has a citizen initiative process, you could support organizations that push for changes directly on the ballot through the initiative process. But what reforms should we push for?

Campaign Spending Limits

Gray Davis might never have devolved into such a money-grubbing pig if he hadn't been constantly worried about being outspent in a political campaign by someone like multi-millionaire Al Checchi. If we want campaigns to be contests of ideas instead of dollars, the best thing to do would be to set a limit on how much each candidate can spend and then let the best man or woman win. That way, the candidates who stand up to special interests wouldn't be outspent by a four- or five-to-one ratio by the candidates who are groomed for office by the fat cats.

A recent poll found that 87 percent of Americans support this basic idea of spending limits to promote fairness in campaigns.[2] Unfortunately, the United States Supreme Court does not. The Court struck down a mandatory spending limit that Congress had passed in the wake of the Watergate scandal that led to Richard Nixon's resignation. Although they didn't have the decency to sign their names to the decision, a majority of justices argued, in the case *Buckley v. Valeo,* that spending money on campaign ads is the same thing as free speech. That's rubbish of course. Supreme Court justices are, after all, politically appointed. What they are really saying is that powerful interests with enough money to buy speech get to talk and the rest of us get to shut up and listen.

This isn't the first time the courts got something wrong. Over history, the Supreme Court has upheld slavery, rejected women's right to vote, thrown out the minimum wage, and ruled that a tax on voting was constitutional. Eventually, when people stand up and refuse to accept this nonsense, the Court backs down. Sometimes it takes a constitutional amendment to set things straight, as in the case of the 19th amendment that gave women the right to vote and the 24th amendment that banned the poll tax.

In 1997, the Vermont legislature decided to challenge the Supreme Court's ruling by passing a law with mandatory campaign spending limits. Lower courts upheld the concept of spending limits and sent the case to the Supreme Court to review. In June 2006, the Court rejected Vermont's law in a splintered opinion. Three justices (Ginsberg, Souter, Stevens) held that both spending limits and contribution limits should be constitutional. Three justices (Kennedy, Scalia, Thomas) held that neither should be constitutional. The other three took a middle position, saying that precedent dictated that no spending limits would be upheld by the current Court and that even some contribution limits would be struck down. You might have thought that given the difficulty the justices had agreeing among themselves about what the Constitution says, they would have deferred out of judicial modesty to the State of Vermont to try things its own way. You'd have been wrong.

In May 2006, Duf Sundheim, then chair of the California Republican Party, suggested a United States constitutional amendment to overrule the courts and allow mandatory campaign spending limits and limits on candidates using their own personal wealth to overwhelm their opponents. Senator Arlen Specter of Pennsylvania has introduced such an amendment many times in the U.S. Congress. Former Senators Bill Bradley and Fritz Hollings pushed for campaign spending amendments to the Constitution when they were in office. Given the Supreme Court's continued intransigence, perhaps the time has come to take these men up on their suggestions.

Until we either knock some sense into the U.S. Supreme Court or pass a constitutional amendment, there are two things we can do to reduce the role of big bucks in campaigns. We can put limits on the money that candidates can raise from each donor, even if not setting upper bounds on what they can spend, and we can provide candidates who want to abide by spending limits with a way to compete with those who don't through a system of public financing of campaigns.

Contribution Limits

The courts have ruled that we can pass laws that limit both the amount and the source of contributions raised by candidates, parties, and political action committees. As of 2006, 37 states set some sort of limit on contributions by individuals to candidates. If we set contribution limits low enough, candidates who rely on $10 and $25 contributions from a large number of ordinary citizens can compete with those who cater to the small number of citizens who typically give $500 and more. How many of us can give the current limit of $22,300 to a candidate running for governor of California or even $2,200 to a presidential candidate? Most of us can't give anywhere close to these amounts.

Had California established low limits on campaign contributions, Arianna Huffington and Tom McClintock would have raised more from their donors than Arnold Schwarzenegger or Cruz Bustamante during the recall campaign. The playing field would have been more level and, to the extent that one candidate had more money, it would truly be because they had more public support. But setting high contribution limits, like California does, still gives candidates who can score the backing of a handful of wealthy donors more influence than those who go out and really generate public support. Candidates like Tom McClintock and Arianna Huffington might have more supporters than candidates like Bustamante and Schwarzenegger, but under high contribution limits, these grassroots candidates will continue to be blown away by big money interests.

Banning Corporate Contributions

One of the oldest types of campaign finance reform is to ban corporations from making political contributions from their shareholder funds. The federal government did this in 1907 and many states have also banned direct corporate contributions. California has not. The U.S. Supreme Court has upheld this campaign restriction because corporate treasuries are amassed with the aid of favorable state laws and have little or no correlation to the public's support for the corporation's political ideas.[3]

Some people think that when we ban corporate contributions, we ought to also ban contributions from labor unions. Federal law bans both corporate and labor union contributions to candidates and parties. But the Supreme Court has said that "the funds available for a union's political activities more accurately reflect members' support for the organization's political views than does a corporation's general treasury" because workers can decide not to contribute dues to a labor union's political activities. While there's plenty of evidence that unions outspend consumer, taxpayer, and environmental interests in California and elsewhere, it's simply not the case that labor gives anywhere near what corporations do.

Of course, people who support corporate ideology are still free to express their political opinions just like the rest of us. They can form a political committee and fund it with their own dollars, not their customers' dollars. This helps ensure that the money spent on politics truly represents the beliefs of those spending it. When I fill up with a tank of gas at Chevron, for instance, I have no intention of supporting Chevron/Texaco's candidate for governor. But unless we ban corporate contributions, Chevron/Texaco can take part of the money it gets from my gas purchase and give it to a candidate or political party. Stopping this is a no-brainer. Banning corporate treasury contributions does not ban the people of a corporation from supporting pro-corporate candidates, but it would create a more fair balance between corporate, labor, and other interests.

Reining in the Millionaire Candidates

The problem with only limiting contribution sizes and banning corporate contributions is that it makes it easier for a personally rich candidate to dramatically outgun a candidate who has to go out and raise every dollar from someone else. California saw millionaire candidates even before there were contribution limits. Remember Al Checchi and Jane Harmon?

But, it was easier for the Gray Davis type candidates to compete against them when California had no contribution limits. The 2006 Democratic primary race for governor was between two millionaires, Steve Westly and Phil Angelides. Westly put more than $35 million of his own money into funding his failed attempt to win the Democratic nomination. Phil Angelides beat him with the help of a $10 million independent expenditure by his friend and business partner, developer Angelo Tsakopoulos, and Angelo's daughter Eleni. By prohibiting spending limits, the Supreme Court has forced us to pick one of two choices: either we accept a system of contribution limits where millionaires have an unfair advantage in their own campaigns or we accept a system with no limits where millionaires can buy campaigns for their friends.

Some choice.

But, given the predicament, there are good reasons to choose a system that makes it easier for millionaires to run themselves, and harder for them to buy elections for their buddies.

Millionaires don't always make the best candidates. Remember Bill Simon and Al Checci? And independent expenditures don't always help a candidate nearly as much as money that the candidate can control.

This means that a millionaire's money isn't usually as effectively spent on their own campaign or on an independent expenditure as it would be if they gave it to some career politician who shared their political agenda. In addition, when candidates entirely fund their own campaigns, at least they aren't beholden to anyone else. Unfortunately, what we have right now in California, and most states, is a system that both allows millionaires to spend wads of money on their own campaigns (witness Steve Westly and Steve Poizner) *and* turn around and raise huge amounts from private interests (witness Arnold Schwarzenegger and Phil Angelides).

Voters in Oregon enacted a ballot initiative in November 2006 that sets limits on the amount of money that any candidate can spend on their own campaign. The law is facing battles in the Oregon courts. This may be an opportunity for the Supreme Court to revisit its past mistakes and get it right this time. Other states should do the same thing, even if judges resist. Eventually, courts will get the point.

Public Financing of Campaigns

The first time I heard this idea, I thought it was crazy. The gist of it is to give politicians our hard earned tax dollars to run their campaigns. Huh?

Turns out, it makes a lot of sense—if it's done right. Citizens in Arizona and Maine have blazed the trail with an innovative reform idea that they call clean money. Qualified candidates who voluntarily agree to go cold turkey on taking private contributions get a lump sum of cash from the government to run their campaign. Non-serious candidates, like the stripper Mary Carey in the California recall, and extremists have a hard time qualifying because it takes more than signatures on a petition to qualify for clean money. Candidates have to go ask hundreds, sometimes thousands, of constituents to give them $5. That demonstrates that they have enough real support to participate in the clean money program.

If another candidate rejects the clean money system and tries to outspend somebody who is playing by the rules, the clean candidate gets additional funds from the government to match the spending of their opponent. While this doesn't get rid of the unnecessary attack ads, it at least gives each side the opportunity to respond.

George Steffes, who has been lobbying for business interests in Sacramento for nearly 40 years, explained why he has come to believe in public financing of campaigns:

> The thing that really changed me was that I grew up in a system where constituents supported the candidate. I was always for private financing because it was a test of whether candidates could get people to follow them. Today, constituents have little to do with the financing of campaigns. The upshot is that the average person thinks the government is for sale or for rent. That's a major reason to try public financing.

Steffes added that citizens' perceptions are right, saying too many politicians really:

> are corrupted. You hear 'em saying one after another, 'I can take their money and it doesn't affect my vote.' And after a while you just want to throw up.[4]

In Arizona, more candidates are running and there are fewer uncontested races since public financing of campaigns went into effect. The candidates are increasingly from more diverse backgrounds.

Observers in Maine credit the passage of prescription drug reform and new laws to crack down on arsenic and mercury in the environment with the fact that legislators are now more willing to stand up to industry lobbyists due to Maine's clean money system.

Recall proponent and anti-tax activist Ted Costa has suggested a system of awarding public funds to political parties, but only if those parties require their candidates to abide by a strict code of conduct. Costa is not one to waste tax dollars, but he sees the value in getting politicians off the special interest dole.

Connecticut enacted a clean money program in 2005 after Connecticut Governor Roland resigned and went to prison as part of a corruption scandal. It will go into effect for 2008. New

Mexico has a clean money program for its state Public Regulation Commission and recently extended the idea to local elections in Albuquerque and judicial races. North Carolina has a successful program of full public financing for judicial elections as well and New Jersey has started a pilot program for legislative races.

While paying for campaigns out of public funds isn't free, when you add it all up it's usually only about five to six bucks a year for each of us. Remembering that old adage, "You get what you pay for," regular citizens are probably a lot better off buying the politicians ourselves rather than letting someone else buy them. We'd more than make up the cost of a public financing system through savings in the special tax breaks, budget earmarks, and wasteful contracts that lobbyists win for their clients with the help of well-placed campaign contributions.

Reining in Electioneering Groups

Apologists for big money in politics try to drum up opposition to contribution and spending limits, as well as to public financing systems, by pointing out that they aren't 100 percent effective. It's a little bit like saying that we should give up on building levees and flood control systems because we saw in New Orleans that sometimes they can fail.

Fat cats can get around campaign finance laws that limit what candidates can raise or spend by giving money to outside electioneering groups instead of candidates. We saw lots of this in the 2004 presidential election. In the general election, both John Kerry and President Bush received 100 percent public financing for their own campaigns. Although both of them had raised gobs in the primaries, neither one raised a dime for their campaigns in the fall of 2004. Instead, fat cats like George Soros on the left and T. Boone Pickens on the right funded outfits like the Media Fund and the Swift Boat Veterans for Truth. These groups acted independently of the candidates, but still used big money to shovel out the same negative TV ads that we've grown to expect from the politicians themselves.

Big money fans like to argue that the contribution limits and clean money systems simply drive campaign funds underground, because often the disclosure requirements for these outside groups aren't as strong as disclosure rules for candidates. But money will go underground to avoid disclosure as easily as it will to avoid limits on contributions. As was the case in Kevin Shelley's campaign for secretary of state (see chapter 14), donors try to evade disclosure laws even if there are no contribution limits.

As shown in chapter 9, for instance, Ameriquest funneled its money to support the anti-union Proposition 75 through a variety of ballot committees so as to hide the true source of the funds. They did this even though it would have been perfectly legal for them to give the money straight into the Prop 75 Committee.

If disclosure of a contribution is actually effective because it causes the candidate or ballot committee to lose support when voters find out about it, the donor will try to avoid disclosure.

So, campaign finance limits aren't the problem with money going underground. The problem is laws that allow that money to stay underground. The solution is simple—require better disclosure of the funding for these outside groups.

The other thing to recognize is that these outside campaigns sometimes backfire, or at least don't work out as well as the big money boys hope. Just as Arnold found that his supposedly independent Citizens to Save California group was not nearly as effective as his California Recovery Team, candidates always prefer to have money coming into a committee that they can control 100 percent. Moving it away from the candidate makes it less useful to the candidate as well as the donor who seeks access and influence. Even if there was nothing to do about these outside groups, we'd still be better off with them than with no limits on money going straight to candidates.

But, luckily, there are some things we can do.

One reform is to place limits on contributions to outside electioneering groups, just as we place limits on candidate committees. It's fine for any group to raise its voice about an election issue, but they shouldn't be able to play by different rules than the candidates. Federal law has long applied contribution limits to political action committees that run so-called independent expenditures that tell people to vote for or against a candidate. Big donors got around this in the last election by funding ads that simply promoted or attacked a candidate, but didn't tell people how to vote. Reformers are currently working to close this loophole by applying contribution limits to any group that is spending money to actively promote, support, oppose, or attack a candidate.

Clean money systems can also deal with outside electioneering groups in the same way they deal with a candidate who is trying to unfairly buy an election. When an outside group attacks a candidate, clean money systems give the candidate additional public funds so that they can respond. Sometimes just knowing that a candidate will have the chance to answer a false attack provides a reason not to sling the mud in the first place.

Tighter Ethics Enforcement

Changing campaign finance laws can go a long way toward influencing what sort of person runs for office in the first place. Regular folks are more likely to run when they know they have a shot against the special interests with deep pockets. But even if we had a different, more honest, set of people getting elected, we'd still have problems when they ran into conflicts between their personal financial interests and their public duty.

One no-brainer reform would be to ban our statewide and legislative candidates from receiving outside income. This would eliminate the type of conflict we saw with Arnold's veto of the dietary supplement bill while he had a personal stake in the supplement makers' ads in bodybuilding magazines (chapter 10).

Another easy reform is to ban all gifts to elected officials. There's simply no good reason to allow a lobbyist or a corporate CEO to give legislators tickets to sporting events or to buy them fancy dinners. The gifts, outlined in chapter 3, from the California Chamber of Commerce to officials in the Schwarzenegger administration are just greasing the skids for special interest favors. Citizens should demand an end to the practice. We could make an exception for friends and relatives who have exchanged holiday or birthday gifts with an official before they run for office, but there's no need to allow lobbyists or other power brokers to wine and dine our public officials. Politicians get higher salaries than most of us, and they can afford to buy their own supper.

Finally, as we saw with the Joint Legislative Audit Committee's foot-dragging in the Kevin Shelley investigation, there is an inherent conflict of interest in having politicians enforce ethics rules. Every state, including California, needs an independent agency that has the ability to subpoena witnesses in public hearings to get to the bottom of any alleged ethics violations.

Colorado voters enacted a ballot initiative in November 2006 to tighten ethics rules in their state. North Carolina is considering changes after a scandal involving its legislative leadership. Other states should join the trend.

Repairing the Recall

When campaign finance laws and ethics rules fail to keep out the bad apples, citizens in California still have the recall to fall back on. Most other states either have no recall process or recall systems that are nearly impossible to use. They should consider catching up with the time-tested idea of recalling politicians as the most fundamental way to hold them accountable.

California could stand to tune up its recall process. While things worked out in the last election, the potential to have a winner who receives only a low plurality is a real problem. Tom McClintock faced a lot of unfair pressure to drop out during the recall by Republicans who feared he would drain votes away from Arnold Schwarzenegger. But everyone has a right to run for office.

California could make its recall work better by using either a runoff election or an Instant Runoff Voting system like San Francisco has adopted. Instant runoffs ensure a winner with majority support and do so in only one election, saving the time and trouble of a traditional runoff. Come to think of it, we should be looking at Instant Runoff Voting for non-recall elections as well.

We should also do something to ensure that recalls can succeed without the support of millionaires like Darrell Issa. Given that a majority of Californians really did want to recall Gray Davis, Issa arguably did the state a big favor by his willingness to drop a couple million dollars of his own money to qualify the recall. But it shouldn't have to happen that way. Instead, we should create a way for citizens to circulate recall petitions online and lower signature thresholds to levels that can be reached without huge sums of money going for paid petitioning gatherers. Then, we should ban huge contributions to recall campaigns.

Improving the Initiative

The initiative process is another tool of the early 20th century populists that serves as a final check and balance when private interests like the Union Pacific Railroad or modern day pharmaceutical companies get too much power in the legislature. Only 24 states currently have the initiative process. Those that don't should consider adopting it.

Unfortunately, the tool needs sharpening. Powerful interests now use the same techniques to defeat citizen initiatives that they use to defeat pro-citizen candidates—they attack them with expensive TV ads.

Citizens should respond by applying the same campaign finance rules to ballot initiatives as we do to candidates. So far, the courts have resisted these attempts, striking down both contribution limits and bans on corporate contributions to ballot campaigns. But Professor Rick Hasen has noted that the Supreme Court's thinking has evolved significantly in the past ten years and it may now be ready to support such reforms.

I attended a hearing of the Ninth Circuit Court of Appeals in 1997 that considered a Montana law that banned corporate contributions to ballot campaigns. A lower court had found that corporate money had not corrupted the initiative process in Montana. But one judge on the Ninth Circuit noted that the Supreme Court has found corporate money to be inherently corrupting in candidate campaigns[5] and that the same logic should apply to ballot initiatives. A second judge said that she thought corporate money could corrupt the initiative process, but wasn't ready to overturn the judge below her who ruled that it had not in this particular circumstance. Only one of the three judges held that corporate money should always be allowed in ballot campaigns.[6] California would be a logical state to test the courts' thinking on this once again.

As with the recall, it has become so expensive to qualify a ballot initiative in California that increasingly only millionaires and special interests are able to use the process. Citizens have been priced out of the game. California should lead the country in adopting an online signature gathering process with a longer time period for circulation that would make it easier for volunteer citizen efforts to get ideas in front of the voters. Alternatively, we could consider a system such as Arizona and Maine use to qualify clean money candidates by qualifying ballot questions based on the collection of a significant number of $5 contributions by citizens as an alternate route to getting a higher number of signatures alone. Initiatives that qualified for this route could also receive public funds to respond to any attack ads funded by large contributions.

Don't Wait for Arnold or Other Politicians

The bottom line is that so far Arnold has not lived up to the promise of sweeping the special interests from Sacramento. He's tried to do some good things, but he's also opposed serious reform efforts and made matters worse by blowing holes in our already weak campaign finance system.

We may have been naïve to hope that any politician would really take on the task of reforming government.

This may be something that citizens have to do for ourselves. Fortunately, there are a lot of steps we can take that would reduce the role of big money in politics. While Republicans and Democrats will play blame games 'til the cows come home about whose fault it is, the rest of us should get busy working to clean things up. If we don't want the politicians to sell us out, we may just have to take matters into our own hands. The one promise you know you can trust is one you make to yourself.

APPENDIX A

News release from TheRestofUs.org on June 24, 2004, the day the FPPC adopted its rules concerning fundraising limits on candidate-controlled ballot committees

Get Big Money Out of California's Ballot Questions

Californians should pay close attention to what regulators at the Fair Political Practices Commission (FPPC) do about big money in ballot campaigns, according to TheRestofUs.org, a nonpartisan watchdog.

"Big money is distorting and corrupting California's ballot initiative process," said Derek Cressman, director of TheRestofUs.org. "The initiative is for citizens to use when wealthy private interests prevent the legislature from protecting the public interest. There's a problem when those same private interests, like Indian casinos, can then turn around and influence ballot measures through big money campaigns."

There are additional concerns when candidates control ballot measure campaigns. For example:

1) Governor Schwarzenegger's staff are suggesting that he will raise some $20 million, possibly from Indian tribes, to defeat two ballot measures dealing with gambling on this fall's ballot.

2) Lieutenant Governor Cruz Bustamante was fined by the FPPC for taking unlimited contributions (largely from Indian tribes) into an old candidate committee that he then transferred into his ballot committee against Proposition 54. But nothing to date would have prevented Bustamante from soliciting unlimited contributions directly into that ballot committee. Indeed, his committee did receive direct contributions from:
   - The Santa Rosa Rancheria for $478,000
   - Jerry Perenchio for $100,000
   - AFCSME for $200,000
   - Angelo Tsakopoulos's AKT Development Corporation for $45,000

3) Arnold Schwarzenegger's committee to support

Proposition 49 in 2002, which helped position him to run for governor, received contributions from:

- The Emulex Corporation for $60,000 plus at least another $320,000 from its CEO Paul Folino
- Richard Santullie, CEO of Net-Jets Corporation for at least $100,000
- Todd Wagner of Dallas, Texas for at least $600,000
- Jerry Perenchio of Univision for at least $1,000,000
- Conexant Systems for $50,000
- The Morongo Band of Indians for $25,000
- The Yucaipa Companies LLC for $100,000
- Developer Alex Spanos for $100,000.

4) Arnold Schwarzenegger and Steve Westly's Committee to Support Propositions 57 and 58 received contributions from:
   - Western Manufactured Housing Companies for $50,000
   - Kaiser Foundation Health Plan for $150,000
   - The California Building Industry Association for $50,000
   - Anheuser-Busch for $100,000.

According to Cressman, there are at least two serious problems for our democracy with contributions this massive:

First, wealthy interests can easily drown out the voices of the rest of us in public debate about ballot measures, creating an un-level playing field for public policy decisions. It is particularly troubling when corporations or tribes use state-conferred advantages that allow them to accumulate massive amounts of money to distort the political process.

Second, many donors who give to ballot committees that are controlled by candidates, future candidates, and officeholders, have business pending before the state of California or other private interests at stake dealing with state action or regulation. They could easily gain privileged access and favorable treatment by public officials by giving such huge amounts to ballot campaigns either controlled by or prominently featuring those elected officials.

On Friday, the FPPC has the opportunity to do something about the second problem by counting contributions to a candidate-controlled ballot committee as contributions to the candidate that are already limited by current law and by requiring all ballot committees that use candidates as spokespersons to abide by candidate contribution limits.

The first problem is more vexing and would require action by the legislature and approval by the courts. Some courts have indicated that they would uphold a ban on corporate contributions to all ballot committees, whether or not they are tied to a candidate. The California legislature could pass such a law. The courts could also go further and reverse their previous rulings that struck down commonsense contribution limits to ballot measure committees. But, the courts cannot do this unless a state such as California or a local government enacts limits that can create a test case.

"The FPPC cannot solve all of our problems with money in ballot initiatives this Friday. But it could take a step in the right direction by limiting what candidates can raise for initiatives," concluded Ned Wigglesworth, a researcher for TheRestofUs.org.

#-#-#

APPENDIX B

TheRestofUs.org complaint to the California Fair Political Practices Commission.

February 7, 2005

Steven Russo
Chief of Enforcement
Fair Political Practices Commission
428 J Street, Suite 620
Sacramento, CA 95814

Dear Mr. Russo:

I am the Director of TheRestofUs.org, a nonprofit organization dedicated to raising awareness of the role of big money in politics. In the course of my duties I have been following the role of a so-called "independent" political committee that is working with Governor Arnold Schwarzenegger to promote the governor's agenda with certain ballot measures likely to be voted on later this year. I believe the committee is being used by the governor and his agents to illegally bypass the FPPC's rules restricting campaign contributions to candidate-controlled ballot measure committees. Specifically, I allege that the Citizens to Save California Committee is, both in fact and for purposes of the Fair Political Practices Act and the Regulations of the Fair Political Practices Commission. controlled by Governor Arnold Schwarzenegger; and is raising contributions in amounts greater than the $22,300 allowed under FPPC regulation 18530.9 for a candidate-controlled ballot measure committee. Please consider this a formal request that the Fair Political Practices Commission investigate these allegations pursuant to FPPC regulation 18360(b).

Governor Schwarzenegger has a re-election committee, Californians for Schwarzenegger—2006, registration no. 1261585. This committee raised $1.38 million in 2004. He also has a candidate-controlled ballot measure committee, Governor Schwarzenegger's California Recovery Team, registration no. 1261406. Both these committees are subject to a contribution limit of $22,300.

Citizens to Save California (CSC) is a general purpose recipient committee, registration no. 127022. Its board members include Allan Zaremberg, president of the California Chamber of Commerce; R. William Hauck, president of the California Business Roundtable; Joel Fox, the former chief policy consultant to Arnold Schwarzenegger's 2003 gubernatorial campaign and president of the Small Business Action Committee; and Jon Coupal, president of the Howard Jarvis Taxpayers Association.

In its fundraising literature, CSC has described itself as "an independent committee supporting Governor Schwarzenegger's reform agenda." (LATimes 2/4/2005- http://www.latimes.com/news/local/la-me-money4feb04,1,5534881.story) In press accounts, its political consultant, Rick Claussen, has stated that "(T)he governor laid out an agenda in the State of the State speech" and that CSC's "desire is to help him achieve that agenda." (LATimes, 1/12/2004- http://www.latimes.com/news/local/la-me-money12jan12,1,4619679.story)

Governor Schwarzenegger has announced his intention to pursue a series of ballot measures if the state legislature does not take sufficient action on his agenda. This agenda includes action on redistricting, state spending, state pension plans, and merit-based pay for teachers. (OCRegister 2/3/2005- http://www.ocregister.com/ocr/2005/02/03/sections/region_state/region_state/article_396725.php) These initiatives would be on the ballot in a special election in November 2005. (San Diego Union Tribune, 1/28/2005) - http://www.signonsandiego.com/uniontrib/20050128/news_1n28arnold.html)

These initiatives are being prepared and filed by CSC. The initiatives deal with redistricting, state spending (Hauck and Zaremberg), state pension plans (Coupal), and one to increase the power of the governor to reorganize and streamline the executive branch (Fox). These and other facts about the CSC can be found on the Chamber of Commerce website, at http://www.calchamber.com/headlines/index/cfm?id=507&action&=detail&navidd=269.The Chamber has stated it will pursue those measures that best advance the governor's agenda.

Governor Schwarzenegger has announced his intention to raise $50 million to pursue his ballot agenda. (LA Times 1/29/2005 - http://www.latimes.com/news/local/la-me-arnold29jan29,0,1699289.story, Orange County Register 2/3/2005) He has also indicated that he will pursue these donations from around the country, and that likely donors would include people who could "contribute $10,000 or $20,000 or $50,000 or be in charge of raising $500,000 from smaller donors." (LATimes 1/29/2005) The governor has indicated that he considers himself part of the CSC by his statement that "I feel it's wise not to just rely on the same people that we normally go to." (LA Times 1/29/05, emphasis added.)

The governor has already begun these fundraising efforts, speaking at a series of fundraising lunches around the state at which William Zaremberg has also spoken. The official invitation for at least one of these fundraisers was issued on Schwarzenegger campaign stationery. (LATimes 2/4/2005) Although the invitations are careful to state that the CSC is not "controlled" by the governor, the governor has been quoted as stating that he "will help them with fundraising, and I will help them to endorse it and to do TV campaigns, because it is according to my agenda." (SJ Mercury News 2/5/2005 http://www.mercurynews.com/mld/mercurynews/news/10824985.htm)

Jon Coupal has said that the CSC will take guidance about what the governor wants through signals he has sent in the legislature and in his speeches. (LA Times 2/4/05) Joel Fox has said that the CSC will "certainly talk to the governor's office. We can get a feel of where the governor is going to go.

He's the big king on the chessboard. Wherever he moves, a lot of things move with him." (LA Times 1/12/05) These statements clearly indicate that Arnold Schwarzenegger is controlling CSC.

The governor also has stated that he is abiding by the letter of the law, though whether he is abiding by its spirit is "a matter of opinion." (SJ Mercury News 2/5/2005) However, we believe he is failing to abide by the letter of the law, as well as its spirit. A candidate controls a ballot measure committee if he or his staff participates in decisions regarding its fundraising methods, its strategy decisions, its decisions regarding what measures the committee will support or oppose, and development of communications. (*Ferguson* Advice Letter, FPPC no. A-86044; *Trimbur* Advice Letter, FPPC no. A-00-067.) There is no doubt here that CSC is coordinating with the governor's office on strategy decisions and fundraising.

Surely the FPPC will not allow the governor to undermine completely the regulation on candidate-controlled ballot measure committees by having an "independent" group glued to his hip, telling the group publicly everything he wants them to do, and procuring the funding for them to do his bidding. The fact that much of this is being played out in public does not make it any less nefarious. Moreover, we as citizens have no access now to the records of the CSC's expenditures, and no way of knowing whether spending decisions, like those for fundraising, are being coordinated with the governor's office. Nor do we have access to other documents that may uncover further evidence of control.

CSC has indicated that it can raise money in unlimited amounts to pursue the governor's agenda. (LATimes 2/4/2005) Governor Schwarzenegger has announced his intention to raise money in amounts of at least $50,000. The actions and statements of Governor Schwarzenegger and CSC demonstrate that despite its protestations of independence, CSC is controlled by Governor Schwarzenegger. By pursuing and collecting contributions in amounts greater than that allowed for a candidate or candidate-controlled committee, CSC and Governor Schwarzenegger have violated section 18530.9 of the regulations of the Fair Political Practices Commission.

I look forward to a prompt and thorough investigation of this matter.

Sincerely,

Derek Cressman
Director

APPENDIX C

CONTACT PHONE NUMBERS FOR SOME DONORS PROFILED IN THIS BOOK

This information is taken from major donor reports filed with the California secretary of state.

Ameriquest: 714-564-0600
Donald Bren (Irvine Company): 949-717-4646
Jerry Perenchio: 310-556-7610
William Armstead Robinson: 707-769-0437
Alex Spanos: 209-478-7965
Angelo Tsakopoulos: 916-383-2500
Christy Walton (WAL-Mart): 415-389-6800

END NOTES

Notes to Introduction

1. "Move to Recall Governor Spins California Into Political Turmoil," *Washington Post*, June 10, 2003.
2. "Source, Schwarzenegger Won't Run for Governor," *Fox News,* July 28, 2003.
3. Campaign quote recounted in "Governor Goes Fund Raising Despite Pledge of Reform," *San Francisco Chronicle*, February 6, 2004.
4. "Schwarzenegger Gets Egged Before Campaign Speech," *Fox News*, September 4, 2003.
5. "One Man's Special Interests," *California Insider Weblog* at SacBee.com, August 25, 2003.
6. "Financially, the Recall Was Business as Usual," *Los Angeles Times*, October 10, 2003.
7. "Schwarzenegger Woos Key Corporate Donors; He Vowed Not To Take Money From Anyone," *San Francisco Chronicle*, September 7, 2003.
8. "Schwarzenegger Woos Key Corporate Donors; He Vowed Not to Take Money From Anyone," *San Francisco Chronicle*, September 7, 2003.
9. "Opponents Claim Momentum Before Vote," *San Diego Union Tribune*, October 5, 2005.
10. Poll by *USA Today/CNN/Gallup,* September 28, 2003.
11. "Governor is Focus of Ethics Complaint," *Los Angeles Times*, July 19, 2005.
12. "Survey: Recall Electrified Electorate," *Los Angeles Times*, October 16, 2003.
13. "Survey: Recall Electrified Electorate," *Los Angeles Times*, October 16, 2003.
14. Transcript of Schwarzenegger's acceptance speech provided by *Associated Press*, October 8, 2003.
15. Inaugural address excerpted from *CNN.com*, November 17, 2003.

Notes to Chapter 1 – The Predecessor

1. Dave McCuan, Political Science Professor at Sonoma State University in a note to the author June 12, 2006.
2. "Gray Davis for Governor TV Spots," *Campaigns and Elections*, July 1, 1998.
3. "Gray Davis for Governor TV Spots," *Campaigns and Elections*, July 1, 1998.
4. "Davis Wins Heralded California Governorship," CNN.com, November 3, 1998.
5. "Davis' Nonstop Cash Machine Many Big Donors Have Interests in Governor's Decisions," *San Francisco Chronicle*, May 19, 2002.
6. "Davis' Nonstop Cash Machine Many Big Donors Have Interests in Governor's Decisions," *San Francisco Chronicle*, May 19, 2002.
7. Data in this chart was downloaded from the National Institute of Money in State Politics on May 16, 2006. The Institute codes as many contributions to economic sector as it can and then uses a database to calculate totals. The Institute claims that it has 100 percent of data entered from the 2000 cycle, 95 percent from the 2002 cycle, and 90 percent from the 2004 cycle. There are many contributions that are coded as unknown, and many contributions that are given by political parties that do not have the donors to those parties included. Many business and labor groups give money to the parties in addition to contributing directly to candidates, so these numbers only tell part of the whole picture.
8. "Davis' Nonstop Cash Machine Many Big Donors Have Interests in Governor's Decisions," *San Francisco Chronicle*, May 19, 2002.
9. "Citigroup Donating Big Sums to Davis," *Associated Press*, August 13, 2002.
10. "California's Gray Politics," *The Nation*, August 1, 2002.
11. "Modest Donor Squeezed out of Governor's Race," *Los Angeles Times*, February 28, 2002.
12. "Modest Donor Squeezed out of Governor's Race," *Los Angeles Times*, February 28, 2002.
13. "Davis' Nonstop Cash Machine, Many Big Donors Have Interests in Governor's Decisions," *San Francisco Chronicle*, May 19, 2002.

14. "Governor Overreaches Again on Fund Raising." *San Francisco Chronicle*, November 20, 2000.
15. "McCain Criticizes Gov. Davis' Fund Raising / He says goal of $26 million is 'disgraceful' and calls for reform," *San Francisco Chronicle*, March 9, 2001.
16. "Enron, Preaching Deregulation, Worked the Statehouse Circuit," *New York Times*, February 9, 2003.
17. "Enron, Brash, Bold, Beaten," *Sacramento Bee*, November 29, 2001.
18. "New Documents Suggest Enron's Lay, Skilling, Washington Lobbyist Knew About Company's Trading Schemes In CA," *DissidentVoice.org*, June 7, 2004.
19. News release by CALPIRG, June 22, 2001.
20. "California's Gray Politics," *The Nation*, August 19, 2002.
21. "Why Vote at All? That's the Question," *Sacramento Bee*, March 29, 2002.
22. "California's Gray Politics," *The Nation*, August 19, 2002.
23. "California's Gray Politics," *The Nation*, August 19, 2002.
24. "Gray Skies From Now On; Dreary California governor an early bet for presidential nomination," in Canada's *National Post*, November 9, 2002.

Notes to Chapter 2 – Total Recall

1. Schrag is quoted in "Internet Puts the E in Recall," by Nick Shulz, *Los Angeles Times*, June 19, 2003.
2. "What is the History of Recall Elections," by Joshua Spivak, *History News Network*, September 1, 2003.
3. "What is the History of Recall Elections," by Joshua Spivak, *History News Network*, September 1, 2003.
4. "What is the History of Recall Elections," by Joshua Spivak, *History News Network*, September 1, 2003.
5. "Why did California Adopt the Recall?" by Joshua Spivak, *History News Network*, September 15, 2003.
6. "Why did California Adopt the Recall?" by Joshua Spivak, *History News Network*, September 15, 2003.
7. "On Historical Scale, This Batch Carries Weight," *San Diego Union Tribune*, October 3, 2003.
8. "Move to Recall Governor Spins California into Political Turmoil," *Washington Post*, June 10, 2003.
9. "Davis Recall: Be Careful What You Ask For," *Los Angeles Times*, June 4, 2003.
10. "Issa Was Charged in San Jose Car Theft," *San Francisco Chronicle*, June 25, 2003.
11. "Move to Recall Governor Spins California into Political Turmoil," *Washington Post*, June 10, 2003.
12. "Recall Drive at 40 percent of First Goal," *Los Angeles Times*, June 25, 2003.
13. Poll by the Public Policy Institute of California.
14. Human Events website, August, 2003.
15. "A Timeline of the California Recall," *USA Today* Website visited February 17, 2006.
16. "The Recall—A Minefield in California Election Law," *San Diego Union Tribune*, June 19, 2003.
17. "Crowded Ballot May Lead to Delays, Disarray, Experts Say," *Los Angeles Times*, August 28, 2003.
18. "Voter Initiatives Leave California Little Wiggle Room; Governor Has Little Budget Discretion," *Washington Post*, August 13, 2003.
19. "Do Better Next Time," *Los Angeles Times*, August 17, 2003.
20. "Actor Rejects Need to Identify All Donors Now," *San Jose Mercury News*, October 4, 2003.
21. "Actor Rejects Need to Identify All Donors Now," *San Jose Mercury News*, October 4,

2003.
22. All of the donations reported on this page are from "Financially, the Recall Was Business as Usual," *Los Angeles Times*, October 10, 2003.
23. "Developer and Environmental Scofflaw Gives Big To Schwarzenegger," *Associated Press*, September 29, 2003.
24. "Recall – Corporate Donations Defended," *Sacramento Bee,* August 27, 2003.
25. "Recall – Corporate Donations Defended," *Sacramento Bee,* August 27, 2003.
26. "Money Trail Tells a Story," *Santa Maria Times*, October 3, 2003.
27. "California Campaign Gifts Spur Lawsuit," *Washington Post*, September 5, 2003.
28. ""Bustamante Contribution Maneuvering Sparks Controversy," *Contra Costa Times*, September 5, 2005.
29. "Indian Campaign Donations in the Spotlight; One-fifth of all Recall Money—$6.7 million—Has Come from Tribes," *San Francisco Chronicle*, September 24, 2005 and "Tribes' Assertive Role in Race May Return to Haunt Them," *Copley News*, October 7, 2003.
30. "Indian Campaign Donations in the Spotlight; One-fifth of all Recall Money—$6.7 million—Has Come from Tribes," *San Francisco Chronicle*, September 24, 2005.
31. "Tribes' Assertive Role in Race May Return to Haunt Them," *Copley News*, October 7, 2003.
32. *Recall, California's Political Earthquake*, M.E. Sharpe, 2004, p. 75.
33. "Tribes' Assertive Role in Race May Return to Haunt Them," *Copley News*, October 7, 2003.
34. "Schwarzenegger's Own $8 Million Went to Fund Recall Campaign," *Wall Street Journal*, October 8, 2003.
35. "California Recall Adds Fuel to Electronic Voting Debate," *Associated Press*, August 13, 2003.
36. "Ounce of Prevention," *Sacramento Bee*, September 16, 2003.
37. "Delaying the California Recall," *New York Times*, September 16, 2003.
38. "The Vote Must Go On," *New York Times*, September 17, 2003.
39. "Court Ruling Clears Way for Pivotal Debate," *Christian Science Monitor*, September 24, 2003.
40. *Recall, California's Political Earthquake,* M.E. Sharpe, 2004. p. 119.
41. "Survey: Recall Electrified Electorate," *Sacramento Bee*, October 16, 2003.
42. "Politics as It Was Meant to Be," *Los Angeles Times*, August 17, 2003.
43. "Recall May Be Dizzying, But it Portends a Revolution in Governance," *Los Angeles Times*, August 17, 2003.
44. "Recall as Reform Politics," *Washington Post,* August 16, 2003.
45. Exit poll of 5,205 voters conducted by the *Los Angeles Times.*

Notes to Chapter 3 – The Moneymoon

1. "President Schwarzenegger?" *CBS News,* October 29, 2004.
2. "Should the Constitution be Amended for Arnold," *USA Today*, December 3, 2004.
3. "Unruffled Governor Vows to Repay Loan," *Los Angeles Times*, January 28, 2004.
4. "Governor's Loan for Recall Ruled Illegal," *Los Angeles Times*, January 27, 2004.
5. "Donors to Governor Get Posts of Prestige," *San Diego Union Tribune*, August 28, 2006.
6. "Senate Investigates Schwarzenegger Campaign Contribution," *Associated Press*, March 30, 2005.
7. "Schwarzenegger Rakes in Funds from Special Interests," *Scripps-McClatchy News Service*, June 22, 2004.
8. "Tickets to Schwarzenegger Fundraiser in New York City Will Cost $500,000," *Los Angeles Times,* February 4, 2004.
9. "Tickets to Schwarzenegger Fundraiser in New York City Will Cost $500,000," *Los Angeles*

Times, February 4, 2004.
10. *Recall, California's Political Earthquake*, M.E. Sharpe, 2004. p. 87.
11. "Gifts Flow, as Does the Access," *Los Angeles Times*, November 7, 2004.
12. "Gifts Flow, as Does the Access," *Los Angeles Times*, November 7, 2004.
13. "Gifts Flow, as Does the Access," *Los Angeles Times*, November 7, 2004.
14. "Gifts Flow, as Does the Access," *Los Angeles Times*, November 7, 2004.
15. "Nonprofit Groups' Donations Scrutinized," *Los Angeles Times*, August 28, 2005.
16. "Schwarzenegger Says He May Campaign for Bush in Ohio," *Associated Press*, September 2, 2004.
17. "Workers Compensation in California," Institute of Governmental Studies at UC Berkeley, http://www.igs.berkeley.edu/library/htWorkersCompensation.htm.
18. "Drug Companies Give Big After Schwarzenegger Vetos," *Associated Press*, March 11, 2004.
19. "Term Limits Pit Allies Against One Another," *Los Angeles Times*, May 31, 2006.
20. "Governor Faults Prop 70 Backers," *Los Angeles Times*, October 5, 2004.
21. Ad recounted in the *Los Angeles Times*, November 13, 2004.

Notes to Chapter 4 – Reinventing the Cruz Loophole

1. FPPC news release, August 28, 2003.
2. "FPPC Unlikely to Act on Fund-Raising," *Los Angeles Times*, September 4, 2003.
3. "Bustamante Faces Suit Over Large Donations," *Sacramento Bee*, September 3, 2003.
4. "Bustamante Faces Suit Over Large Donations," *Sacramento Bee*, September 3, 2003.
5. "Bustamante to Shift Disputed Donations," *Sacramento Bee*, September 7, 2003.
6. "Prop 54 Sponsor Concedes Passage Now Unlikely," *Los Angeles Times*, September 7, 2003.
7. "Bustamante to Shift Disputed Donations," *Sacramento Bee*, September 7, 2003.
8. "Bustamante Contribution Maneuvering Sparks Controversy," *Contra Costa Times,* September 5, 2003.
9. "Bustamante Faces Suit Over Large Donations," *Sacramento Bee*, September 3, 2003.
10. "Critics: FPPC Lacks Teeth," *Sacramento Bee,* December 27, 2004.
11. "Bustamante Agrees to Largest Ever Campaign Violation Fine," *Associated Press,* April 14, 2004.
12. "Bustamante Agrees to Largest Ever Campaign Violation Fine," *Associated Press,* April 14, 2004.
13. "Governor is Raising Funds Faster Than Davis," *Los Angeles Times*, February 15, 2004.
14. *Contra Costa Times*, as cited in *Democracy's Daily Posts* on June 23, 2004.
15. "Campaign Loophole Closed; Panel Limits Funds for Candidates' Ballot Measures," *San Jose Mercury News*, June 26, 2004.
16. "Election Funding Limits Added," *Sacramento Bee*, June 26, 2004.
17. "Schwarzenegger Must Alter His Fundraising Style," *Sacramento Bee*, November 16, 2004.

Notes to Chapter 5 – Saving California's Corporate Citizens

1. "Special Election Would Test Governor's Power, Voters' Patience," *Associated Press*, January 17, 2005.
2. "Governor Walks a Fine Line on Boundaries," *New York Times*, January 5, 2005.
3. "Governor Seeks Outside Donors for Campaign," *Los Angeles Times*, January 29, 2005.
4. "Groups to Aid Gov's Push for Reforms," *Los Angeles Times,* January 12, 2005.
5. "Groups to Aid Gov's Push for Reforms," *Los Angeles Times,* January 12, 2005.
6. "Groups to Aid Gov's Push for Reforms," *Los Angeles Times,* January 12, 2005.

7. "Groups to Aid Gov's Push for Reforms," *Los Angeles Times,* January 12, 2005.
8. "Governor's Tie to Fund Drive Questioned," *Los Angeles Times,* February 4, 2005.
9. "Schwarzenegger Banking on Star Power," *San Jose Mercury News,* February 5, 2005.
10. "Governor's Tie to Fund Drive Questioned," *Los Angeles Times,* February 4, 2005.
11. "Trying to Shore Up Limits on Fundraising," *Los Angeles Times,* January 19, 2005.
12. "Big Ticket Drive Supports Gov's Agenda," *Los Angeles Times,* February 9, 2004.
13. "Big Ticket Drive Supports Gov's Agenda," *Los Angeles Times*, February 9, 2004.
14. "Governor Seeks Outside Donors for Campaign," *Los Angeles Times*, January 29, 2005.
15. "Bush Denounces Petition Gathering Groups," *Tallahassee Democrat*, February 7, 2006.
16. "Bush Denounces Petition Gathering Groups," *Tallahassee Democrat*, February 7, 2006.
17. "Bush Denounces Petition Gathering Groups," *Tallahassee Democrat*, February 7, 2006.
18. "A Matter of Context," *The Patriot Ledger*, May 26, 2005.
19. "Schwarzenegger to Go On Road to Raise Funds," *Los Angeles Times,* February 25, 2005.

Notes to Chapter 6 – The Lawsuit

1. "Schwarzenegger Banking on Star Power," *San Jose Mercury News,* February 5, 2005.
2. "Rethinking the Unconstitutionality of Contribution and Expenditure Limits in Ballot Measure Campaigns," Loyola Law Professor Richard Hasen, Legal Studies Paper No. 2004-26 available at http://ssrn.com/abstract=621321.
3. "Business Group in Agreement with Governor," *San Diego Union Tribune*, March 17, 2005.
4. "Business Group in Agreement with Governor," *San Diego Union Tribune*, March 17, 2005.
5. Wilson is quoted by Thomas Elias in the *Daily Midway Driller*, February 28, 2005.
6. CALPIRG *amicus* brief filed February 22, 2005, in California Superior Court, page 6.
7. Campaign Legal Center *amicus* brief filed February 18, 2005, in California Superior Court, page 1.
8. CALPIRG *amicus* brief, page 4.
9. "Ruling Puts Limits on Ballot Measures on Hold," *San Francisco Chronicle*, March 25, 2005.
10. "The Money Tree," *Los Angeles City Beat*, April 7, 2005.

Notes to Chapter 7 – Recovering from Reform

1. "Governor's Team Taking Reins," *Sacramento Bee*, March 30, 2005.
2. "Governor's Team Taking Reins," *Sacramento Bee*, March 30, 2005.
3. "Governor Digs Fixing Potholes, San Jose Crews Destroy Part of Road for Staged Event," *San Francisco Chronicle*, May 27, 2005.
4. "Governor Fails to Curb Big Money," *Los Angeles Times*, February 21, 2005.
5. "Governor Collects Millions for Election," San *Francisco Chronicle,* April 22, 2005.
6. "Schwarzenegger Prepares to Do Battle in California," *Washington Post,* March 28, 2005.
7. California Government Code section 85316.
8. California Government Code section 82015.
9. Declaration of Raymond Strother, president of the Washington, D.C., political consulting firm Duffy Strother, May 14, 2005.
10. "Schwarzenegger to Go On Road to Raise Funds," *Los Angeles Times,* February 25, 2005.
11. "Governor's Election May Hinge on Special Vote," *San Francisco Chronicle*, March 6, 2005.
12. Dan Walters, in his *Sacramento Bee* Column, May 17, 2005.

Notes to Chapter 8 – Arnold v. The Rest of Us

1. California Government Code section 425.16(a).

2. Final ruling of Judge Shelleyanne Chang in *TheRestofUs.org v. Schwarzenegger*, page 7.
3. Subsection 425.17 (d)(2) of California Government Code.
4. Citizens to Save California Special Motion to Strike, June 15, 2005.
5. Citizens to Save California Special Motion to Strike, June 15, 2005.
6. Declaration of Allan Zaremberg in Support of Special Motion to Strike, May 9, 2005.
7. Declaration of Marty Wilson in Opposition to Motion for Preliminary Injunction, June 7, 2005.
8. California Government Code section 82007.
9. California Government Code section 82016.
10. Ruling of Judge Shelleyanne Chang in *TheRestofUs.org v Schwarzenegger*, page 10.
11. KCRA website, September 8, 2005.
12. "GOP in a Fighting Mood," *Sacramento Bee*, September 19, 2005.

Notes to Chapter 9 – Plutocracy Run Amok

1. "Governor's Allies Test Curb on Fundraising," *Los Angeles Times*, February 10, 2005.
2. "Schwarzenegger Prepares to Do Battle in California," *Washington Post*, March 28, 2005.
3. "Nurse is Asked How She Got Into Screening," *Los Angeles Times*, February 23, 2005.
4. "Gov's Donor Under Fire From State," *Los Angeles Times*, June 20, 2005.
5. "California Governor Bypassed Charities, Gave Cash Back to Noe," *Toledo Blade*, September 3, 2005.
6. "Governor to Mine Bastions of GOP for Cash," *San Francisco Chronicle*, February 17, 2005.
7. "Failed State," *New Republic*, September 5, 2005.
8. "Panel Discusses Fixing the Initiative Process," *San Francisco Chronicle*, April 21, 2005.
9. "Secret Donors Behind Union Dues Initiative," *San Francisco Chronicle*, May 3, 2005.
10. "Union Calls off Ameriquest Protest," *Orange County Register,* June 8, 2005.
11. "Ambassador Nominee's Company is Scrutinized," *Los Angeles Times*, August 7, 2005.
12. "Ameriquest's Giant Payout," *ABC News*, June 25, 2006.
13. "Governor Relents on Sped Up Remapping," *Los Angeles Times*, April 28, 2005.
14. "Arnold Scorned by Backer Over Shift in Redistricting," *Los Angeles Daily News*, April 29, 2005.
15. "Governor Readies Special Election to Attack Legislature, Unions," *Los Angeles Times*, May 17, 2005.
16. "Special Election Ballot Taking Shape," *Los Angeles Times*, May 11, 2005.
17. "Governor Readies Special Election to Attack Legislature, Unions," *Los Angeles Times*, May 17, 2005.
18. "Governor Readies Special Election to Attack Legislature, Unions," *Los Angeles Times*, May 17, 2005.
19. "Governor to Mine GOP Bastions for Cash," *San Francisco Chronicle,* May 17, 2005.

Notes to Chapter 10 – Arnold's Second Job

1. "Schwarzenegger Says He Will End Relationship with Magazines," *Associated Press*, July 15, 2005.
2. "Governor to Quit 2nd Job," *San Francisco Chronicle*, July 16, 2005.
3. "Governor to be Paid $8 Million by Fitness Magazines," *Los Angeles Times*, July 14, 2005.
4. As noted in the bill analysis and summary by the legislative analyst for SB 1630.
5. "Pumping Him Up," *San Francisco Chronicle,* January 16, 2005.
6. "Governor is Focus of Ethics Complaint," *Los Angeles Times*, July 19, 2005.
7. "Pumping Him Up," *San Francisco Chronicle*, January 16, 2005, recounts the 1996 quote from the *Los Angeles Times* in 1996.

8. "Pumping Him Up," *San Francisco Chronicle*, January 16, 2005.
9. "Schwarzenegger Faces New Battle," *Financial Times*, July 14, 2005.
10. "Governor Won't Give up Second Job," *San Francisco Chronicle*, July 15, 2005.
11. "Schwarzenegger Faulted for Lucrative Deal With Fitness Magazines," *Associated Press*, July 14, 2005.
12. "Governor to Keep Outside Job With Muscle Magazines," *San Jose Mercury News*, July 15, 2005.
13. "Part of the Problem – Shady Deals in the City of Angels," *Democracy's Daily Posts*, March 23, 2005.
14. "Governor to Keep Outside Job With Muscle Magazines," *San Jose Mercury News*, July 15, 2005.
15. "Speaker Defends Consulting Work, But Says He May Drop It," *Associated Press*, March 23, 2005.
16. "Furor Over Salary Boost," *Los Angeles Daily News*, May 30, 2005.
17. "Tabloid's Deal with Woman Shielded Schwarzenegger," *Los Angeles Times*, August 12, 2005.
18. *Fantastic, The Life of Arnold Schwarzenegger*, St. Martins Press, 2005.
19. *Fantastic, The Life of Arnold Schwarzenegger*, St. Martins Press, 2005.
20. *Fantastic, The Life of Arnold Schwarzenegger*, St. Martins Press, 2005.

Notes to Chapter 11 – The Not-so-Special Election

1. "Redistricting Measure Could Drop Off Ballot," *San Francisco Chronicle*, July 7, 2005.
2. "Dems' Ethics Suit Means 'Now We Go To War'," *San Francisco Chronicle*, July 21, 2005.
3. "The Governor Must Retreat to Advance," *Los Angeles Times,* July 23, 2005.
4. "Dems' Ethics Suit Means 'Now We Go To War'," *San Francisco Chronicle*, July 21, 2005.
5. "Prop 77 Foes Want Soft Money to Fight Initiative," *Associated Press*, August 17, 2005.
6. Dissenting opinion of FEC Commissioner Scott Thomas to Advisory Opinion 2005-10.
7. "Governor Cashing in on Rolling Stones," *San Francisco Chronicle*, August 11, 2005.
8. "$100k to Watch Stones Concert with Gov," KGO-TV, August 11, 2005.
9. "Governor to President: Stay Away Until After Vote," *San Francisco Chronicle,* September 21, 2005.
10. "Governor to President: Stay Away Until After Vote," *San Francisco Chronicle,* September 21, 2005.
11. "Arnold Act II," *Orange County Register*, September 17, 2005.
12. "$300 Million Price Tag on Initiative Battles," *San Francisco Chronicle*, November 2, 2005.
13. "Drug Firms Gave Money to Some Who Endorsed Prop 78," *Los Angeles Times*, November 4, 2005.
14. Quoted by William Bennett, Californian.com, September 17, 2005.
15. Results downloaded from California Secretary of State's Website, March 28, 2006.
16. According to Dan Weintraub, *Sacramento Bee*, March 8, 2005.
17. "Saga of the Special Election," *Sacramento Bee*, November 13, 2005.

Notes to Chapter 12 – The Second Moneymoon

1. "Even Top Dems Help Governor with Turnaround," *San Francisco Chronicle*, August 31, 2006.
2. "Governor's New Chief of Staff Piles it On," *San Francisco Chronicle*, February 5, 2006.
3. "Governor's New Chief of Staff Piles it On," *San Francisco Chronicle*, February 5, 2006.
4. "Governor's New Chief of Staff Piles it On," *San Francisco Chronicle*, February 5, 2006.
5. "Governor's Campaign Reports Debt," *Los Angeles Times*, February 1, 2006.

6. "Governor's New Chief of Staff Piles it On," *San Francisco Chronicle*, February 5, 2006.
7. "Gov's Gift to PUC Official Questioned," *Los Angeles Times,* February 3, 2006.
8. "Gov's Gift to PUC Official Questioned," *Los Angeles Times,* February 3, 2006.
9. "Big Business Lobbies Hard for Video Licensing Bill," *San Francisco Chronicle*, August 28, 2006.
10. "Big Business Lobbies Hard for Video Licensing Bill," *San Francisco Chronicle*, August 28, 2006.
11. "Governor Drops Freeway Fees to Accelerate Fiber Optic Lines," *Sacramento Bee,* January 7, 2007.
12. "Governor's Cause Gets Gift after He Signed Law," *Los Angeles Times,* March 22, 2007.
13. "Governor: Go Slow in Fight on Warming," *San Francisco Chronicle*, April 12, 2006.
14. "Schwarzenegger's Green Credential's Questioned," *Los Angeles Times*, April 13, 2007.
15. "Schwarzenegger's Green Credential's Questioned," *Los Angeles Times*, April 13, 2007.
16. "Redistricting Reform Might Live to See Another Day," *Sacramento Bee*, November 29, 2005.
17. "Senate Seeks to Yield Power on Redistricting," *Los Angeles Times*, August, 17, 2006.
18. "State Redistricting Proposal Succumbs in Legislative Limbo," *San Francisco Chronicle*, August 18, 2006.
19. "Legislative Leaders Fail to Live Up to Promise," *Sacramento Bee*, August 20, 2006.
20. "State Redistricting Proposal Succumbs in Legislative Limbo," *San Francisco Chronicle*, August 18, 2006.
21. "11th Hour Bills Receive Little Scrutiny," *Los Angeles Times*, September 2, 2006.
22. "11th Hour Bills Receive Little Scrutiny," *Los Angeles Times*, September 2, 2006.
23. "11th Hour Bills Receive Little Scrutiny," *Los Angeles Times*, September 2, 2006.
24. "Divorce Info Bill Secrecy Spurs Dispute," *San Diego Union Tribune*, February 24, 2006.
25. "Pledging Muddles Campaign Finance Picture," *Orange County Register*, August 30, 2006.
26. "Checks Roll in as Laws Roll Out," *Los Angeles Times*, August 31, 2006.
27. "Checks Roll in as Laws Roll Out," *Los Angeles Times*, August 31, 2006.
28. "It's Open Season on Lobbyists Donations," *San Francisco Chronicle*, August 9, 2006.
29. "With Bills in the Balance, Arnold Hauls in Checks," *Los Angeles Times*, September 11, 2006.
30. "Gov Ups the Stakes," *Sacramento Bee,* March 4, 2007.

Notes to Chapter 13 – The 2006 Elections

1. "Steve Westly, Combination of Business and Politics Featured in Campaign," *San Francisco Chronicle*, May 28, 2006.
2. "Steve Westly, Combination of Business and Politics Featured in Campaign," *San Francisco Chronicle*, May 28, 2006.
3. "Steve Westly, Combination of Business and Politics Featured in Campaign," *San Francisco Chronicle*, May 28, 2006.
4. "Steve Westly, Combination of Business and Politics Featured in Campaign," *San Francisco Chronicle*, May 28, 2006.
5. "Tsakopoulos Cash Carries Controversy," *Sacramento Bee*, June 4, 2006.
6. "Foes Remain on the Offensive," *Los Angeles Times*, May 30, 2006.
7. "Foes Remain on the Offensive," *Los Angeles Times*, May 30, 2006.
8. "Foes Remain on the Offensive," *Los Angeles Times*, May 30, 2006.
9. "Foes Remain on the Offensive," *Los Angeles Times*, May 30, 2006.
10. "Tsakopoulos Cash Carries Controversy," *Sacramento Bee*, June 4, 2006.
11. "Democrats' Primary Election Spending Tops $60 Million," *San Jose Mercury News*, May 26, 2006.
12. "Angelides Mailers Use Preschool Issue to Skirt Campaign Contribution Limits," *Los Angeles Times,* June 2, 2006.

13. "Revealing the Reiner Commission Operation," New West Notes in *LA Weekly*, March 7, 2006.
14. "Revealing the Reiner Commission Operation," New West Notes in *LA Weekly*, March 7, 2006.
15. "Reiner Not Exiting Political Stage," *Sacramento Bee*, June 11, 2006.
16. "Giving a False Stamp of Approval with Mailers," *Los Angeles Times*, June 13, 2006.
17. "Giving a False Stamp of Approval with Mailers," *Los Angeles Times*, June 13, 2006.
18. "Giving a False Stamp of Approval with Mailers," *Los Angeles Times*, June 13, 2006.
19. "Moderate Republican PAC Has Forged Close Ties with Schwarzenegger," *Associated Press*, March 18, 2006.
20. "Moderate Republican PAC Has Forged Close Ties with Schwarzenegger," *Associated Press*, March 18, 2006.
21. "With Bills in the Balance, Arnold Hauls in the Checks," *Los Angeles Times*, September 11, 2006.
22. "Unions Will Spend Big to Defeat Governor," *San Francisco Chronicle*, September 20, 2006.
23. "Schwarzenegger Raises $113 million for campaign," *Associated Press,* November 4, 2007.
24. "Governor's Supreme Motive: Success," *San Jose Mercury News*, October 25, 2006.
25. "Schwarzenegger on Track to Break Fundraising Records," KXTV, November 2, 2006.
26. "Schwarzenegger on Track to Break Fundraising Records," KXTV, November 2, 2006.
27. "Schwarzenegger on Track to Break Fundraising Records," KXTV, November 2, 2006.
28. "Tribes Rolling Dice with Republicans," *Contra Costa Times*, October 27, 2006.
29. "Parties use County, State Committees to Skirt Donation Caps," *Capitol Weekly*, November 2, 2006.
30. "Parties use County, State Committees to Skirt Donation Caps," *Capitol Weekly*, November 2, 2006.
31. "Parties use County, State Committees to Skirt Donation Caps," *Capitol Weekly*, November 2, 2006.
32. "Campaign Cash Flows Around Rules," *Los Angeles Times*, October 20, 2006.
33. "Tribes Rolling Dice with Republicans," *Contra Costa Times*, October 27, 2006.
34. "Parties use County, State Committees to Skirt Donation Caps," *Capitol Weekly*, November 2, 2006.
35. "Outside Money Feared in Races," *Sacramento Bee*, September 13, 2006.
36. "Campaign Cash Flows Around Rules," *Los Angeles Times*, October 20, 2006.
37. "Governor, Angelides Seize Ballot Initiatives as Ammunition," *MediaNews*, August 13, 2006.
38. "Deep Pockets Carry the Day," *Los Angeles Times,* November 9, 2006.
39. "Tobacco and Oil Ballot Questions Draw Big Money," *San Francisco Chronicle,* September 12, 2007.
40. "Tobacco and Oil Ballot Issues Draw Big Money," *San Francisco Chronicle*, September 12, 2007.
41. "Deep Pockets Carry the Day," *Los Angeles Times,* November 9, 2006.
42. "Tobacco and Oil Initiatives Draw Big Money," *San Francisco Chronicle,* September 13, 2006.
43. "Donations Lag for Initiative on Campaign Finance," *San Francisco Chronicle*, September 21, 2006.
44. "Public Financing is the Right Idea, but Prop 89 is the Wrong Way to Do It," *Los Angeles Times*, September 14, 2006.
45. "Public Opinion Polls Concerning Presidential Public Financing 1972–2000," Campaign Finance Institute, 2005.
46. "Big Campaign Donations Growing Say Groups Favoring Reform," *Associated Press*, September 20, 2006.

47. "War Chests Crushed My TV," *Los Angeles Times*, November 6, 2006.
48. "$500 Million in Campaign Spending So Far Stuns Campaign Limit Supporters," *San Francisco Chronicle,* October 27, 2006.
49. "Cemex Aids Arnold with Check," *Los Angeles Daily News*, December 19, 2006.

Notes to Chapter 14 – What Arnold's Done Right

1. "Precursor to Prop 77 'Orchestrated Well'," *Sacramento Bee*, October 19, 2005.
2. *Competitive Districts in California – A Case Study of California's Redistricting in the 1990s*, February 21, 2005, the Rose Institute of State and Local Government at Claremont McKenna College.
3. "Precursor to Prop 77 'Orchestrated Well'," *Sacramento Bee*, October 19, 2005.
4. "GOP Fears a Redistricting Backfire," *Los Angeles Times*, February 8, 2005.
5. "GOP Fears a Redistricting Backfire," *Los Angeles Times*, February 8, 2005.
6. "GOP Fears a Redistricting Backfire," *Los Angeles Times*, February 8, 2005.
7. "GOP Fears a Redistricting Backfire," *Los Angeles Times*, February 8, 2005.
8. "GOP Fears a Redistricting Backfire," *Los Angeles Times*, February 8, 2005.
9. "Schwarzenegger and Common Cause: Strange Bedfellows?" *Associated Press*, February 21, 2005.
10. "Schwarzenegger and Common Cause: Strange Bedfellows?" *Associated Press*, February 21, 2005.
11. "The Politicians Are Lying to You About Prop 77," *Sacramento Bee*, November 3, 2005.
12. "Secretary of State Shelley Received Dubious Donations," *San Francisco Chronicle*, August 8, 2004.
13. "Shelley Ends Contracts of 15 Consultants," *Associated Press*, September 24, 2005.
14. "Criminal Charges Filed Against S.F.. Official," *San Francisco Chronicle*, April 8, 2005.
15. "Indignant Shelley Denies Wrongdoing," *San Francisco Chronicle*, August 26, 2004.
16. "Money Laundering, the Worst Campaign Finance Violation," *San Francisco Chronicle*, August 23, 2004.
17. "Indignant Shelley Denies Wrongdoing," *San Francisco Chronicle*, August 26, 2004.
18. "What He Knew and When He Knew It," *San Francisco Chronicle*, August 22, 2004.
19. "Shelley's Sad Defense," *San Francisco Chronicle*, August 26, 2004.
20. "Shelley's Consultants Schmoozed On the Job," *San Jose Mercury News*, September 22, 2004.
21. From the State Auditor's report, "Office of the Secretary of State: Clear and Appropriate Direction Is Lacking in Its Implementation of the Federal Help America Vote Act," executive summary, December 2004.
22. "2003 Donation to Shelley Raising Question of Impropriety," *San Jose Mercury News*, October 1, 2004.
23. "Shelley Took Check in his Office, Donor Says," *San Francisco Chronicle*, September 30, 2004.
24. "Shelley Took Check in his Office, Donor Says," *San Francisco Chronicle*, September 30, 2004.
25. "What He Knew and When He Knew It," *San Francisco Chronicle*, August 22, 2004.
26. "2003 Donation to Shelley Raising Question of Impropriety," *San Jose Mercury News*, October 1, 2004.
27. "Shelley Must Resign," *Sacramento Bee*, September 23, 2005.
28. "Shelley's a No Show at Hearing on Use of U.S. Voter Funds," *San Francisco Chronicle*, January 11, 2005.
29. "Deal may be in the works for Shelley," CBS5.com, January 21, 2005.
30. "Kevin Shelley vows a vigorous fight to keep his job," *San Jose Mercury News*, January 27, 2005.

31. "Timing of Bush's Fundraiser is Bad for Governor's Agenda," George Skelton in the *Los Angeles Times*, October 20, 2005.
32. "Perata Bill Seen as Foiling Donation Probes," *San Francisco Chronicle*, February 15, 2005.
33. "FBI Probes Lobbyist Ties to Perata," *San Francisco Chronicle*, November 19, 2004.

Notes to Chapter 15 – Ideas for Improvement

1. "Low Voter Turnout Raises Questions for November," *Associated Press*, June 7, 2006.
2. Poll conducted by Lake Research Partners on behalf of the National Voting Rights Institute, December 5-9, 2005.
3. See *Austin v. Michigan Chamber of Commerce*, issued March 27, 1990, by the U.S. Supreme Court.
4. "Public Financing of Campaigns is the Right Idea," *Los Angeles Times,* September 14, 2006.
5. See *Austin v. Michigan Chamber of Commerce.*
6. See *Montana Chamber of Commerce v. Argenbright.*

Index

A

B

C

I

J

K

L

M

N

O

P

Acknowledgements

Ned Wigglesworth, my partner in crime at TheRestofUs.org, provided much of the original research contained in this book as well as significant edits, suggestions, and encouragement. I'm forever grateful.

Thanks to the Arkay Foundation for offering general support to the Poplar Institute and to Harry Lonsdale and Dan Meek for providing funding to publish this book.

This work is largely a compilation of stories researched and broken by a host of reporters working at the *Associated Press, Los Angeles Times, Sacramento Bee, San Diego Union Tribune, San Jose Mercury News, Orange County Register, and San Francisco Chronicle.* Mainstream newspapers have a bad rap these days, some of it deserved, but they have done a reasonably good job of reporting problems of money in California politics. Perhaps having a celebrity governor has helped, but whatever the reason, these reporters and their editors have my gratitude. I would list them all but for fear of forgetting some from the list. By shining a light on the often dismal story of money in politics, they are helping citizens hold elected officials accountable and make democracy work a little better.

I owe a special debt to Bob Stern, not only for a lifetime's work on campaign finance reform, but also for providing important suggestions after reviewing an early draft. Thanks also to Paul Ryan, Adam Lioz, Debra Kaplan, Nick Penniman, Gary Kalman, and Dave McCuan for providing helpful comments after reviewing all or parts of the book.

Thanks to those in the book trade who have helped, often at pro bono or discounted rates, including my editor Walter Kleine and cover designer Brion Sausser. Thanks also to agent Robert Shephard for providing initial encouragement.

It has become almost trite for authors to thank their spouses in acknowledgement sections, but in this case it is certainly warranted. My wife, Deniz Tuncer, not only did more than her share of childcare duty while I worked weekends and nights on this book, she is also a trained editor and provided excellent copy edits to the final manuscript. Thanks are also in order for family members Jodi and Rachel Cressman.

I would further like to thank all of those who have served to inspire and educate me in the field of campaign finance reform and who have worked so hard to make things better. These include Craig McDonald, John Bonifaz, Brenda Wright, Nick Nyhart, Susan Anderson, Micah Sifry, Deb Ross, Jim Knox, Chellie Pingree, Pete Maysmith, Jon Goldin-Dubois, Ellen Miller, Trevor Potter, Meredith McGehee, Tony Miller, Susan Lerner, Janice Thompson, Cindi Canary, Mike McCabe, Trent Lang, Jo Sedita, Granny D, Jon Motl, C.B. Pearson, Joan Claybrook, Lloyd Leonard, Miles Rapoport, Rick Hasen, Stuart Comstock-Gay, John Rauh, Joan and Jay Mandle, Adonal Foyle, Julie Peters, David Wood, Bill Wood, Julia Hutchins, Elena Nunez, Margie Alt, Wendy Wendlandt, and Gene Karpinski. This book is dedicated in memory of Susan Birmingham, who recruited me to take my first job on democracy issues in 1995 and who in the course of her lifetime inspired a legion of activists to take on the challenge of making the world a slightly better place.

Onward!

About the Author

Derek Cressman is a senior fellow at The Poplar Institute, a think tank devoted to government accountability, and a consultant to good government groups working across the country. From 2003–2006, he founded and ran TheRestofUs.org, a nonpartisan watchdog of the role of money in politics that monitored Arnold Schwarzenegger's campaign fundraising more closely than anyone.

Cressman is one of the nation's leading experts on applying spending and contribution limits to big money in politics with experience in researching and analyzing data, drafting legislation, creating and implementing strategies to enact reforms into law, defending campaign finance statutes from legal challenge, and enforcing the law. Both the U.S. Senate and federal courts have relied upon Cressman's expert testimony regarding campaign finance reform. He has helped craft campaign finance and ethics ballot initiatives in four states.

Cressman has been quoted in *The New York Times, USA*

Today, Associated Press, Los Angeles Times, CNN Headline News, San Francisco Chronicle, Sacramento Bee, San Jose Mercury News, San Diego Union Tribune, Orange County Register and numerous other news outlets. His columns about money in politics have appeared in the *San Francisco Chronicle, The Christian Science Monitor, Cleveland Plain Dealer, The Hill, Minuteman Media, The Oregonian, Albuquerque Tribune, Orlando Sentinel, Tompaine.com,* and the *Washington Times* among other publications.

Cressman has worked professionally on democracy issues since 1995 when he served as the State Public Interest Research Groups (PIRGs) Democracy Program Director. With the PIRGs, Cressman helped write and edit many reports on money in politics, including *Soft Money Shuffle, Carpetbagger Cash, Pushing the Limit—The Impact of Raising Federal Limits on Contributions to Campaigns, Lone Star Election Laws, Look Who's Not Coming to Washington,* and *Contribution Limits and Competitiveness.* In 2005, Cressman authored two reports examining democracy in Ohio, *Safe Seats, Dangerous Democracy* and *Making Safe Seats Safer.* He authored sections for the *Encyclopedia of the Supreme Court,* published by Facts on File (2004) and the *Initiative and Referendum Almanac,* by Carolina Academic Press (2003).

In 2001, Mr. Cressman served as an election observer in Somaliland, Africa, with the Initiative and Referendum Institute.

Cressman graduated *cum laude* from Williams College where he won the Richard M. Krouse prize in political science. After growing up in Colorado Springs, Colorado, and residing for five years in Washington, D.C., he now lives with his wife and family in Sacramento, California.